Book Design & Production:
Columbus Publishing Lab
www.ColumbusPublishingLab.com

Paperback ISBN: 978-1-63337-987-9
E-Book ISBN: 978-1-63337-612-0

Printed in the United States of America
1 3 5 7 9 10 8 6 4 2

"Zorba," I said, "you think you're a wonderful Sinbad the Sailor, and you talk big because you've knocked about the world a bit. But you've seen nothing, nothing at all. Not a thing, you poor fool! Nor have I, mind you. The world's much vaster than we think. We travel, crossing whole countries and seas and yet we've never pushed our noses past the doorstep of our own home."

—Nikos Kazantzakis, from *Zorba the Greek*

A Lot of World to See

memoir: 1958–1964

Judith Lee Jones

Wayne Johnson and Wynema Linn

Preface
Tryon, Oklahoma
September 14, 1934

Dearest Wynema,

" ... the high school kids are planning to go to the State Fair on Friday ... can you get off school that day ... and will your folks let you go?"

Lovingly Yours,
Wayne Johnson, Esq. (seventeen-year-old farm boy)

During the year 1934, before and after the letter to Wynema was written (she was barely fourteen), the world churned. President Paul von Hindenburg of Germany died at age eighty-six, on August 2. Hitler had been appointed Chancellor the year before, and now began his deadly consolidation of power. Japan continued its appropriation of China, desperate for the natural resources it needed for war and survival. Closer to home, FDR, now in his second year as President, still knee-deep in the Great Depression, made worse by drought and the relentless Dust Bowl, used his Fireside Chats by radio to bring hope to fellow Americans. Oklahoma, the home of desperate "Okies" in search of jobs, food, homes—that dear battered state—had two F2 tornados in September. A massive dust storm on May 11 was among the worst recorded. But if you are in love, and you have grown up on a farm in Lincoln County with unending financial crises, tornados, and dust storms, who are you thinking of?

Wynema.

She graduated from Cushing High School when she was fifteen and enrolled in Draughon's Business College in Tulsa. It was a relief, a pause, from a life determined by each new oil field boom: leaving school mid-semester to find herself the new girl again in Oklahoma, Texas, Louisiana, Illinois. At least for most of the Depression they had Shell Company houses to live in, and cash. Her father, Jess had steady, dangerous work, and a bad temper if he was drinking, but he also insisted his children play a musical instrument. The piano came naturally for Wynema. At nine she began playing for church services in Oklahoma: Chandler, Drumright, Cushing, Shawnee; and in Salem, Illinois; Rodessa, Louisiana. The best of times were when she was joined by her younger brother Jess; lending his fine baritone voice to her soprano, they became part of their transient communities through their shared love of music.

Wynema, although somewhat shy, or wary, of strangers, was a seasoned performer by twelve years of age when she met Wayne at the drugstore in Tryon, Oklahoma. He was fifteen, handsome, played tennis, basketball, baseball, and had also won the county prize for penmanship one year. Although she rarely spoke to him in chance meetings (she just couldn't think of what to say, she told me), there was an unvoiced understanding.

In July 1938, on the courthouse steps in Chandler, a fight broke out between Wynema's parents. Yelling, cursing. No one remembers the cause of that particular eruption; they occurred often...maybe lack of money (five children, ages ranging from eighteen to four). But that display was a last straw for Wynema—and Wayne. He decided they would marry that weekend. It was the beginning of their new life. Wynema told me many times how long it took her to understand she could read all day, and no one cared, especially her new husband. (Her favorite book at the time, which remained so all her life, was *Anna Karenina*.) Wayne was a reader too.

Two years later, in 1940, my grandfather Jess Linn and his brothers built a house on the edge of the Salem, Illinois oil field. There was work for Wayne that summer: Cleaning debris and other odd jobs gave him good money between his teaching assignments and finishing college. Poor Wynema, in labor two days. With just a sheet strung across the doorway for privacy and the kitchen table prepared for the delivery. All went well and soon thereafter the three of us left Illinois for Oklahoma, where Wayne taught in a one-room schoolhouse. Sometimes mom's brothers lived with us, Jess, or Bob or young Toss. There was a piano, sheet music, and singing.

"When you wish upon a star/Makes no difference where you are..."

Jess Linn, third from left, Mens Quartet
Central State College, 1942

1
August 6, 1958
Houston

Racing down Bellaire Boulevard in my 1956 yellow Chevrolet convertible trying to find Fats Domino or Jerry Lee Lewis on the radio, I pretend I am Ava Gardner: sexy, aloof, independent. I dream of places I want to go, what I want to do. If I'm not speeding around Houston, I'm in my bedroom reading and hoping Mom won't open the door while I'm trying to plan my life. So far, the best I can do is avoid the choices Mom and Dad have in mind. Such as: secretarial school. Just great. The worst typist to graduate from Bellaire High. And college? Not my dream. Although my best friends are leaving next week for Baylor and Texas Tech.

Every time I drive somewhere in my convertible, all by myself, I feel like I am leaving too. Dad gave me the car two summers ago, just in time to move from Houston to Oklahoma City. Dad led the way, speeding and smoking, and probably dreaming of his new business opportunity. My sister Linda and I followed in my convertible, trying to keep up with him, yet stay within the speed limit. Mother was last in our caravan with my younger sisters, Janet and Beth. That was a horrible day because I didn't want to leave my friends. I had cried all night, my eyes were swollen, and I fell asleep every time we stopped for gas and snacks.

At Putnam City High School my car became a minor celebrity, I became best friends with a girl from Estonia who guided me to good books, and I made an F in cooking class.

Within nine weeks we moved back to Texas. We had a weekend farm house outside of Houston to live in while Dad and Mom began yet another business. Linda and I began high school there, I met my cute boyfriend Gene, and we loved living in the country (a pecan orchard, a stream, grandparents on the property). At Thanksgiving we helped Grandma Lee make wild muscadine jelly. Grandma and I drove around old dirt roads with the top down. She is just like me. We are happy driving anywhere. Christmas Eve we wrapped presents with yarn string and comic strip paper, singing silly songs, and laughing. My Grandpa taught me how to drive his Plymouth with a stick shift.

But on a sad New Year's Day, 1957, we moved again, from the farm to a rental house in Houston. My old high school, my old friends, everything seemed different. Now I missed the friends I had met months ago in Oklahoma. At least I had my snug home to dream in, my yellow convertible, Elvis, and the Five Satins singing "In the Still of the Night."

My dreams float in and out of my bedroom window according to the book I'm reading or a movie I've just seen or even a song Mom might play on the piano. "On the *rue de la Paix*, there was once a cabaret" comes to mind. This is my imaginary discussion about my wild dream with Wayne and Wynema, my parents:

Judy, exactly what is it that you want to do?

Well, Dad, I ... I'd like to go to Paris....

PARIS? France? What in the hell do you want to go to Paris for?

Well, I ... I saw that movie, *The Last Time I Saw Paris*, with Elizabeth Taylor and Van Johnson, and I .... Well, Dad, remember in *Little Women* when Jo goes to New York to be a writer? You know ... I just thought I would go to Paris and write and—

Oh, for Christ's SAKE! What is the matter with you, Judy?

I think that is how it would go. (But you never know. Dad said he dreamed of being a sports announcer when he was a kid because he loved basketball and baseball so much.) Anyway, I would never ever breathe a word of wanting to be a writer in Paris, or an actress, or a dancer—to be *An American in Paris*. When I wash dishes, I dream of being Ava Gardner as Lady Brett Ashley in *The Sun Also Rises*. Drinking wine in Paris, bullfights in Spain.

I want to be far away and find a romantic, handsome man and fall in love for a few days. I love being with my boyfriend Gene, all naked and breathless in the back seat of his green Chevy. But I've never gone all the way with anyone. I don't want children, and surprises happen, and I would be mortified if I became pregnant. I have three younger sisters and I can't stand taking care of them, so sex all the way is out of the question. I am interested in what making love is, but I don't have friends who know about sex except my mom, and I would never ask her about how you do it.

Even though we don't talk about sex, Mom and I sit up late together when the house gets quiet, and read our books. We go to old movies, and she taught me how to dance the Charleston and we can hop around all evening to Pete Fountain records. Mom named me after Judy Garland because she is mom's favorite singer.

I know Hawaiian dances too. It's because in 1950 a terrible thing happened. My Uncle Jess died in his Navy plane off the coast of Oahu, and his wife and my cousins came to live with us. Aunt Jo taught me the hula and that started me being on stage. I've been a dancer in our school musicals for the last eight years. Even though Mom says she doesn't know what to do with me, and I don't either, she admits to reading me a thousand and one fairy tales (dancing princesses) that could have put some fantastical ideas in my head.

All I know is this: I barely passed typing, and I don't like being in school, and maybe I do want to live in Paris and write and explore. I've read about it in books and seen old movies, and I think the purpose of reading and seeing movies is to show you other parts of the world, and help you discover things you never thought about before.

I wish I could go visit Dad's parents on the farm in Oklahoma. I can think when it's quiet. There is a tall cedar tree in their front yard, and Grandma and Pa-Pa and I sit underneath it after chores and dinner. We wait for a breeze to come by, swat mosquitoes and flies, listen to cicadas hum. We search for the first star. No one says a thing.

If I dared, I would tell Dad that the first time I thought about Paris was in Grandma Johnson's bedroom. She keeps a blue glass bottle of *An Evening in Paris* perfume on her vanity. I've been dreaming about Paris since I could read the label.

2

Mom whips the car into the Shamrock Hotel parking garage. This hotel is famous. Glenn McCarthy built it in 1949 after he made lots of money striking oil all over Texas. My dad went to the opening on St. Patrick's Day. We learned about it in the movie *Giant*. James Dean played Jett Rink, the character based on Mr. McCarthy. Poor James Dean. That was his last movie, and I was so sad when he died.

Mom and I get out of the car and don't say a thing. We are here for a beauty contest. The winner will receive a six-week contract to dance at the Sands Hotel and Casino in Las Vegas. Mom's friend called early this morning to tell her I should enter it. I glance at Mom and think this is the craziest thing, but she looks so calm. My dress gets stuck to my back, I can smell Arid under my arms, and my black patent leather high heels suck on my feet. I want to cool off in the gift shop, but Mom says NO, we are late to the beauty contest. We walk into a room with no windows, and girls are powdering their noses and rummaging through their make-up kits. Mom and I find two chairs together; she lights up a cigarette, then winks at me.

A Mr. Charlie Evans introduces himself and five other judges. I know his name because he writes a column called "Night and Day" for the *Houston Chronicle*. He wrote about our neighbors, Coach Harold Lahar and his wife Dottie. Harold is head football coach for the University of Houston and is always in the news during football season. Mr. Evans walks around the crowded room handing out a form to fill out. I can see his hair is thin on top when he leans over; he's skinny too, but has a friendly smile. I write my name, Judy Johnson, that I am 5'9", weigh 125 pounds and yes, I want to be a dancer at the Sands Hotel in Las Vegas.

Then we wait.

I begin tingling all over. I listen to the first group of girls introduce themselves. They don't speak up and my body, or part of me, feels like I am flush to the ceiling, hovering, nervously deciding what I have to do. I am in the fourth group. Mom squeezes my hand, and I walk up smiling. I look at each judge like my high school drama teacher, Mr. Pickett, would have wanted. I don't mumble when I tell them my name; I smile, I turn, and I pose with my best model imitation. My legs shake. My mouth feels frozen. But I keep sucking in my stomach and trying to keep my shoulders from hunching up to my ears. I keep saying to myself, *be a dancer, be a far-away dancer.*

Our turn is over and we find our seats. I fidget. My hands are clammy. I need a cold Grapette, or at least some ice chips to put down the front of my dress. I think maybe I will win. I have been on stage a lot. Dancing the hula, in piano recitals, and I was very good in a scene from *Born Yesterday*.

Mom pushes hair off my forehead and squeezes my hand. Maybe I am dreaming all this. Four hours ago I was reading *Silver Screen* magazine about Elvis Presley and babysitting our neighbor's kids, Lolly and Billy, with no premonition of an adventure. I look sideways at mother. She does the strangest things. I remember how she pinned gardenias and carnations in my hair every morning before school. During class I would think of her when the fragrance floated around my face. Now this. Sitting next to me smoking a cigarette, cool as can be.

The room is quiet. Finally, Mr. Evans stands up and smiles and nods and says, "*Thank You. Thank you.*" to all the contestants. He pauses, clears his throat, looks around the room, and then loudly announces the new Texas Copa Girls.

"Miss Kathy Martin and... Miss Judy Johnson!"

Even though I felt I was going to win, I jolt out of my seat because winning is completely different from sitting next to mother hoping I would win. In a split second the whole summer of creeping around the house trying to think of a plan vanishes. I have won a six-week contract to dance at the Sands Hotel and Casino for $150 a week. I find Kathy across the room, with no mother beside her. She has an aloof look, like Marlene Dietrich, but we hug anyway. Kathy and I are asked to pose for photos. We stand close together and she is taller than me, exotic looking, with black eyeliner curling up like a cat's eye.

Afterwards (I can't keep from staring at her—pale white face, black hair and eyes), she whispers, "We're on a grand adventure!"

We are scheduled to leave in seven days.

Kathy has been at Southern Methodist University this past year, living in a rented room. She designs her clothes and in high school won a contest and modeled at Foley's department store. Best of all, she loves poetry like I do and wants to live in Paris and study fashion. Since she is my first friend that loves Paris, we talk on the phone every day, and as soon as we hang up I want to call her again, just to hear her laugh.

The day we leave, my Grandma Lee starts joking about how I might end up marrying a big movie star out in Las Vegas and reminds me that Frank Sinatra is a single man now. She always teases me about boyfriends and getting married. I say I would like to be a movie star, but I'm not going anywhere to get married. She rolls her eyes like always. She says, "Have a good time. I might drive out and live with you." Grandma tells us about meeting Grandpa at a barn dance where he played the guitar and she danced all evening.

Grandma Johnson and I spoke on her party-line phone, and we had a good connection and I could hear her for once. Unlike Grandma Lee, she is not excited about me going to Las Vegas and clucked a lot like her chickens.

"Save money from each paycheck."

"Yes'm."

"Be a good girl."

"Yes'm."

She said she owes me a letter and she will send it to me soon.

"Yes'm."

My grandmother lives on the farm with her body and soul rooted in the Oklahoma soil by day, but by night she explores the moon and stars and planets with the new binoculars Dad bought her for Christmas.

For seven days I've been excited about going to Nevada and I never really thought about saying goodby to my sisters. We pack the car with my blue-and-black marbled Samsonite luggage Mom and Dad gave me for high school graduation, and as suddenly as I had won the contest last Tuesday, we back out of the driveway. I wave to my family. My youngest sister Beth looks so cute and her little face so sweet, and even Janet and Linda look different. Not for half an hour, until I see signs to the airport, can I speak without a lump in my throat.

3
Las Vegas

Kathy and I leave Houston on Continental Airlines. We lift off and I watch the small squares and rectangles of Houston lawns and streets disappear through the haze of clouds. I know, or feel, or am, or seem to be, disappearing too.

We are transfixed by clouds outside our window. "Like a dream," Kathy says.

Yes.

While we look out at the blue sky Kathy says, "My collection of Madame Alexander dolls began my dreaming of living in France."

I answer with, "The words to a song, 'the last time I saw Paris, our hearts were young and gay' captured my imagination." And we begin another conversation about our daydreams, our beginnings, with each other. Kathy was born in New Orleans during a hurricane. I was born in Illinois on the edge of an oil field. Only when the plane descends do we stop talking.

We change in Phoenix to Bonanza Airlines. Clouds disappear and mountain peaks reach up and scare the crap out of me. The plane bounces up, then feels like it's falling in space. Grandma Lee's adventure stories float around me, a wagon topples over in the Caney river, clothes and food and blankets escape downstream. She always warns us to be careful of deep water, mean people, and train tracks. She never mentioned anything about bouncing over mountaintops. The plane squeezes through our downward path. Scraggly mesquite bushes, sandy spaces rush into view.

Hot desert air smacks me in the face. Careful not to stumble, we lean our way down the steps, the aluminum railing hot to the touch. In the distance, I see silver heat waves, whirling mirages that disappear into the sand.

A short, suntanned man walks up to Kathy and me and introduces himself as Al Freeman, the Sands publicity director. He has startling white teeth, a gold necklace, and a loose shirt, and keeps saying "hey babe" over and over.

When we wheel out of the parking lot he starts tapping me on my shoulder and on my thigh and I keep smiling and shrugging and scooting as far away from him as I can. Out the car window I watch leaping, flying tumbleweeds travel down the road with us. I have to push Mr. Freeman's hand off my leg about ten times.

He checks us into the Sans Souci Motel across from the Sands and tells us to meet him in the Garden Room in an hour, so he can introduce us to our boss, Mr. Jack Entratter. I say "yessir" and take the key he gives me. Within minutes of entering our new room, it is full of our suitcases and clothes and our books and magazines and us laughing! I feel like jumping on the beds but I don't. I look around…no kitchen, no dishes to wash, no cooking grits in the morning, no nothing except…we don't know. No one to tell us what to do or not to do, except our new boss.

We brush our teeth, fluff our hair, put on lipstick, and walk outside and look at the Sands Hotel across the street. It is the color of the desert. The marquee says, "Jack Entratter presents the Beautiful Copa Girls." Marguerite Piazza and Louis Armstrong are both performing at our hotel for a week.

Inside the Sands, we stand in the lobby and look and listen and watch. Men in long-sleeved white dress shirts and cute bow ties and black slacks stand behind green felt half-moon-shaped tables; playing cards are being slapped down or flipped over; silver dollars and poker chips clink and make music everywhere. Bells and buzzers are going off, and ladies in short, black dresses with white ruffled aprons and black mesh hose in high heels carry trays of drinks and cigarettes. It sounds and seems just like Playland Park in Houston, and my boyfriend winning me stuffed animals and aluminum coins with our names printed on them.

Meeting Mr. Entratter took about ten , and I was glad to leave because he is tall and asked a lot of questions and acts like a boss, and the whole time I was fidgety and hoped he liked me. He wanted to know if I had ever been on stage before. Yes. Five piano recitals, three dance recitals, two high school plays, and I danced the hula every year in the school talent show. He laughed and so did Mr. Al Freeman and our stage manager, Harold Dubrow.

The next morning, Kathy and I start our first day at work. I'm thinking we will get on stage and dance hard for hours and learn our routine. I am so excited I can hardly breathe when we find our way through the heavy velvet curtains into the Copa Room. It is dark, quiet, and shadowy, with cigarette smoke curling up through an overhead light. Four or five girls are slouched in chairs with their legs propped up on tables. A red-headed girl sits with her head tilted back, puffing on a cigarette, blowing smoke rings in the air. Each ring skims over the stage railing, wobbles in the one beam of overhead light and falls apart. I admire how they dissolve over the stage, then ask her if she is from Texas.

"Hell, no," she answers. Then adds after another puff, "This whole Texas Copa thing is a crock of shit, too."

I nod in agreement. "I'm Judy."

"Gloria."

Her eyes are green like my mom's. She cusses like mom too.

Barely half of us are from Texas. Linda and Coralynn are from Dallas. For this show they are going to be models like Kathy and wear sequined dresses and mink coats. Joan is from Houston and was a cheerleader at Rice University. Collette has coal black hair, a creamy white complexion, blue violet eyes, and thick black eyelashes like Elizabeth Taylor's. She is from Utah and has years of ballet training. I can tell by watching while she does pique turns on stage. Arlene has translucent skin and light reddish-blond hair. She is sweet and seems a little sad; she gazes over my shoulder when she talks. Arlene looks like a Storybook Doll, except for the fact that she smokes.

I visit with the piano player. He picks out tunes, chuckles when someone cusses or complains, and doesn't flick off his cigarette ash till it almost reaches his lips. I ask him if he knows "The Gypsy," and he picks out the melody. He knows a little of "Alice Blue Gown." I tell him those are pieces that Mom played a lot. He arches his eyebrows and nods with the cigarette pressed between his lips and the ash just about ready to fall.

When Bob and Renne, the choreographers, appear, the girls stub out their cigarettes and find their places on stage. I edge to the back. Renee begins humming and counting and snapping her fingers, marking time. She has short, curly blond hair, shapely legs, bags under her eyes, and wears short shorts and mesh hose and heels. From behind she has a nice figure, but when she turns around her stomach sticks out too much. She looks old, probably forty. She has a foreign accent or something.

"GladyousegirlsarehereJudyyou'rethedancer?" She takes a drag on her cigarette.

I can't understand her. "Yes ma'am." There is laughing and I know next time to call her Renne.

She hisses out smoke and says, still clinching the cigarette between her teeth, "Firstfourcounts."

We begin rehearsals. I follow the girls in front of me. Renne changes combinations, steps, counts, positions with every puff of her cigarette.

She tells the piano player to start, stop, then start again. She hisses at her assistant, Bob, who hisses back.

On the break, when I sit with the piano player he hums "… in a quaint caravan there's a lady they call THE GYPSY. She can look in the future…" I like sitting next to him and listening to old songs. By the end of the afternoon, I am comfortable in the Copa Room, and I already know it is an easy job.

At five o'clock when Kathy and I walk outside the Sands and over to our motel room, the sun is so bright and the mountains so big that our six hours in rehearsal seem like a dream. I can hardly believe we have earned money for sitting around most of the afternoon.

On our third day in Las Vegas we move into our garage apartment on San Francisco Street, a block from the Sahara. We have a pullout couch in the living room, and a bedroom, kitchen, and bathroom. My favorite spot, though, is at the top of the stairs on our landing. We have enough room to sit outside and dangle our legs and dream our dreams as we marvel at the ever-changing colors of the mountains in the east.

If we are hungry, we skip over to Foxy's and get a free dish of pickles and cauliflower and peppers when we order a Coke. We agree that our thirty-minute walk to work doesn't take long at all. We could catch the bus, but we walk and talk and we are at the Sands in no time. We talk about the Copa girls. We like Gloria. She tells jokes, and even though she cusses a lot, we can tell she is tender-hearted. Charlotte is funny too. She will be a model like Kathy, with a mink coat to walk around in. But she learns all the dances in case someone can't make the show. Charlotte is our line captain and the swing girl.

Our conversations always return to fashion and Paris. Kathy's aunt is a buyer for Neiman Marcus and showed Kathy how to sew the new dresses. Kathy wears a rhinestone pin like a necklace, across her forehead! Like a princess from India. She isn't afraid to do things like that. I could wear a flower in my hair, but not something dangling in the middle of my forehead. She knows about Paris "because my boyfriend from South America lived there and told me all about it." So each day we walk down the Strip and tell stories, interrupting each other with many questions and finding ourselves at rehearsals before we know it.

After a week of rehearsals, we still don't have a set routine and opening night with Jerry Lewis is in five days. Renne has to stop for a smoke every ten minutes. And then forgets what she did before the smoke break. It's maddening. Charlotte and Gloria remember everything, and I don't know why they aren't in charge of choreography.

On the way home today we start talking again about boyfriends. Kathy asks me, "Have you gone all the way with someone?"

Just the question scares the crap out of me. I am full of guilt and embarrassment and can barely say "No." Heck, I've never talked to anyone about sex except my girlfriend Sheila in junior high. And at the time I didn't believe what she told me. That a boy would want to put his mouth on a girl's breast and nibble and suck on it! But then I found out in high school that it did happen, and I liked it a lot.

I tell Kathy how much I love being with my boyfriend, getting naked and his hands moving over my face, my mouth, my breasts, pressing on my stomach and finally, at last, to the most private, eager part of me, but we never ever went all the way. I wanted to have sex with him. We spent hours in his old Chevy on deserted Galveston beaches or way out in moonlit pastures with cattle bumping each other as they walked around outside of the car while we gasped for air. Just describing to Kathy about being naked with him makes me feel faint, and guilty, and like I might get pregnant just talking about it.

Kathy stops to tell me, "Judy, you can have sex without having a baby." But that's a mystery too. How?

Walking down the Strip, deep in stories about Kathy having sex is about as daring as actually doing it. I barely notice the cars and taxis on the strip, or the busses chugging to a stop, or the vacant spaces between the Desert Inn and the Riviera where we always hope for tumbleweed to appear. I have to tell myself to watch out for the curb, watch every step I take, so I won't stumble.

Kathy says it is perfectly "natural" to have sex with someone you love. She made love with her boyfriend and says that even if you aren't married, it doesn't mean you aren't a nice girl. She loved him and still does, but he went back to Argentina and she doesn't hear from him now. She said she was happier than ever having someone to love and be close to; to be near him made her tremble. Kathy has tears running down her face, and I know she misses him a lot.

I felt tingly with Gene, him touching me like he did, but we are just kids. Is that the real "being in love"?

I have read *Lady Chatterley's Lover.* We had to sneak a copy around, deathly afraid of our parents discovering it under the bed while we were in school. It seems everything about sex has to be a big mysterious secret, which makes me more curious than ever.

Kathy and I stand at the corner of San Francisco Street, notice that Mitzi Gaynor will be starring there soon, and decide to keep walking and talking about sex, boyfriends, sexy movies, and our favorite movie stars. I like Jennifer Jones in *Duel in the Sun.* I want to be sexy like the character Jennifer Jones plays, but I think it's hard to do. You have to drink and tilt your head back and whisper out smoke, and pose with a long cigarette holder, like Ava Gardner. When I try to drink or smoke, I choke and cough every time. Kathy says smoking is awful. I agree.

By the time we finish talking, it is almost seven in the evening. I sit on top of the steps looking east. Kathy takes a shower. She cried off her eye makeup telling me about her boyfriend. My brain is thick with new thoughts, soggy, swirling like a heavy Houston rain. I sit and hold onto the far mountains and think of our stories. Now, with Kathy, I feel at ease talking about sex and boyfriends and our dreams of going to France. She understands me, and I understand her. I have a good feeling when I am with Kathy. It is a little like being happy when I am at Grandma Johnson's farm. When I can walk to the big pond with my dog Beauty and read Zane Grey stories all day out in the sunshine, grasshoppers humming, buttercups snug all over the pasture, and song birds hopping about.

4

Yesterday was strange. It all started right after our long walk home from rehearsals. Kathy went out to buy mascara. I sat on the steps writing postcards to my sisters and thinking for an hour or two, studying how the foothills seemed to creep into the dark purple desert. Then Kathy came back with the mascara and a very handsome young man from Sweden. The two of them were holding hands and kissing and laughing. Kathy seemed very happy, and I think partly because they had been drinking wine. They said he had a friend for me to meet, and so Kathy and I went inside to put on dresses. The three of us walked to the Riviera, where my date was waiting for us.

He was from Italy. His uncle in New York City had brought him to the United States to visit. He had sexy brown eyes and just the right mouth, with a curve in his lower lip. His accent made me fall in love with him almost immediately. I couldn't resist staring at his face, listening hard to his voice, and trying to decipher what he was saying, which actually didn't matter that much to me at all. It was enough to just figure out a word here and there. We laughed, and I instantly felt we could walk together and be quiet and have an understanding too. I liked the way he looked at me so intently, polite and calm. His name was Joky and his uncle, Mr. Gambino, had sent him to Las Vegas so he could see all the big stars. He loved New York, he told me, and he had a lot of family there. Or I think that's what he said. I told him my family was big too. I said it was a shame he couldn't swing by Oklahoma and Texas and see cowboys. That made us laugh. Texas! Bang! Bang!

It was about 9:30 p.m. and the air was fresh and perfect and made you want to walk for hours up and down the Strip. But we walked to the Stardust. The Stardust had opened in July, and even in Rome, Joky had heard about the fabulous sign. I think it's the biggest sign in the world. We could have spread out a picnic blanket and had fun looking at the thousands of rippling lights, a Busby Berkeley vaudeville show of changing colors, but of course we didn't. We went inside and sat in the lounge and all ordered something to drink. We wanted to see some of the English and French dancers in the Lido, but they must have been getting ready for the next show. I wanted to see Lelani Kele's Hawaiian revue, but they weren't on either. I tried to tell everyone how good the Hawaiian dancers are, and that my aunt Jo had taught me the hula when I was ten. Joky said he worked on *films* in Rome. He definitely didn't say movies. I told him about my three sisters and about Grandma and Grandpa Johnson and their farm in Oklahoma. He loved that my Grandma Lee was a Cherokee Indian. He kept saying, "Ok-La-Ho-Ma" as if it were something strange, but I liked how he said it, over and over, like a poem.

After a while he started holding my hand. Later, on the street, he put his arm around my shoulders and kissed me right there. I liked that. We started back to our apartment and I knew long before we got to San Francisco Street that this was it. I was going to go to bed with him. All the way.

Kathy and her Swedish friend crossed over the Strip and said they were going to the Sahara to catch Louis Prima and Keely Smith. Joky and I walked together very slowly. I was lightheaded thinking about having sex, a little scared, but certain this was it. I was over all the big notions that had kept me from doing it. I mean, there's ways to have sex and not get pregnant. I know that now. I just don't know exactly what you do, but I thought Joky should know. And I no longer think you're bad if you do it either. It helped, too, that I was a long way from my mother.

When we got to my apartment we sat out on the top steps for a while kissing and becoming familiar with each other. He said he liked how I felt, looking right into my eyes and pressing his hands over my breasts. Honestly, my insides moved, I couldn't close my mouth, my breath stayed inside me. I liked him finding out about me, with my clothes on. It felt so good I could hardly wait to go inside and pull out the sofa bed and get started, even though I'd only known him for six hours.

We went inside. I kept thinking over and over, oh shit I'm going to do it. Once he started tracing my eyebrows, then my lips with his finger, and whispering things I couldn't understand in his nice accent, I didn't have much control any more. In no time my clothes were off.

Our hands and arms and legs were all tangled up, and he was kissing me along my neck. Having all that space in a bed was new. More room than in the back seat of a car. Just as he was pressing hard against me, I had this thought that maybe he should know it was my first time. He got confused when I eased away and asked him to stop, that I had something to say. He thought I didn't want to go on, that he had done something wrong. Sitting there cross-legged and completely naked—quite forward of me, and probably not all that convincing—I told him that I had not gone all the way with a man before. As much as we had puzzled through our stumbling English/Italian conversations, somehow he understood my mumbling, my slight embarrassment, the way I was pointing at him, signaling number one, my first. He chuckled, shaking his head, and taking my face in his hands, he mumbled to himself in Italian. I wished I knew what he was saying. I think it was tender, though. We went on. I found out about having sex. That it can hurt a little, like running and falling down and skinning a knee, even though at the same time you're having fun, free as can be.

I was very happy with Joky cuddled next to me, with his arm around me. I was about to ask him if he had read *Lady Chatterley's Lover*, but before I could, the craziest thing happened. Someone knocked on the door. It was the only time since Kathy and I had moved in over a week ago that anyone had ever knocked on the door. Not to mention that it was about five in the morning.

"Kathy?" I asked.

"No," a male voice answered. If it had been my mother, my father, my uncles, it couldn't have been any worse. I knew his voice, his tanned face, his blue-green eyes, thick, black eyelashes, his beautiful white teeth, his sandy, tousled hair. I knew the feel of his rough, baseball-calloused hands on me, my thighs, our naked bodies together. "No. It's Gene," he said.

I opened the door an inch. I could see his mouth, part of it. I could have licked his lip. An eye.

"You can't come in."

"Why not?"

"Because," I whispered. "My girlfriend and her boyfriend are asleep on the sofa bed."

Wait, I would come out. I would get my key. I turned to Joky and made a face and grimaced and whispered, "boyfriend from Texas." I put my finger to my lips, "quiet, quiet, shhhh." I said to go down the steps in a little while. He raised his eyebrows. Did he understand?

"Texas....Boyfriend."

I don't know why, maybe because they were close at hand, but I put on my see-through, baby-doll frilly pajamas, gave my bewildered man from Italy a quick kiss goodbye, and walked outside. First, it was cool in the dark in my thin shorties. But it helped me clear my head, form more of a story. Gene seemed confused but I stuck to my big fat lie, taking his hand, pecking his cheek, acting light-hearted and carefree as if no one in Las Vegas would think a thing about us walking around in almost daylight, and me in my ruffled pale pink pj's.

I chattered on, trying to convince Gene that I felt bubbly and lively and not at all dumbstruck and horrified at his terrible timing. While Gene had been driving around Las Vegas looking for my apartment, I was having sex with an Italian stranger. How could he have appeared just when I had done it...without him? It should have been him. Instead, there I was, scrambling to make sense to Gene, knowing that I was as unintelligible to him in English as I had been to Joky.

Gene kissed me and asked, "Do you want to get married?"

"Of course not," I answered quickly. "I'm working."

He knew I never wanted to get married. He didn't either. He was going to the university, where he belonged, to be a writer and an athlete and the best student ever.

If we had been at home he probably would have gotten mad at my answer. But we were far from our deserted beach in Galveston, far from his green souped-up Chevy with its steamed up car windows.

Gold and pink started showing around the mountains. We walked back to the apartment. His friends were waiting for him and we kissed and the car door closed and he disappeared in the soft morning light.

5

Mail came today from Grandma Johnson in Tryon. She says she is late answering my letter of two months ago. She says she can hardly believe I'm old enough to be away from home.

In her letter, Grandma brings up a lot of memories. She reminds me of how I used to scold Papa for saying "ain't" until I found out it was fun to say (only if my mom and dad weren't around). And she remembers how I begged to sit in the back of the pickup truck so I could see the sky good and let the hot air rush through my sweaty hair. I loved riding in that old bouncy truck, watching pink Oklahoma clouds float happy and high above the summer heat. Grandma says I looked free and as happy as a wild bird sitting in the truck bed. I could talk to both of them through the back window of the cab, shout out what I saw, maybe a turtle, or bunches of tall golden wildflowers, or monster grasshoppers whizzing by. Papa had to check on his herd of cattle every other day. He had one lot out past the Tryon cemetery and through four pastures and gates. Linda and I took turns jumping out of the truck and fussing with wire hooks to swing the gates open so Papa could drive on through. We were careful not to step in fresh cow patties.

Grandma ends her letter by telling about Papa. She says he has bought a new buckskin horse that's real nice and gentle and loves to work with cattle. She doesn't say his name, though. I can see Papa with his cowboy hat on, nice and tall on the new horse. I wouldn't be a bit surprised if he rode across Oklahoma and Colorado and New Mexico clear into Nevada, just like in his Zane Grey books. He did ride into New Mexico once to round up wild horses. He told us about it one night while we were on the old squeaky spring bed under the summer stars. Linda and me, Grandma and Papa. We loved being outside in the night with the lightning bugs rising up to the millions of stars overhead, our stories tangled up with frog croaks and thundering crickets. I'm glad the letter came because I've felt different since I made love with Joky. So much has happened in two weeks.

Mom is here. I can't stop talking. I'm afraid she'll see right into my mind and know I've had sex. Ever since she got here I've been blabbering about how wonderful our apartment is, telling her about each of the Copa girls, our routine, our costumes, Pauline the seamstress, and Harold the stage manager. I made a big mistake telling her that Arlene had dated Frank Sinatra. But I had just heard Arlene talking about him a few days ago and I thought it was interesting. But mom doesn't approve of Frank Sinatra, and the look on her face scared the crap out of me. Although I am very glad to see her, I'm worried she'll think I look different and guess the truth. I just smile and hold her hand and hope and pretend we are having a good time.

We went to the drugstore earlier today and bought cosmetics. All the things Charlotte said I needed. Odd-shaped sponges, pancake makeup in ivory, a pot of deep rose rouge. Erace to conceal the bags under my eyes. Charlotte said she never saw a seventeen-year-old girl with dark shadows like I have. Grandma Lee always tells me it's her Indian part coming out, that my eye bags are just like hers. I doubt Erace can get rid of them, but I bought it anyway. Also, black Maybelline eyeliner, eyelash curler, black mascara, Revlon Fire and Ice bright red lipstick, lip gloss, and false eyelashes. Charlotte cut and shaped the eyelashes and gave me the Johnsons Surgical Glue to stick them on with. I have a jar of Albolene cold cream to wipe off all the mistakes I make fixing my new face.

Mom likes Las Vegas a little. We walked behind the Sands pool to her room in the Hialeah building where the gardens are a beautiful surprise, since outside the hotels the desert pushes onto the sidewalks and streets wherever it can. Mom named all the blooming trees and shrubbery, all the hardy flowers spilling out their bright colors. And earlier she watched Jerry Lewis rehearse. She sat in the back booth in the Copa Room and since she is a pianist and sang in many choirs, she found it a thrilling two hours. She was impressed with Mr. Lewis's musical knowledge, how serious he was. There was no semblance of the comic artist we know. She said he is a "perfectionist" and professional in his exchanges with the musicians.

Mom seems a lot younger out here. She might be wearing more makeup. For the first time I notice Mom has a great figure for being thirty-eight with four kids. It's funny. She looks different to me after two weeks. I hope I look exactly the same to her. She bought me a new cocktail dress to wear tomorrow night—it's white, with a scooped neckline, sleeveless, and rhinestones across the bodice. It is straight, not too too tight, and has a slender belt dotted with rhinestones. It is almost sexy.

Harold called out "five minutes" into our dressing room and we started rushing around, looking in the mirror one last time, dabbing on a bit of powder or applying more lip liner or rouge. We were smacking our lips together, using tissues to wipe bits of lip gloss off our teeth, and then fastening each other's rhinestone necklaces. It was like getting ready for the prom, but much more fun. Our costumes are lots sexier than any puffy prom dress. They look sort of like white bathing suits, but are made of a shiny material and covered in rhinestones. The bottom has white fluffy fur around it, which ends in a silly tail on our butts. Our white furry hats are shaped like our white furry muffs, but about half the size. The hats sit at a slight angle. It takes a lot of bobby pins to keep them on tight. Our muffs go on our right arms, so we point to the audience with our left hands when we sing, "Gimme a little kiss and I'll give it right back to you!" Mr. Entratter wants us to look sexy but "wholesome" and I think we do, like Cyd Charisse, one of my other favorite movie star dancers.

Pauline fixed everyone's costume to show off bosoms. One girl needed six falsies on both sides of her bra to push her breasts together for a sexy cleavage. When Pauline finished with our costumes we all looked sexy, fake or not. I wear a g-string. It feels funny at first but we have to have them. We can't wear regular panties underneath our costume because they would show, so I have to act like it's normal to have this patch of triangle cloth covering my privates and a string up my butt. Our mesh pantyhose come in two parts, which Pauline has to cut for us. We put one hose on at a time and hitch them together. Kathy's dress is too big, it's pinned together in the back with huge safety pins. It isn't comfortable, and although it's all covered by the fur coat, she doesn't feel glamorous in it. She should though. She is the tallest showgirl and her smile and beauty command the stage.

When I walked down the stairs from the dressing room for the 8p.m. opening show with Jerry Lewis, I had to hold on to the banister. Even though I've been wearing high heels to rehearsal for a week, I didn't want to trip going down to the stage. As it was, I felt each stair step through my high heels, my mesh hose on my toes, the fur tail on my costume bumping against the back of my legs. I felt the sparkle in my earrings and the shine in my lip gloss.

Downstairs, the whole backstage was lit up and full of new people. Men were checking light and sound equipment, worrying with the curtains, joking and telling us how good we looked. Harold looked distracted and nervous as usual, but told us all to "break a leg" and that we were beautiful. Antonio Morelli and his orchestra were warming up; Joe the piano player was in a tux and no cigarette; Steve, our production singer, was clearing his throat; and even some of the chorus girls were stretching and warming up, but not me. I was flushed and loose and ready. I double-checked that my seams were still straight, and I borrowed a bobby-pin from Pauline and stuck it in the front of my furry white hat where it felt wobbly.

The lights backstage went down, and we picked our way over the mess of cables on the floor and got in line, standing in the dark, between the curtains of the "Sands Hotel, A Place in the Sun," and waited. Just a few feet in front of the curtain, in the Copa Room, people were laughing, waiters were taking plates from tables, ice clinked in drinks, and the smell of cigarette smoke drifted in to us. Mom was sitting in the audience with Mr. Evans, who had come from Houston for the show. Then the production singer announced, "Ladies and Gentlemen, Jack Entratter presents the bee-yoo-ti-ful Texas Copa Girls!" The music began, Charlotte started counting, the overhead lights jumped on stage, and there we were. In a second my mouth hurt from smiling so big. I made eye contact with the front row audience, and everyone I looked at looked back at me and smiled.

I wiggled, I pointed and sang, "Gimme a little kiss, won-cha huh? And I'll give it right back to you!" I sang to the couple right in front of me, and they both winked.

We had a problem in the first show. We were bunched up wrong when we did our high kicks diagonally across stage. First, we form two short lines, one behind the other, lock arms and hands behind each other's backs, and then, with a step, kick, step, step, kick, we move across stage, which isn't that easy in high heels. One girl hissed between her teeth, "Get the fuck out of my face," which scared the hell out of me, but I kept right on counting, kicking, and smiling. Our number was over so quickly I couldn't believe it. I wanted to dance and sing more.

Our midnight show was perfect. Maybe, I thought, I'll become a famous dancer like Ann Miller or Juliet Prowse. I would love to dance on stage for the rest of my life. Mr. Lewis made everyone laugh. We can hear the whole show up in our dressing room. Mom and I held hands and walked around the casino like best friends. She told me Mr. Evans thought we were beautiful onstage and that she did, too. Mr. Evans is going to write about our opening for his column. I will have my name in the *Houston Chronicle* again.

I met Mom for breakfast in the Garden Room the day she left for home. She had been wondering why we were named the Texas Copa Girls. Just about that time Al Freeman walked in and came over to ask if Mom had enjoyed her visit. He pulled out a chair and joined us and I asked him about the Texas Copa girl name. It was a long answer but that's how he is. It's his job as public relations man to know all about Las Vegas.

First, he said "Copa" comes from the Copa Room in New York City, where Mr. Entratter used to work. The owners of the Sands thought it would be a good idea to have the same famous name in Nevada. Secondly, Al said, one of the owners of the Sands, Mr. Jake Freedman, was from Galveston where, it turns out, he owned part of the famous Balinese Room there. (I've seen the Balinese Room a million times, sticking way out into the Gulf of Mexico, right across from the beautiful Hotel Galvez.) So, they linked Texas and Copa together and hoped to get some publicity that would bring in more people to the Sands.

The only thing is, Mr. Jake Freedman died this past January. I felt really sorry about that because I think if he were still alive we would have lots to talk about and not just Galveston. Al said Mr. Freedman had a lot of friends in the military and was very patriotic, and I could have told him about my uncles and cousins who were in the military and we probably would have been friends.

Once Al started talking about Mr. Freedman, we learned a lot. Kathy had told me a day or so ago that atomic bomb tests go on around here, but I had no idea how many or how long this testing has been going on until today. Al said that they've had lots of famous people out here watching atomic bomb tests. The Sands has been completely full at times with bomb watchers. Just three years ago John Cameron Swayze was here, as was our mayor from Houston, Roy Hofheinz, to watch the largest atomic explosion test ever seen in America. Al told us that he remembers it so well because the bomb didn't go off like it was supposed to and for three days the hotel reservations got all jammed up and it was a nightmare for him and Mr. Freedman.

Once I ask Al about something, he starts talking fast and I learn a lot. Right now, this month and next, lots of atomic bomb tests are going on because President Eisenhower has to sign a treaty with the Russians and our bomb people have to finish up their work before the signing.

Mom and I always held hands and we didn't have one cross word in four days. I do have a job now and even though I'm not in college, I am paying my own way and learning new things: If we wait until midnight to eat at the Chuck Wagon buffet, it's very cheap. Do not put too much glue on the false eyelashes or you'll have a big mess. We were sad finding out that a lot of taxes are taken out of our paycheck that we weren't expecting and also, it's scary to discover that according to Charlotte, we are barely an hour's drive from the atomic bomb site.

6

Kathy and I have performed in twenty-one shows since we opened with Mr. Jerry Lewis. It's the first evening that I can sit in the lounge and order a drink like everyone else. I'm eighteen today. Kathy and I order glasses of Manischewitz wine, but I don't like it.

The Copa girls gave me a birthday card that has blond chorus line dancers on the front. They surprised me with a red and white striped cotton robe to wear in the dressing room. I also had birthday cards from my sisters and Grandma Lee. The cards came addressed to me, c/o Sands Hotel (back stage), Las Vegas, Nevada. Although I certainly know that I am here at the Sands, when I pick up my mail, it seems like someone else's.

Mr. Weisberg and Mr. Kandel, two of our casino bosses, stopped at our table to ask me why I was in the lounge. For ten days I've been sitting at a table in the postcard section, reading and watching guests and cocktail waitresses and famous stars like Jimmy Durante and Lucille Ball walk by. I tell them I can be in the lounge since I am eighteen today. They wish me a happy birthday and join us for a while. Mr. Charlie Kandel always seems like he knows a joke he's not telling. The casino bosses have the job of watching the dealers and the customers to make sure the money is safe. There are a lot of casino bosses but I only know the ones who work at night.

After the second show I change lickety-split from my furry, white-tailed costume to my white cocktail dress with sparkles, and hurry downstairs. Kathy and I sit in the lounge again and listen to Red Norvo play the xylophone. That xylophone zings and sighs, Red's hands fly, and

I listen and watch the bartenders and the cocktail waitresses at work. In no time it is two in the morning, yet I'm not ready to walk home. Sitting in the postcard section for ten days seems like a dream tonight.

We don't stop over at the Sahara to see Louis Prima and Keely Smith, like we usually do. We have a drama lesson tomorrow afternoon.

Mr. Benno Schneider, Kim Novak's drama coach at Columbia Studios, flies over from Hollywood every couple of weeks to teach us acting. For our first lesson we used short scripts that we read with partners, like an audition for a play. Not all of the Copa girls came to class, so it was almost like a private lesson. Our second class was improvisations. He gave us a scene and a character and we made up the dialogue. We did the same things in Mr. Pickett's classes.

Mr. Schneider is small, with thin, dark-gray hair. He looks right into your eyes when he talks. He doesn't like a Texas drawl. He can't understand it. We must work on diction. He says I have a Midwestern sound and not too much of a drawl, but my voice doesn't project. Mr. Pickett said the same thing. The sound of my voice doesn't match how tall I am. I am too tall to be squeaky and breathy. I have to stand up straight and learn to breathe correctly and have voice control.

Since Mr. Schneider is a famous acting coach, there is no cussing in class the way we do in the dressing room. We want to impress him, and maybe he will select one of us for a screen test. We're completely different in acting class than we are in our real life, on stage. Most of the Copa girls came dressed in warm clothes today, straight wool skirts, cashmere sweaters, little makeup and no false eyelashes. We are having cool weather, but I think it's to show this coach we can look serious. We are the same age as college drama students. Even though I wore blue jeans and a shirt, I hope he notices that I have been trained by a famous drama coach (well, famous in a Houston high school), and I am speaking up now and trying to be the best in class.

Nick the Greek, or Mr. Nicholas Dandolos, is a famous gambler who is staying at the Sands. Whenever he comes to Las Vegas, he is a big attraction because people like to watch him gamble. He likes company for dinner, so Kathy and I have been appointed his dates in the Garden Room for tonight. Our dinner will be free.

Nick the Greek is tall. His hair is dark with streaks of gray. He is very handsome but he must be in his sixties, at least. He's sophisticated like Cary Grant. Nick is from the island of Crete. When he was young like us he "studied philosophers like Plato and Socrates." He thinks we need to study the Greek philosophers also. I say, "I will, Mr. Dandolos." Poker is his favorite game; it's his main job. He's won a lot of money and lost a lot of money. I would hate to have that kind of work. He likes betting on horse racing too. I tell him that my Grandpa Johnson raced his quarter horses in Oklahoma and people bet on their favorites. It was just on old dirt roads, though, not on a track. I could listen to Mr. Dandolos all night because he tells us about the casinos in Monte Carlo and Venice and Paris and beautiful yachts and cruise ships. Kathy and I tell him we want to live in Paris and he said the nicest thing: "I am certain you will, Mademoiselles." I want to hug him for that, but we just shake hands in the nicest way and excuse ourselves to get ready for the midnight show.

Kathy has a date after the second show, so I walk home alone— alone except for the stars overhead, all the billboards announcing new performers, and then the shadow of the mountains in the far distance. I never get tired of their company. I think about Nick the Greek and Paris and working at the Sands and how I like walking home in the dark. I think about how Kathy and I love sitting in the lounge and listening to Morrie and his Violins, and talking about our plans. She wants to go back to college and study art, but I just want to stay here and meet famous people and dance two shows a night and have fun. I don't ever want to leave the Sands until I go to Paris.

Renne calls a rehearsal. She isn't changing our dance steps or any other basics, but she is going to have Kathy and the other showgirls walk around in a different direction. While Renne and Charlotte are working with the showgirls, someone walks in from the casino and into the Copa Room through the velvet curtains. He, Mr. Sammy Davis Jr., begins mimicking showgirls, holding out his arms, twisting and tiptoeing his way through the tables as if he were wearing high heels.

"Hey, Renne! How do I look? Charlotte! You're so lov-ee-ly today!"

He tosses his head, pouts his lips, bats his eyelashes. The whole grumpy, sleepy, shadowy Copa Room comes alive. We laugh. He does too. His small, wiry frame, his smile, his good-natured teasing lights up the rehearsal.

"Gloria! Arlene! Ladies, Ladies!" He hops on stage, looks at me quizzically. "What's your name?"

"Judy."

"JU-Day, JU-Day JU-Day," he says over and over in a big performance. He makes a fuss and teases me even more when I say I am from Texas. Big drawling TEXAS. He teases Renne too. He taps a few steps, laughs at himself. He tells us all that he is going to be at the Sands in a few weeks, that we will have a party, have some fun. And then he is tiptoeing through the tables, hands on his hips and being silly until he disappears through the curtains into the casino. Everyone acts like it was normal to have Sammy Davis walk through rehearsals, but it wasn't for me. He is the first big star that has asked my name.

•

Harold tells us, "Sammy has parties for Copa girls, stage hands, orchestra people. He has movies too, with popcorn and sodas. He's just like that because, a few years ago, Sammy, his father, and uncle—the Will Mastin Trio—weren't allowed in the casino and they were the headliners in the Copa Room." They couldn't stay at the Sands either. The Sands had a policy that people of color weren't allowed in the hotel. But Lena Horne and Marlene Dietrich and other big stars objected and marched on the Strip and finally that changed. So Sammy has an understanding of "unimportant" people and does these nice things for us.

7

Kathy and I have moved to a place behind the Colonial Hotel, several blocks off the strip. It's the cheapest studio apartment we could find between the Sands and the Desert Inn. We're right in the desert, too, with nothing separating us from the sand and the tumbleweeds blowing in from the mountains. I can't see the mountains unless I walk out into the dirt street and stretch.

We didn't want to move from San Francisco Street. We liked having a lot of room, but it costs too much. A lot of things have happened since we started getting our paychecks. I forgot about saving for the rent the first week we were paid—and the second week. Kathy, too. I bought a black velvet very tight skirt and a pink cashmere sweater with a lace collar and tiny rhinestone buttons. I bought a pair of high heels that are clear plastic with rhinestones on top, like movie stars wear. I have three new red lipsticks and another lipstick brush for my purse. I also bought a portable record player and joined the Columbia Record club. I joined the Classics Book Club, and in a few weeks I should get three books, Plato, Socrates, and Aristotle, which only cost a few dollars. I hope I see Nick the Greek again soon, so I can tell him I'll have books on philosophy like he suggested.

Kathy and I had fun shopping here and there and enjoying our paychecks until we realized we had quite a bit of money due for the October rent. So we gave our notice and turned in our keys and moved to a less expensive and smaller place. For six weeks we have passed a sign advertising cheap rooms at the Country Club Apartments. We had no problem getting the room since it's so crummy: a motel set in the middle of nowhere, just mesquite bushes and sand blowing, with no one around until you walk up to the Strip.

I will miss our San Francisco Street home, the long walk up and down the Strip each day and night, stopping off at the Stardust to see Leilani Kelly and her Polynesian dancers, or going over to see Keely Smith and Louis Prima at the Sahara. Now, no more perch at the top of my steps to watch the stars slowing fading when night turns to morning.

Now that I am a dancer in Las Vegas and have made love with Joky, I didn't think I'd be going to a slumber party. But last night Gloria had a sleepover for all the Copa girls: Arlene, Linda, Coralyn, Joyce, Collette, Jackie, Charlotte, Joan, Kathy, and me. At 2 a.m., right when we got off work, four of us jammed into a car to go to Gloria's.

It was sort of a grown-up slumber party, not like the one I'd been to in high school, where we walked up and down the streets at 3 a.m. in our shorty pajamas. It's because we're older and more serious. I'm eighteen; Kathy, Linda, and Colette are twenty; Joan, Joyce, and Arlene are a little older; and Charlotte is twenty-seven and has two kids. We stayed inside, and sat around Gloria's coffee table and had popcorn and Cokes and wine, and everyone told their own stories, just like my family does.

Arlene told us that Frank Sinatra called her about a month ago to see how she was doing, and she got his new album, *Only the Lonely*, in the mail the other day. I guess when Arlene listens to it she feels pretty alone. She felt important being his girlfriend and met a lot of famous people and now, that's over. But she can't help seeing pictures of him in the newspaper or the magazines, with each new girlfriend. I think Arlene is lots prettier than Juliet Prowse anyway. We agree that Mr. Sinatra probably sings "Angel Eyes" to every girl he dates.

Charlotte said she saw Frank (she calls him Frank) and Ava Gardner at the Sands a few years ago. They were walking around the pool arm in arm. She said there's no one like Ava. I said Ava was beautiful in *Show Boat* with hardly any makeup on. And Charlotte said Ava didn't have to wear makeup, that her skin is beautiful, her eyes as green as can be, and she is slender. We couldn't decide which movie she was best in, *Show Boat* or *Mogambo* or *The Sun Also Rises*. I think it's hard to decide about her acting when her face is what you notice most of all.

While we were talking about Ava, I forgot all about Arlene and how sad she was. She must feel about Frank how he felt about Ava once.

Coralyn is dating a cute guy named Mickey Callan, who is trying to break into the movies. He's filming a western now, and he did star as Riff in *West Side Story* on Broadway. Coralyn should be a movie star too. She has a face like Virginia Mayo and has been very good in our acting classes. We talk about how we all want to be movie stars and hope Mr. Benno Schneider gives us a chance to take screen tests. He probably can't tell yet who is a good actress, since we've only had a few classes. I think I'm pretty good.

Charlotte has been performing since she was a little kid, starting out dancing in shows at the Community Opera House in St. Louis. When she was old enough, she headed to Broadway and found a place to stay at the Capitol Hotel, a residence for show business girls across the street from Madison Square Garden. She got a job right away at a famous New York City nightclub, the Latin Quarter, which was a good thing since she had only forty dollars when she left St. Louis. She told us the most exciting job she had was as a dancer in Mike Todd's *Peep Show*. It was a honest-to-goodness Broadway musical that opened at the Winter Garden in June of 1950 and ran nine months. Charlotte said there is nothing like performing on Broadway. She can't believe Mike Todd is dead. It's all we have read about for months, about how his plane crashed and Elizabeth Taylor is a widow now with her little baby. It's just awful. For some reason you think famous people don't die, or can't die, like ordinary people do.

Linda mentioned that when the weather is good, Al Freeman is going to take us waterskiing on Lake Mead. I told everyone how awful I am at water skiing and that I would be scared to death to go, since Lake Mead is really deep. I remembered, then, a true family tragedy that happened when Hoover Dam was being built. I told the girls about Grandma Lee's youngest brother, John, who was killed working on the dam. He fell out the back of a pickup truck that was bringing workers home after their shift. The truck behind them couldn't stop in time and he was run over. It was a terrible time for Grandma Lee. John's widow needed Grandma Lee to come to Hoover Dam to testify to the insurance company so she could collect a little money. Grandma Lee scraped up enough cash to get there. Grandma said her brother and his wife barely made ends meet, even though he was a laborer and his wife ran a small whorehouse. I didn't know if I should tell that part, but it was the real story. John's widow used the insurance money to improve the whorehouse, which made some of our family unhappy. But not Grandma Lee. She knew how tough times could get.

Grandma Lee grew up around Collinsville, Oklahoma, across the Caney River from Will Roger's family. Will Rogers had a love for travel in airplanes, did rope tricks, made jokes about politicians and the government, and he was a Cherokee. He died in Alaska in a plane crash.

I fell asleep in Gloria's living room, remembering family stories of how people died, and of the reunions in Collinsville, with Grandma's cousins, the Victorys, the Barnetts, and the Davises. I couldn't ever remember all the names. But I remember the green trees, a forest it seemed, the men and their dark braids, the women with husky voices, laughing, spreading food over long rough tables: fried chicken, potato salad, and good sweet iced tea or lemonade and sometimes Grapette in tubs of cold water. Grandma Lee's cousins owned the farm. We kids played tag for hours, fell asleep on spread blankets listening to ghost stories, swatting mosquitoes, watching fireflies sending light signals among the tall trees.

From Cora Lee Linn's memorabilia, Hoover Dam

8

Arlene, Joyce, Kathy, and I walk into the lounge after the first show. It is empty except for one table where Mr. Entratter and Mr. Gary Cooper are sitting together, having drinks, and we are invited to sit with them. I keep pinching myself and trying not to stare at Mr. High Noon himself. Mr. Cooper is too handsome, just like in the movies, but friendly as can be, like Sammy Davis Jr.

Mr. Cooper and Miss Rita Hayworth are filming a western movie called *They Came to Cordura* not far from here.

Mr. Cooper tells us, "Rita isn't playing a glamour girl," and he thinks "she is terrific in the part." He says, "I'm plain worn out from running and jumping around," and he is glad to be out of the desert and into his nice room at the Sands. They began filming in another state, but the weather was so bad they moved the whole thing to Nevada.

Mickey Callan, Coralyn's boyfriend, is also in the movie, and Mr. Cooper assures us that Mickey Callan is a fine young actor. My mind can't settle down while I listen to Mr. Cooper's comments, as if we are friends. I nod at his words, astonished at his famous face. This isn't normal. At the same moment I am thinking of Papa Johnson, who reads every western story there is, and I have to write him about meeting Mr. Cooper. And that gets me to thinking of the many times I watched Papa in the Tryon Café, shaking his tobacco out of the little string cloth bag into the thin slip of paper, rolling it back and forth a few times, then licking spit on the rolled-up ready-to-go cigarette, and just that second, I wonder, what is real? Sitting here in this lounge with a movie star or the picture in my head of Papa at the Café, rolling a cigarette one-handed?

Even though it is strange and confusing sitting across from him, Mr. Cooper sure isn't stuck-up. When we excuse ourselves to go back on stage for the second show, Mr. Cooper stands up. That's how polite he is. Two hours later, when we are back in the lounge again, we spot him strolling out of the Garden Room, trailing behind his wife, Rocky, and his daughter, who is our age. He could have walked right by us without an acknowledgement and we wouldn't have thought a thing about it, but instead, he turns his head and winks at us before going into the casino with his family.

Later, I wish I had asked Mr. Cooper if he reads Zane Grey like Papa does. I hope the movie theatre in Tryon is back working again so Papa can see Gary Cooper's new movie. The last time we were in Tryon and got to go to a cowboy movie on a Friday night, smoke came out of the projection room and we had to leave before the bad guys got caught.

Wedding photo of my grandparents, Bill and Winnie Johnson, 1915.

9

I have sad news…for me. Kathy is moving to Hollywood! She's tired of walking around the stage in the mink coat and the sequined dress that doesn't fit. She says she's ready for a change, and her new friends that worked as extras in *South Pacific* say she will find plenty of work. Everybody is surprised and especially me. Kathy isn't afraid of moving since she can stay in an apartment with one of Joyce's friends until she finds her own place. But I like Las Vegas and I am happy my mom found me this job.

Kathy says she might take classes at UCLA and also find out about work in costumes and makeup. She does have a hundred-dollar bill to take with her. I know that. I have one too.

That's because one night Arlene hurried into the Garden Room and motioned for us to come to the Lounge. She pointed to where several of the girls were sitting with a loud, boisterous man and said, "He's giving away hundred-dollar bills!" That sounded crazy to me, but it was true. He was hailing every person who came by, mumbling nonsense, swaying in his chair, waving hundred-dollar bills that were scattered over the table, floating to the floor. "Here you go, ladies," he said and handed us each a hundred-dollar bill. Whether it was right or wrong, we wanted the money, and we kept it.

We went to the bank the next day and paid for a safety deposit box to keep our money in. It was a bright, sunny, windy day. A loose sheet of newspaper was dipping and flying like a kite, up and over our heads. I had the bill in my hand and the wind came along and grabbed it, and it skipped down the sidewalk. I chased that bill for several minutes before I caught it high up in the air. Kathy and I laughed so hard we were breathless when we got to the bank.

I've been telling Kathy I'll be just fine on my own, and she has to write to me as soon as she finds a place. Mr. Entratter said Mr. Benno Schneider thinks I should have a screen test, so maybe I will get to see her in Hollywood someday. She leaves on the bus in three days. Kathy gave me her beautiful green velvet cocktail dress with the scooped neck and full skirt. I have always admired it. She says she won't need it now.

10

Miss Judy Garland begins her two-week engagement here at the Sands this evening, and everything is topsy-turvy in preparation for her show. New curtains have been rigged to screen Miss Garland's exits and entrances. Harold and Pauline have both warned us several times there is to be no talking backstage or outside of our dressing room. No visiting with stage hands before or after our number. Everyone seems snappier, walking stiffly and putting on their very best manners. No one can slip into the back of the Copa Room to watch the show—no one—don't even ask. Harold has been very firm and very nervous. We can't even watch from backstage. No watching her show. Period.

It's the first time Miss Garland has ever played at the Sands, so no one knows her very well. Last year when she came to Las Vegas, she played next door at the Flamingo. She travels all over the United States singing, and even in Europe. Harold says that she has been working so hard she has a sore throat that won't go away. She's been married three times and has three little kids to take care of too. Mom says no one can sing like Judy Garland.

Frank Sinatra is bringing half of Hollywood here for Miss Garland's opening. I like that he's doing this for her. I think he's doing it because he's struggled with his career like Miss Garland, and he wants to make her feel better. They both have been sad over their marriages too—sad over someone leaving them. You have to have friends when bad things happen to you, or you might just stay sad for way too long. I was thinking about all this after Harold told us about not causing any noise or anything that might bother Miss Garland backstage. But tonight I will walk up and down the same steps Miss Judy Garland does, and I am going to be on the same stage as she is, and our dressing room probably isn't fifty feet from Judy Garland's. It's unbelievable, but true.

I could have reached down and touched Debbie Reynolds. Or Frank Sinatra. Or Mr. and Mrs. Dean Martin. Louella Parsons was sitting right in front of me. And Gary Cooper! Oh my god. Right in front of me, first table, center, all of them. And David Niven.

Mr. Sinatra did exactly what he said he would do. He brought all the big stars in for Miss Garland's opening night. I can see why everyone was nervous. If I were Miss Garland, I would be nervous too. The stage hands and the musicians, the waiters, just everyone was all over themselves. I didn't get to see any of it, but Harold told us she had as big an opening as he's ever seen here in Las Vegas. Harold said at the end of her show she asked Dean Martin and Frank Sinatra to come up on stage and sing with her, and they did, for almost twenty minutes. Dean Martin was being silly and dancing and kicking his legs up, and Mr. Sinatra had a good time too. The Copa Room was sold out, every table, every chair, snug up against the walls, all six hundred spaces.

I've been dancing here for over a month, and tonight was the best. The only way it could have been better would be if Mom could have been here. Mom never thought when she named me after Judy Garland that I would be in a show with her.

I think that when Miss Garland sings, her heart comes flying out of her voice with every song.

Inside my head I keep hearing her singing, "clang clang clang went the trolley…" That's how it was here at the Sands tonight: clanging! And my heart keeps skipping beats.

Every night I beg Rudy, the maître d', to please, please, please, let me sit or stand in the back of the Copa Room to see Judy Garland's show. Every night he's said, "NO. Come back later." I told him I had to see her perform; I was named after Judy Garland! He laughed. He said so were thousands of other girls. And I said, "But they don't work here like me."

"Okay. After the midnight show, change quickly, before the second act is over. Be here before her music begins."

I was. I flew after our number, out of my costume, mesh hose, off with the earrings and necklace, pins and hat off my head, hung everything up, wiggled into my own hose, my dress, high heels in hand, and flew down the stairs, out the side door, into the casino, through the slot machine aisles, and over to the Copa Room. Second act were taking their bows.

Rudy escorted me through the velvet curtains. Threatened me: "Don't move, don't breathe, don't get out of the shadows." It seemed as if the audience heard him too. They were quiet, hushed. No loud talking or laughing or drinks clinking. Just cigarette smoke hanging in the air, waiting.

She walked out into the light, through her tunnel of curtains backstage. She walked like the Tin Man, stiff. Her hair wasn't nice, too short and choppy. Her face was puffy, swollen, like she had been crying. I thought her makeup was bad too. She looked very small, and sad, tired. She said "Good evening" or something and people sort of laughed and she smiled and people started clapping, then cheering, and I don't know why but I had a big burn in my throat and my eyes stung and then Miss Garland started singing. She just started singing like her old self. We all started breathing together, and Miss Garland sang songs from her movies. Her voice tremulous, powerful, clear. She smiled at us while she walked awkwardly around the stage. Then she leaned over her microphone to sing to the people ringside, and I felt tears running down my face and I didn't move once. When Miss Garland sings a song, whether a happy or a sad song, I feel a longing in me, something lonesome, like when I am at the farm and I'm happy to be there, but I know I will have to leave.

This evening, about seven minutes before our show, I scrambled out of the dressing room to run into our bathroom and I nearly knocked Miss Garland right off her feet. She was in her bathrobe, going into our restroom. I didn't realize it was her right away because she wasn't supposed to be there. Everything has been arranged so no one will disturb her, so why was she was about to go into our bathroom? I felt very big and tall next to her. She is very small.

"Oh Miss Garland," I said. "I'm so sorry. Excuse me."

She just shook her head a little and laughed.

"Please, Miss Garland, go right in."

"Oh, no, honey," she said softly. "You go on stage in a few minutes. You first."

I went inside. I closed the bathroom door. The door looked strange, mud green. I realized I had almost stepped on Miss Judy Garland. Was I in the right bathroom? Yes. Yes, I was. I washed my hands, got back outside. She was still there.

"Miss Garland, my name is Judy. My mother named me after you."

She smiled. She said something.

"My mother loves to hear you sing. I do too."

"Thank you, dear. Tell your mother thank you."

I stepped out of her way. She went into our bathroom and I went into our dressing room and said to the girls, "Judy Garland is in our bathroom," but no one looked up. They were all busy, pinning headdresses, putting on high heels, talking. The dressing room was very bright. I got my costume off the hanger and stepped into my rhinestones and fluffy tail, slipped into my high heels, pinned on my furry white headdress, put my muff on my right arm, checked my lip gloss and made sure my seams weren't twisted. I told myself that as soon as we finished our number I was going to call my mom.

Frank Sinatra, Dean Martin, Sammy Davis Jr., Joey Bishop, and Peter Lawford are all in the lounge, in the casino, on stage in the Copa Room. The whole hotel is crazy and it's made me nervous. I would rather have stayed up in the dressing room between shows until everything is back to normal, but our job is to put on a nice cocktail dress and sit around in the lounge or the Garden Room, or just walk around the casino after each performance. Just as I am walking past the Lounge toward the Garden Room I notice Mr. Entratter motioning me to sit down. I know I look dumbstruck, but Mr. Entratter just smiles and gestures again for me to sit down right next to Mr. Sinatra, who is at the head of several tables that have been pushed together. I don't want to sit there because Mr. Sinatra is so famous he scares me, and I feel tongue-tied, can't breathe, but I sit down and smile politely.

Mr. Sinatra's face is five or six inches from mine, but he leans in closer. I feel my face get red. His eyes are really blue, just like all the magazines say. For a brief, very brief, second, I think of him in *High Society,* and I want to say how much I liked him in that movie, but he leans even closer and barely moving his mouth he says, "Baby, when you got a bod like that you odda pass it around as much as possible."

I suck in my breath and hold it. I keep looking at him thinking, that isn't nice. I don't answer. I notice he looks a little old, that there are lines in his cheeks. He asks me, "How old are you?" He says this in a nice voice, not at all like how he sounded before. I tell him I'm eighteen.

He jerks his head around and looks up at Mr. Entratter, who is standing on the other side of the table talking to Peter Lawford. "Hey, Jack, Jack," he calls out. "This gal odda be in college. She's the same age as my daughter. Jack, did you hear me? She odda be in college."

During the last days of her engagement, Miss Garland got sick and couldn't work. Now Sammy Davis Jr. and the Will Mastin Trio are taking her place. Mr. Davis goes around smiling, laughing, joking, and being nice to everyone. He's just the opposite of Mr. Lewis, who was strictly business all the time and never funny unless he was on stage. Mr. Davis, though, is always the same, funny and kind. I think Sammy Davis Jr. could walk on stage without ever rehearsing, with no orchestra, and put on a show that makes you cry, and sing, and laugh and dance. There's no difference in his personality, on stage or off. He carries all his sad feelings right on stage or backstage when he's joking with us, right before we go on stage, and then he acts like a magician, and *poof*! a little tap step, and like that he's made you happy.

Charlotte and I have coffee and pie together in the Garden Room between shows. She hopes Mr. Entratter lets her off to go home for Christmas and see her kids in Missouri. Arlene joins us. She says she's feeling sad and doesn't know why. I know why I feel down.

The first night I sat in the lounge without Kathy, I looked around and missed her. Neither one of us liked having a drink and always moved to the Garden Room if the lounge was too noisy. We liked sitting in the restaurant, where it was quiet. She has been in Hollywood over a week. She hasn't written me yet.

11

Tonight we were all sitting in the lounge with Mr. Martin and then one by one, Charlotte and Gloria and Collette left, then even the pit bosses, Charlie and Eric, went home. It was 4 a.m. and the lounge was empty. Security guards I'd never seen before were on duty. A few people were holding drinks, standing at a nearby craps table. Mr. Martin and I kept talking.

A fan wandered over and asked Mr. Martin to autograph a napkin and a Sands place card. He responded, as always, "With pleasure." I liked listening to the casino sounds and to Mr. Martin talking casually to me as if I were a friend. I asked him questions about working with Mr. Lewis and it almost felt natural when I looked at him and he twisted his drink glass around in his hands. He offered to take me home. "Oh no," I said right away. "It's just a short walk." But he insisted.

So Dean Martin drove me home in his sports car. We had been in the lounge for nearly three hours, and suddenly we were sitting together in his car. It was unbelievable for me, but he sang a little of "That's Amore," and he made me laugh because he made silly faces while he was singing. As we pulled up in the dark to my motel room, I saw that it looked like a rundown farm shed. He leaned over and pecked me on the cheek before I got out, and observed that it was a pretty crummy-looking place to live. I agreed and remembered to say, "Thank you for the ride home."

Inside my apartment, I put on my scratchy waltzes I ordered from the Record Club, opened the door carefully to see if any sun was pushing light over the mountains, and could hardly believe that Dean Martin had said to me, right in the space outside my door, "Good night, Judy." That he had opened his car door for me. That he had kissed my cheek. That he had acted silly in the car and sang to me. Already it seems impossible, and I knew I wouldn't walk into the dressing room and tell the girls that Dean Martin had taken me home. They would tease me. When I walk into the dressing room and everyone is busy applying Albolene cold cream to their faces, and hair curlers are spilling everywhere, I'll be quiet. I'll sit down and listen to the usual "fuck you" and "move over" and joking that goes on every night, but I'll feel different. I'll put on my eyelashes, mascara, lip liner, lipstick, and lip gloss and hope I get to visit with Dean Martin again.

We have started rehearsals for our new show with Nat King Cole, which opens November 15. We have two numbers to learn and I don't like either one of them. For one, because I have "good balance," according to Renne, I walk on a wooden circus ball. It is about two feet high, very heavy and cumbersome to work on. Harold, or someone backstage, has to help me get up on it each day. I find my balance, step carefully backwards or forwards to move the ball across stage, or downstage, keep my arms gracefully relaxed, watch where I am going with a forced smile, and all the while I'm thinking, I don't like this.

There are good things, though. Dean Martin has driven me home to my shed in the desert three nights in a row. He sings in the car; I ask for another verse. I want to reach over and touch his face to make sure he's real, but I never do. As soon as we get to the Country Club "apartments," I jump out of the car, feeling a little bit like Cinderella. I think if he were just a plain person, but funny and with his same personality, I would like him just as much. It is exciting being with him because he's famous, but I think deep down he might just be ordinary, like I am.

Last night I went to dinner with him at the Villa d'Este and I think we both felt the same way about the whole thing. First, Mr. Entratter said Dean had to go to the dinner, and then I was invited by Dean, and I wasn't even hungry.

The restaurant had dim lights. I could barely see my way and we were escorted to a secluded alcove with a long table where six or seven older, unfriendly men sat talking. Unfriendly, or no manners, because they barely acknowledged Dean, and certainly not me. Sometimes they didn't speak English. Said things to each other I didn't understand at all. Worse was how nervous Mr. Entratter appeared and he barely sat down the whole time. He poured water or wine or something from a pitcher. He ordered more bread or cheese and pasta and he was jumpy, waiting on those guys.

Dean and I sat at the end of the table. Dean leaned his chair way back, had a toothpick he fiddled with. I could only study the wall facing me, look pleasant, pick at a cheese plate, drink a Coke, and not understand a word anyone said. I had a strong feeling that Mr. Entratter was not the boss in this room.

We weren't there an hour when Dean said, in his friendly, slow-going way that the two of us needed to get back to the Sands and get ready for the midnight show. No one seemed to care, just nodded. We made our way through the restaurant and outside to the cold night air and into the little sports car and back down the strip.

Dean never said anything, and I sure don't know why we were there.

I did something that made no sense. Dean never asked me to go to his room. But something inside of me, a small curiosity that I didn't understand, led me there. We walked through the casino into the cool morning air and around the swimming pool. At any time I could have said, "I'll go on home," and he would have said, "Okay." I should have done it, because the minute we went inside his suite, we weren't the same. I didn't know what to do. We were only friends, had never kissed on the lips. I had never felt compelled to touch his mouth with my fingers or cover his face with kisses. I was happy sitting in the lounge, talking, or driving home in his car with him singing.

He was fumbling too. He asked, "Do you want to sleep in the front bedroom?" I nodded. "Sure." He walked down to his room and came back with a silky pajama top. I took it and pretended we were just having a slumber party and then he asked if I was alright and I said yes, sure, I'm fine and we hugged. I liked being held. I wanted to have a boyfriend and to feel warm and mushy with someone's arms around me. Mr. Martin has a beautiful, sad face. He went back down the hallway to his room, alone.

I took off my clothes, placed them neatly on a chair, which was not my usual way, put on the pajama top, and got into bed, already wondering how I would leave in the morning. Or should I leave now in the dark? No one would know me anyway. And was I really going to sleep in Dean Martin's front bedroom? I needed a book or magazine to read for a while before I went to sleep. If I could get to sleep. I wished I were back in my apartment playing records. I looked down the hallway towards Dean's room and thought about going there.

In a few minutes, he came walking down the hallway.

"I can't sleep. I have a…I can't sleep. May I sleep with you?" He came into my room just like I wanted him to. "Is it alright?" he asked, his voice small, polite. The words fell on me as if he were singing, as if he were asking me for a simple favor. I said, "Yes," very politely. He slid under the covers, smooth, like his walk, like his smile, as if he didn't want to offend me by making the slightest mistake.

True, I wasn't breathing. I was in bed with someone who was practically a stranger. It wasn't like me to be so lifeless, so still. It wasn't fun, like being with Joky.

This lying in a bed, staring at the ceiling, saying yes to a slow moving body edging on top of me, gently parting my legs, caressing me carefully, with no passion on my part, no goose bumps, no limp knees, no weak, trembling mouth, was a mystery.

Sex with the man inside me wasn't anything like being slippery naked in the front seat of an old souped-up car after a prom, with my formal flung in the back seat, with hose and girdle and strapless bra in a tangled mess, and me, breathless. Gene touching me, his hand slowly moving across my body, felt a hundred times better than this. Why was I in this bed?

It seemed impolite to just lie there and keep my arms around him without feeling, but I couldn't think of what to pretend to do. I was conscious of every small noise, the light down the hall, my clothes over the chair, the sheet sliding off his back, his eyes looking old, his face beautiful. That he was Dean Martin. I had created this. I had wanted to be his girlfriend, to be sexy. I don't know what made me do this.

When the sex was over, he was quiet. I had a little stinging, uncomfortable feeling in my private part, and in my head too. I felt like crying. All I could think of was that I was ready to run all the way back to my apartment in the moonlight. More than anything I knew that I had ruined sitting around with Dean and talking about small things. I told him I might walk home if I couldn't fall asleep. He pushed my hair back from my forehead. I had to bite my tongue so I wouldn't cry like a silly girl.

The next day I was sick and halfway crazy for going to bed with Dean Martin. It was wrong. Especially when I saw his kids running backstage like they did most weekends. And then I saw him chatting with Charlotte in the casino, and I hoped he didn't tell her that I was with him. Everything was fun with Dean Martin until I went to his room. And now I know what I really wanted was a friend to talk to, like Kathy. I was wrong when I said I would be fine if she moved to Hollywood. I'm not okay. I need to talk to her, but there is no phone at her new apartment. If she had been here we would have walked home together, and we would have talked to Dean with the rest of the girls and this wouldn't have happened.

12

Since that night with Dean, I go right downstairs after our number is over. I sit at a table like we are supposed to, stay close to Charlotte or Gloria and Collette. When the crowd leaves the Copa Room after Dean's performance, I scoot around the blackjack tables and, hoping no one will notice, hurry up to the dressing room to read. I've decided I don't like the lounge or the Garden Room without Kathy, and I can't keep working here forever. And what's more, I don't know anything about being like Ava Gardner either. I was so silly last summer. I try to read in my book about Plato but I fall asleep after a few paragraphs. Still, I want to know about important ideas and find out why Nick the Greek thinks we should study philosophy like he did. Right now, I need to figure out why I keep doing things that don't make sense.

Just yesterday, I bought a red sports car, stick shift, that I can't drive. I didn't drive it since I only put a three-hundred dollar down payment on it and have to save another six hundred till it's mine. I don't know why I did that, just walking down the street after rehearsals and seeing a car for nine hundred dollars and buying it. Maybe because I miss my car. Or I liked Dean's sports car. Or because the other night, very cold, walking home at two in the morning, I was scared when I turned off the Strip to walk to my apartment. There are no street lights, and dashing through the dark, forgetting there was no outside light on my door, frantically searching for the key, unlocking the door, opening, entering, slamming the door, turning the latch, all in one breath, I thought that if I had a car, I wouldn't be afraid.

A week before the opening with Nat King Cole I fall from the wooden circus ball during rehearsals and fracture my wrist. Gloria rushes me to her doctor but has to go back to rehearsals. The doctor puts the smallest cast on for me, so I can work. I rest in the afternoon but my wrist hurts a lot and I don't know if that is the reason I cry so much, or because so much has happened. The Texas Copa girls are so sweet and they change their muffs to their left hand so I can go on stage for the 8:15 show. I put on two layers of pancake makeup but my red face and puffy eyes are hard to disguise. We all go out on stage and sing "Gimme a Little Kiss, Won't you huh?" but at the end I feel tears rolling from my eyes and I know I don't look right. Harold meets me as we are coming off stage, said the light man calls down and says I looked awful. Why is my face all streaked? And what in the hell is going on anyway?

Al Freeman called my mom, said she had to come get me. I wouldn't be able to work for weeks with my cast on, and I should be at home, instead of living by myself in Las Vegas.

Mother flew out to help pack my cocktail dresses, portable record player, and three records from the Columbia Record Club, my philosophy books from Doubleday Book Club, and my new soft, pink lace and cashmere sweater. Mr. Entratter hugged us and assured me, and my mother, that I could come back to dance at the Sands whenever I finished college. He reminded us of Mr. Sinatra's suggestion, that I needed to be in college, that I was the same age as his daughter Nancy. The pain in my wrist throbbed, spread into my heart, made my brain soggy, and my eyes watered. But the dreams of being in Paris with Kathy were rolled up tight in the green velvet dress she had given me, packed carefully in my Samsonite luggage, my high school graduation present from Mom and Dad.

My seat is next to the window, the clouds, the sky. I look at the ridges and cliffs below me. I am sad to leave the mountains. I am sorry about missing Mr. Nat King Cole's opening, but I didn't like the new costumes, I didn't like working on the circus ball, and I couldn't tap either. Working at the Sands wasn't the same after Kathy left. No talking about our boyfriends, following a tumbleweed and being silly, and saying, "Oh my gosh, look at the stars tonight."

Sands Copa Room, 1958. Image courtesy of UNLV Special Archives
From left to right: Gloria, Coralynn, Judy, Linda, and Kathy

13
Houston

In Houston I creep around like I did four months ago, searching for a plan. I have a pain that causes me to sleep too much. The more I sleep, the more I wake up feeling sad and lost in this bedroom. Mother asks day after day, when do I think I might get up?

As weeks passed, my wrist and psyche healing at the same painfully slow pace (much to my parents' dismay), I have letters and notes from Charlotte and the Copa girls. I stop sniffling. I sit up in bed and begin conversations with my sisters that I missed so much. My sister Beth makes me laugh when she pats my cheek. Janet holds my hand and sits with me.

At last, Kathy writes to me from Hollywood. "Please call and maybe we should join the USO," and "Perhaps someday, we'll find what we are searching for." She writes, "You are my dearest friend." Everything she says makes me cry and feel better at the same time. She is thinking of returning to Southern Methodist University. She doesn't know that Mr. Entratter said I must have a college degree before I can work at the Sands again. And because of that, I agree to enroll in Central State College in Edmond, Oklahoma. It is the college my father graduated from, and the town I know well from visiting my Grandma Lee and Grandpa Jess many times a year.

Anyway, I had to go somewhere because in the three months I'd been in Las Vegas, everyone and everything at home had changed. Linda takes my car to school and does the shopping and drives Janet and Beth where they need to be. Everything here goes on without me. And it should, because hours go by and I am in Las Vegas watching rehearsals, or walking down the Strip in the moonlight, or by myself in my ramshackle motel room trying to understand *Plato;* other times I am in Oklahoma at my grandparents farm—then I suddenly arrive back here in this strange island, my old bedroom. I am not independent like I was three weeks ago, I have no one to talk to about the strange things that happened to me in Las Vegas, and for sure, I don't want to spend the rest of my days huddling in this room trying to figure life out.

I have to do what everyone wants me to do: go to college.

The holidays revive me. I receive a Christmas card from Collette. I am surprised by the friendly greeting from Joky, the Italian boy I encountered months ago. How did he find my address? With each new card and letter, I say to myself, See? You were there.

"Smile!"

14
January 1959
Oklahoma

I leave Houston on the Atchison, Topeka and Santa Fe. The rattle and music of the train galloping along its train tracks, the monotony and silent passing of miles, and having nothing to do but sit by myself is good. I lean my forehead on the cold windowpane, watch fences, pastures, and Texas fly by. I remember a conversation about Oklahoma, *Ok La Ho Ma*. And my heart beats faster when I see that the Red River swirls and flows beneath our train. Soon enough, I see hints of the Arbuckle Mountains and know that Turner Falls is ahead. I'm only hours away from Edmond and Central State College, and from there another hour to Tryon and my grandparents' farm.

A few years ago, Grandma Lee and Grandpa owned two bars and one restaurant in Edmond. They were busy during the day and night. That meant that when Linda and I and my cousin Donnie visited, we were on our own after Grandma Lee cooked our breakfast: biscuits, eggs, ham, and gravy. We played like gymnasts on the bars in Stephenson Park a short block away. We took pictures with our Brownie camera at the Statue of Liberty on Broadway, walked to Grandma's café for lunch, and went swimming in the afternoon back at the park. In the evening we sat in the movies. We screamed through *Bride of Frankenstein* three times a night for five days. Later it was *Cat People*, a terrifying movie where the cat's paw under the door gave us shivers.

Dad graduated from Central in 1942. Mom took classes, too, but she had me and her waitress job besides. She bundled me up and sat me at a booth while she waited tables. She often told that story of how she worked so Dad could finish school to impress on me the importance of a college degree. She doesn't have to worry about me finishing school. I will work and study and earn a degree and get back to the Sands. Kathy and I have our plans.

Throughout January I feel weak and breathless, still recovering from the fall from the wooden circus ball and struggling with the new routine of college life. Many times a day, rushing and stumbling up the three flights of stairs to my room, 342 Murdaugh Hall, to find a gym uniform or a book, I laugh at my clumsiness, my confusion. The months in Las Vegas seem simple now. Only late at night do I have time to wonder where Charlotte, or Kathy, might be.

If not for the kindness of my perfect new roommate, Sandy, and my new friend Karen, from Chicago, I would never make it through my first tentative weeks as a freshman. Sandy and Karen help me find Monday, Wednesday, and Friday classes. Sandy and Karen guide me to Tuesday-Thursday classes. During the first week, they even escort me to the cafeteria. Mr. Hicks, my drama teacher, says on the first day of class that I will be an extra in *Taming of the Shrew* for their final week of production. I need to be in rehearsal. That relieves Sandy, she with the sparkling eyes behind her glasses, her glossy short brown hair with bangs, her pursed lips always suppressing laughter, and her practical Missouri ways. Also relieved is curly-sandy-haired Karen with her Chicago fast-talking ways and easy bursts of laughter. For a few hours each night I am delivered into the world of actors, a director, the drama department.

Slowly, the routine of dressing, rules, cafeteria hours, notebooks, schedules, names, art supplies, leotards and shoes for modern dance, room keys, and most of all, timeliness, becomes familiar. Once or twice, after listening to the rules, signing in and out of the dorm, I recall my forlorn and solitary studio apartment at Country Club Estates, obscured by sand and tumbleweed, where I came and went at any hour. At least here in the dorm I am safe from my own self, and for a while I have no bother of a boyfriend, nor the stress of one.

There are, however, many stories of sex, after hours in the dorm. Girls I barely know keep us entertained with outrageous talk. Sex at a local drug store. Really? On the counter? No, on the twirling stool. Was he seated? Or was she? And then they did it? How? Those few times, before everyone is loaded with homework, I laugh until I ache. Now I am the audience with mouth and eyes wide open with envy as they tell about climbing down the fire escape outside the dorm windows to meet their boyfriends.

My dorm sisters are not impressed at all when I say I'm from Oklahoma, grew up in Dewey and Bartlesville, and my grandparents own a farm in Tryon. The fact that my uncles and a cousin graduated from Edmond High School doesn't interest them, nor do they care that I have relatives in their home towns of Tahlequah, Cushing, Stroud, Tryon, and Pawhuska. They care little for my family stories.

My best stories, of course, are about being on stage with Judy Garland, Jerry Lewis, and Sammy Davis. But as I describe the Copa Room, or the dressing room, my friends Kathy, Charlotte, and Gloria, the beautiful dancer Collette, all of that seems like make-believe. Less than two months ago I was lonely in my apartment and in daily rehearsals for Nat King Cole's opening. Tonight, I am surrounded by rambunctious girls who keep me laughing, and I love their energy.

But after midnight, in this silent dorm, I remember walking down the Strip at two-thirty in the morning with a dream of living in Paris, and that is not make-believe.

Opening night Sept. 3,1958, Jerry Lewis show

15

Taming of the Shrew is filmed in a large studio with TV cameras rolling around the floor, finding the best shots. Billie Dee plays Kate, and each night I hear her swagger and grovel and coo. Kate is spunky and clever, but in the end she does marry.

The boys in the cast are growing beards for this play and the next, *Oedipus Rex*. Some have full beards, some thin mustaches and goatees, stubbly patches that they hope will shape into something acceptable. When greeting each other in the Student Union, they use Shakespearean-sounding lines. "Out, you rogue!" they say when you need a seat at a table, or a loud "You whoreson, beetle-headed, flap-eared knave!" I'm grateful to Mr. Hicks for adding me to the townspeople. No matter how my mind wanders while we townspeople pretend our conversations, I keep hearing Shakespeare's words.

The few times we have ended early in the evening, some of us walk into town to the Wide Awake Café and have coffee or Cokes and maybe a grilled cheese sandwich to share, then hurry back to the dorm before we are locked out at midnight.

Mom asks, in a letter, if I am enjoying the cold Oklahoma weather. I am. No matter how lazy I am in the mornings, the instant I walk outside the dorm and cold air rushes my face and sucks the breath out of me and my nose turns bright red, I wake up. By the time I get to class, my head has cleared, I'm breathing hard, and I feel good no matter how late I stayed up. So Mom, I do like the snow and cold and, yes, I will watch out for the first lilac bush in bloom and call you like you asked.

Mother will be thirty-nine in July. My baby sister Beth will be five in April, I will be nineteen in September, and Linda and Janet are in the middle. If I were Mom with four kids of all ages, I'd be crazy. It's a wonder she can remember about lilacs blooming in the early spring in Oklahoma. But maybe it's the memory of fragrance and color that keeps her sane.

She writes that Mr. Pickett, now Linda's drama teacher at Bellaire, cast Linda as a model in his spring musical, *Girl Crazy.* She will wear a floor-length, baby-blue satin sheath, silver slippers, rhinestone earrings, a necklace, and bracelets. There's nothing as much fun as being in Mr. Pickett's musicals because you have to be in rehearsal every night whether Mr. Pickett gets to your scene or not.

When mother was ten she played the piano for a church in every oil field town they lived in: Shawnee, Three Sands, Cushing, Stillwater, Tulsa, and even in Tryon. She and her brother Jess sang together in the county chorale. Singing and dancing, lilacs and old Nelson Eddy and Jeanette MacDonald movies—they all remind her of her good times, she says.

Even though the production of *Taming of the Shrew* has been completed, I keep thinking about it. The whole marriage thing keeps me wondering about why men and women have to be tied to marriage. What if a girl wants to have an adventure? Is it possible to have a marriage without it being so depressing for women? I can't see anything but cooking and cleaning and raising kids, and surely there are more interesting things to do in this world. Have women's lives improved since Shakespeare's time?

A day in the life of Dad's mom Grandma Johnson: She starts work before the sun comes up. Down to the barn in the dark, milk cows, carry the pails back up to the house, separate milk and cream, bottle the milk, cook breakfast, wash dishes, clean and sweep kitchen, feed chickens, collect eggs, clean eggs, put in cartons, maybe wall-paper for the day or wash clothes in town, careful not to get caught in the wringers, bring home, hang out on line, fix lunch, starch and iron Grandpa's khakis, overalls, shirts, her dresses, and tablecloths, work in garden, can food, down in the cellar, up, down, do shopping, trade with eggs when short of cash during Depression, check out books at town library, begin dinner, milk cows again, have dinner, clean and wash dishes. After dark, read, cut out poems from *Daily Oklahoman*, sew, clean face with cold cream, brush curly dark hair, put on old nightgown, sleep.

During snow and winter, she makes time to feed the wild birds. They flock to her kitchen door, waiting for black seeds to be flung into the yard. Her winter garden is made up of clicking cardinals, black and white chickadees, red, white, and black woodpeckers, soft gray titmice.

And in late evening, her energy revived in the deep winter, she bundles up and slips outside with her binoculars and travels into the clear night, studying the stars, admiring the secret shadows on a half moon, marveling at Jupiter or Venus or Mars.

She has been to Houston twice to visit us. We have pictures of her floating in the Gulf of Mexico with her arms around my sisters. I see how she and Papa love one another, side by side, carrying in milk pails from the barn, reading quietly in the evenings.

I am not like my mother or grandmother. I could not do what they do.

Galveston with Aunt Oneta, sister Janet, and Grandmother.

16

We are in rehearsals for *Oedipus Rex* by Sophocles. I am the book-holder. I couldn't believe it when Mr. Hicks announced my name. I didn't even know there was such a thing as book-holder. I'm not very good at it yet because I keep reading ahead and when someone drops a line, I'm often on the wrong page. But each night I make fewer mistakes. Once you start reading, though, it's easy to get lost in the words and the story. And our lead actors, LaNelle and Larry, are superb. It's the best play I have ever read.

I never thought that being back stage, standing between the curtains, and following the lines, over and over, night after night, could be so exciting. It's the play. I listen carefully at each rehearsal and always understand something new about the meaning of the words. For instance: never ask if things in life can get worse, because in this play you find out, yes, lots worse.

Mom and Dad will be proud to know that I am the book-holder for this Greek tragedy. No glued on eyelashes or rhinestone necklaces for me.

But speaking of false eyelashes, something dear has come to me, another letter from Kathy. She has been so depressed and she was too lonely in Hollywood and got so mixed up about life that she went back to Texas. Unfortunately, that has made her more depressed, and I know exactly, *exactly*, how she feels because before leaving for Oklahoma, I was the same way.

She says she felt like the girl in the French revue at the Dunes, completely naked, a red spotlight on her, and black gloved hands sliding, dancing all over her body. I remember that show vividly. I was dumbstruck when the curtain pulled back, the long sinuous nude body stretched out, all legs in high heels, a tiny, sparkling g-string (only a suggestion of cover), and then a thumbprint of glitter sprayed on her nipples. I kept gasping, not only at the bodies, but also the dancing. Dramatic, like Cyd Charisse in *An American in Paris,* only in the nude.

Kathy says that in Hollywood she felt naked all the time. She felt sorry, too, for the girls that prostituted themselves to the producers. I think I might be like a prostitute, because last Saturday I spent the afternoon in a motel with a guy I hardly knew. He is cute but not that nice. I don't know why I did it, and every time I think about it I feel like a tramp. Sometimes I am positive that having sex is okay, especially when I listen to the other girls laugh and talk about "making love" experiences so openly. But guilt has paralyzed me too. Am I different from other girls—do they feel brave and free one day—then sink into regret the next?

I need to talk to Kathy about this and a lot of other things. She said she had "deteriorated into nothingness, floating along, not doing anything." I kept reading her words and thinking to myself, yes, yes, that's how I have felt too. She wants me to come back to Las Vegas this summer. But I can't. She doesn't know Mr. Entratter says I must have a college degree before I work again at the Sands. She did ask in her letter if my classes are doors to "an exciting awakening." That's what I want to tell her. I do feel flushed, rushing from the art building (with purple and lavender paint still underneath my nails) anxious to get to philosophy class. And I've had exciting walks with my professor, Mr. Gaddis, and we talk about Zoroaster from Persia and how he believed, thousands of years ago, that people must do and say and think good things. I want to know about ancient teachers, faraway places, and how people keep trying to live better lives.

And I have to tell Kathy about my new friends and how Sandy and

I talk late into the night, and Karen and I exercise and walk on the track, and that I'm book-holder for *Oedipus Rex*. She has to read this play; it is deep, emotional, and tragic. She would love it, I know, just like I do.

Dad makes me so mad. I wrote and asked him if I could have my convertible here at school. "NO," he wrote back. He never owned a car until he had been married a year and was twenty-two years old. What does that mean? That I have to wait four more years for a car? Or get married? If I had my car, I could go see Grandma and Grandpa Johnson. I haven't even seen them yet. He pointed out that I had a car when I was sixteen. But he bought it for me. And I had asked for a bike.

Unfortunately, I wrote in my letter that none of my clothes fit and I need something new for Easter. He replied that I should shop in Tryon or Agra for nice skirts. First, I would have to get there some way, and, second, that was his funny joke since the only thing I've seen in the store at Tryon are jeans, striped overalls, denim work shirts, and the big bonnets that Grandma wears when she's in her garden.

Next, I don't know what he was talking about when he wrote: "You would disappoint us by doing or not doing many things, No. 1, but be honest with yourself and us and we will always get along." Couldn't he address me as Judy? (He thinks it's funny when he calls us by our birth order, numbers 1, 2, 3, and Beth, the youngest, number 4). Then he wrote, "Do unto others as you would have them do unto you." I agree, but what did I say in my letter to get that advice? I don't understand him. He never says things like that when we talk in person.

He had news. Valley Gas made its first deliveries to Trunkline at McAllen yesterday, March 13. That's what he does, connecting gas pipelines across Texas and Oklahoma. I've driven hundreds of miles with Dad, across Texas, visiting the men who work in the field. Maybe he'll make lots of money and buy Linda a car and let me have my convertible back.

He also said he knows April and May, springtime in Oklahoma, will be good to me. I know what he means because I've seen hints of early blossoms on the redbud trees at Grandma Lee's old stone house. Dad loves iris in bloom, and especially grandma Johnson's fragrant roses.

My hope is that when I am honest with him about my grades, he will remember his advice. No matter what I do to outline, use index cards, research something for hours in the library, I cannot make a decent speech in Mr. Graham's class. I'm so terrible that I barely make eye contact with the class while I mumble through whatever our assignment might be. I can speak lines in a play, but I am a fool in speech class. It's a horrible feeling. I think I have a D right now.

A letter from Grandma Johnson! I can come anytime. I can call the service garage in Tryon and tell them where Papa can pick me up. But be careful, roads are icy.

17

Every Sunday I can call home because the rates are lower. And every Sunday Mom asks if I've been to see the memorial Dr. Jesse Hampton made for my uncle Jess, mom's younger brother. Dr. Hampton collects stories and memorabilia of the fallen military men from this area. There are many.

I found the memorial in the basement of Old North Hall. Two students were quietly browsing, carefully looking at photos of Uncle Jess, the *National Geographic* article describing the 1947 mission in the Antarctica he was selected for, military insignia, and the letters from commanding officers, including one from Admiral Byrd. I wanted to tell those students that he was my uncle, and he loved to sing while my mother played the piano, but thinking of the harmony Uncle Jess and my mother made together that last time he was at our home in Bartlesville, the sad remembering of that happy time came full force, and I couldn't speak.

My uncle died in 1950 in his Navy plane during the Korean War. He was only twenty-six. His wife and my three cousins, Kandy, Jess, and Nancy stayed with us until they had a place to live. There isn't anything about that in the glass cases where his white, folded uniform looks freshly starched but forlorn.

Kandy, Jess, and Nancy Linn

Afterward, I walk over to Stephenson Park, which the Civilian Conservation Corp boys built, then to Grandma Lee's old rock house that Grandpa and his brothers built out of Oklahoma redstone. It's still there, and all the fruit trees too. I walk towards town and find the Statue of Liberty where Linda and Donnie and I took dozens of photos one sunny summer day when we were kids.

Now I can tell Mom I visited the display for Uncle Jess. And I'll tell Dad that I'm glad he sent me up here to school (pouting and whining, I recall) and that Central is perfect for me. And where is the Lyttle Restaurant that Mom worked in when Dad was a student here? I'd like to see where I was a baby, watching Mom while she waited on customers. It's hard to imagine Mom at twenty with a baby and being a waitress here in Edmond. That was eighteen years ago. She is still waiting on tables in our kitchen at home.

Mom and Dad are both so right about springtime in Oklahoma. It's silly to think this, but at times I can imagine the whole campus breaking out in a dance. I scrutinize each gray-green leaf bud, imagining what color it will blossom, violet or gray? And I think there must be changes to the redbuds even during the hour I am in Dr. Watkins's English class.

A week or two ago, fretting my way to speech class, I was surprised by the curve of a tree branch. I approached it, thinking it was bleak and gray, but as I was admiring its reach, I noticed the many fuzzy green knobs along its length. What I thought was wintry and grim instead has mossy blue tendrils growing bolder each morning.

If I were a proper observer, I would study one small branch of a particular tree instead of hopping willy-nilly among so many. I should count each leaf nodule, each blossom, and record every pop, every blast of green, even the date when it makes its appearance. I could make a diary of what happens between the time I'm sitting in Union and heading to

Modern Dance. I should compare colors and their ever-changing shades. And why not investigate fragrance? Is it possible that knowing about this lemony iris or Mom's tantalizing lilac could make the world a little better?

I think studying spring should be a two-hour elective, or part of philosophy at least.

I ask, are nine fallen redbuds, hurled off their branch by an indifferent wind and now forming random, swirling patterns on frozen ground, no less a mystery, a delight, than curled roly-polies or spiraling, rising fireflies or a distant arm of the Milky Way?

Oneta, Betty, and Wynema
Springtime in Oklahoma

18
April 16–17, 1959
Mitchell Hall, Central State College

We are in our final rehearsals for *The Diary of Anne Frank.* Billy Dee is Mrs. Frank, and I play Anne's older sister, Margot.

This play is like *Oedipus Rex.* Both stories involve horrible events the characters can't control. Our characters are persecuted because they are Jews, who have a small chance of escaping their circumstances. They must be extraordinarily careful in order to survive. Nevertheless, Anne writes in her diary and lives her life—as much as she can—in a cramped attic. I don't know how she did that. Each night during rehearsal, as we work further into the story, her words find their place, and I always end up thinking, I'll never waste another hour.

Anyone who reads her diary must feel how important it is to live fully, like she wanted to.

We open April 16. Since we must dramatize how noiseless the families had to be to survive, our rehearsals are tense, eerily quiet at times, as we move about while parts of Anne's diary are read over the sound system. I loved being book-holder for *Oedipus,* but having a speaking part has made me more aware of how an actor has to shape each moment on stage in order to stay in character. Every night Mr. Hicks points out a way to make the play, us, better.

The Diary of Anne Frank was a huge success. We felt it from the audience. The hush, the reactions we wanted, the tense emotions. Everything—back stage, props, sound, costumes—every detail worked. I don't want to do anything except act and be in plays. Actors can create a world, and if it works, your audience tells you the whole time. And when you know the audience believes you, there's nothing like it. Mr. Hicks was happy; everyone felt lifted up and carried away.

Amidst all the congratulations and lovely confusion, I glanced around the room and there was a tall man waving frantically to me from the very back of the crowded auditorium. He looked like my father. But that couldn't be. And the woman next to him looked like my Aunt Oneta...and the smaller woman...looked like my Grandmother. I scrambled off stage and made my way towards them, and with not one ounce of control I cried in disbelief, overcome by a feeling of well-being and joy. We hugged and cried and held each other and I didn't understand what was happening to me. I felt proud of being in the play and that the audience had demanded many curtain calls, that dad came, that I felt I had done something good, and my family was there to be with me. Each of their faces seemed etched in light; words floated by and sounds made no sense. I was conscious of my skin, my heart, my breath, and nothing seemed real. I knew that holding them close to me would be locked in my memory forever. It's impossible to understand my dad, the gas pipeline executive who played Hamlet on this same stage.

19
May 1959
Central State College

Since we finished *The Diary of Anne Frank* last month, I've gone crazy. With no rehearsals, no purpose, no focus, I am lost and sad because we are all leaving soon. My roommate Sandy back to Missouri, Karen off to Chicago. The end has come too abruptly. This time last year I finished high school and didn't want to go to college. But now I love being here, and I want everything to slow down. I want to stay at the farm and take a book to the pond and read and listen to summer like I used to do. When we were rehearsing the play, I had energy to do all the good things: write, dance, act, become friends with new people who like the theater. But when it was over, I drifted off. This is how I would describe myself: fat, confused, mean to my friends and family, lacking direction, slovenly, incapable of doing the things that are right and good, a slut. I am tired most of the time, sleep too much during the day, drag myself to classes, and haven't made one good presentation in speech class. I always thought that I was a good friend, but I have not been these last days of the semester.

We had our Drama Awards Banquet. I felt awkward, my feeling of not belonging there, or anywhere, except the farm, overwhelmed me. I was miserable about being a crappy person. Then, out of the blue, my name was called for the Best Supporting Actress award for my role as Margot. I didn't want to seem emotional or corny, but I was. I could barely croak out an understandable "thank you." I had this enormous burn in my throat and felt like a fake, and most of all I wanted, *needed,* to be like everyone there—a real actor. But exactly what was I?

I mumbled and sucked in my breath real hard and swallowed fifteen times, sniffled and quickly got back to my table. I don't remember a thing about the banquet except for those few moments. My brain was in slow motion. Everyone around me was sweet and kind and that made the urge to cry even stronger. Somewhere inside me came the feeling, oh, you are sad because you don't want to leave these actor friends, art friends, philosophers.

I had found a place to be myself.

In the fall I'm going to be a completely different person. I'm going to be serious about my classes, make better grades (I have A's in English, Art, and Philosophy) and I'm not going to fool around with boys because I waste time and feel nauseous getting into scary situations with guys I don't even like. The best thing is that Dr. Watkins says I will have a part-time job as his assistant. I can't wait to tell my parents. And Dr. Watkins says he has enjoyed every essay I have written. "Keep writing," he said.

So much has happened in such a short time, and even though I have been all mixed up a lot and have made many dumb mistakes, I think next year will be better.

Dale McConathy is a senior who has been to almost all our rehearsals this semester. He has always greeted me warmly, even seemed amused, as if he knew all about my life at the Sands and now my attempt to fit in on campus. Many times we have stopped to chat on the way to a class. He compliments me on my choreography for Modern Dance or on a scene in drama class. He makes me feel better. Today I told him that I have my job in the English department with Dr. Watkins next semester. He congratulated me and said that even though he has plans to move to New York City, he will see me in the fall. I say I have plans to live in Paris someday. We hug and say have a good summer and he urges me to buy the novel *Dr. Zhivago* by Boris Pasternak. He said Mr. Pasternak won the Nobel Prize for Literature but wasn't able to leave the Soviet Union to accept it. He says again I must read this book. It's important. I say I will. I will because I want to see Dale in the fall and walk with him and talk about *Dr. Zhivago*, the plays for next year, and about writing, and what classes to take, the teachers not to miss.

20

June 1959
Houston

The first evening at home we sit in the den. Mom and dad have cocktails, me and my three younger sisters have iced tea. We rarely sit with our parents during their cocktail hour, but we do today because I am home from college. Dad volunteers the information that he struggled with an English class at Central. And the professor who gave him an F on a paper was Dr. Grady Watkins, my professor who has offered me the assistant's job in the fall! We find this hard to believe, but he says it's true and mom backs him up.

Later Dad asks, "Judy, do you remember Mr. Thomas, the man in the village who owns the typewriter shop?"

"Yes, I do."

"He wants to talk to you about becoming a contestant in the Miss Houston contest."

"Oh, dad, I don't want to do that."

"Why? You could just talk with him on the phone at least."

I don't want to argue. But at the same time I am thinking, it isn't my idea, or anything I am interested in…a beauty contest. I have been a dancer, but I earned a salary, learned how to live by myself (sort of) and now I will work in the English department at Central. That is what I want to do.

But I speak with Mr. Thomas. He is a member of the Houston Jaycees. He loves theater and does script writing and worked on *Seven Brides for Seven Brothers*. He congratulates me on winning best supporting actress at school and couldn't I just talk with one of his friends about the contest?

Oh, sure. Yes. I could. I am polite. He is dad's friend.

The next day I learn it is part of the Miss America pageant. If you win or place, you might win a scholarship to college. Oh. Still, there is no voice inside me saying, "Judy, be a contestant." No one understands how I feel. Mainly because I can't express how I feel to my parents. Why aren't they happy with the plans I have now? Will they be disappointed in me because I don't want to be in this contest?

I agree to come to a press party and "just meet some young women who are contestants and make new friends." The drive downtown to some crappy party to meet people I don't know puts me in a snotty mood. Inside my head I am sullen, resentful, and feel mean. Outside, I smile, say, "So glad to meet you," shake hands, and try to look friendly and respectful. The contestants, Betty, Linda, Nancy, and JoAnn are beautiful. None of them look like they have eaten tons of food at the school cafeteria three times a day for months. They have tans while I am pimply and pale—Oklahoma-winter color. They are vivacious, but I feel phony and shaky and keep looking around the room for something not there.

After a while, though, it's hard to resist the persistent enthusiasm of the girls who want to be Miss Houston. The contest will be a performance, a show. What will be my "talent"? We speak of bathing suits and costumes. One of the judges, Jess Neely, the head football coach at Rice, is a quiet-spoken gentleman. We talk. I feel a little better and I tell him I know the head football coach at University of Houston. I even tell him I don't want to be in the Miss Houston contest. He grins and says it probably won't be as awful as I think it will be. The way he talks, quietly, with a smile, reminds me of my Grandpa Johnson.

21

Last night at the Western Skies Motel, out on Katy Highway, I won the 1959 Miss Houston Contest. I did the hula, "Little Brown Gal," for my talent, walked around in my bathing suit and my lumpy body and no tan, and answered a question. "How do you feel about states' rights?" I thought what the hell is that? But from my mouth, my throat, my voice came, "I believe in strong states' rights. I think that the stronger the states are, the stronger our country will be." As far as I knew, it was the first I had ever heard the term "states' rights," but I had leaned into the microphone to answer my question. The crowd cheered.

My mom and dad, my sisters Linda, Janet, and Beth, my friends Kay and Bobby and John were there. I had been relaxed, comfortable, without doubt or anxiety, because I never imagined that I would win. Nor did I think of winning. I knew that I was standing next to the girl, the beautiful Linda, who would probably win.

This morning, though, I know I am Miss Houston. I am tucked into the top of page seven, section one of the *Houston Chronicle*. Miss Houston of 1958, gracious and lovely Jan, is placing the rhinestone crown on my head as I hold a bouquet of roses in my lap. The article says I will participate in the Miss Texas contest in July. The *Houston Post* put us on the front page with a note that my measurements are 37-24-38, which I made up.

Last night, when I was announced as the new "Miss Houston," I thought, What? Wait, this isn't right. What about Linda? Or JoAnn with her vivacious personality? Or wait....At the same time, the talk inside my head told me to be nice. Smile. Act excited.

And then the next hour, or more, flashed and rippled by. It was a humid Houston night, dark sky, clouds and palm trees blocking the moonlight. The motel pool was lit from below, and I was aware of the shadows playing tag underwater. My sisters were around me, laughing. I felt strange, not at all ecstatic like I felt when I won the trip to Las Vegas to dance at the Sands.

The evening went by quickly. There were gardenias in bloom on the far side of the pool. A friendly breeze rippled through the palm trees. I didn't hear anything in particular, just followed directions, smiled, posed, and was hypnotized by the shadowy images moving on the bottom of the pool.

Directly under my picture in the *Chronicle* with Miss Houston 1958 is the headline, "Women's Clubs Agree—LADIES SHOULD BE LADIES, NOT BODIES." The General Federation of Women's Clubs meeting in Los Angeles passed resolutions condemning exploitation of feminine appeal, joined in a plea to help stamp out obscene literature, wants laws to control outer space, urges better enforcement of air traffic safety measures, and is concerned about having enough quality water for America's growing population. In the Post I am pictured next to the article, HERTER BLASTS RUSSIAN PLANS FOR W BERLIN. The Reds are smothering German freedom.

Most of the *Chronicle* page, though, lists the movies. One column away from my story is an advertisement for *Some Like It Hot,* with a picture of Marilyn Monroe, Jack Lemmon, and Tony Curtis. It's at the Tidwell Drive-in Theatre. *The Shaggy Dog* and *The Hanging Tree* with Gary Cooper are at the South Main. I need to see Mr. Cooper's movie. And Mike Todd's *Around the World in 80 Days* is at the Delman, at regular one dollar prices. I like being on the same page as the movie stars. Mickey Rooney and his new wife are expecting a baby. He was secretly married in Mexico. Debbie Reynolds is playing everywhere in *The Mating Game,* and the Shepherd Drive-in is having all Marlon Brando movies: *Desiree, A Street Car Named Desire,* and *Viva Zapata.*

My picture would be right next to Marilyn Monroe's except for Mr. Rooney's story and the one on "Fresh Atrocities Reported in Tibet." The Dalai Lama had to escape from Lhasa in March and go to India. And a senior advocate of India's supreme court says the Chinese Communists have slaughtered sixty-thousand Tibetans since 1956. The Communists broke into Tibet in 1951. For some reason, China is trying to destroy Tibet, but a commission is making a report to the UN. The Dalai Lama is twenty-three and will announce later "details of what I think and plan."

Grandma Lee called early this morning. She said she bought three copies of both of the Houston newspapers and has cut out the photos of me holding my bouquet of roses.

22

I have eight weeks before the Miss Texas contest. I have been awarded a year's membership in a workout club, and I exercise daily to get in shape. I have two choreographers to help me with my talent presentation. A Mrs. Patsy Swayze says I will do the hula and a jazz dance. Half of my performance will be to "Little Brown Gal" and then I take off my hula skirt and do a jazz number to the music of "Night Train." Mrs. Swayze (Patsy, she insists) says my skirt and leotard will be red, and I will be terrific. She is a confident person. I go to her home in the Heights almost daily for dance instruction. Her assistant, Larry Berthelot, helps me in the studio a few blocks away.

Between dancing and reducing, I answer calls for "Miss Houston." Photos, interviews for a news column, parties. I am going to represent an ice cream company in a parade in Pasadena. The company will provide an "appropriate Southern Belle costume" for me to wear while waving to the public from a convertible.

An article in the Friday, July 24 *Houston Post*, page ten, section four: "42 Pretty Girls In Miss Texas Pageant." After eight weeks of daily workouts (on my back lifting weights to reduce and firm my butt, lying across revolving wooden spindles to flop off my belly fat, having my insides shaken to pieces by a vibrating belt around my waist) and trying to diet also, I lost seven pounds. Still, my stomach isn't that flat, my midriff is noticeable and my bathing suit straps struggle to up-lift my too-heavy bust. In our group photo I am next to Miss Fort Worth, who is from Houston, and the girl everyone says will win. This has been rumored for two months. She is a classically trained ballerina, svelte, black hair, pretty and confident.

According to the newspaper article we "radiate a fresh, wholesome beauty." And one girl is quoted: "But I am tired. We haven't had more than fifteen minutes to change clothes, and if you're late, points are taken away."

Points. We have points for our behavior, our clothes, our conversations. I was so nervous at the luncheon because one of the judges sat next to me. I listened to everyone around me thoughtfully, watched my table manners, answered direct questions without hesitation, and smiled agreeably. Someone told an appropriate joke. I recalled a silly cartoon I thought was amusing and immediately realized I had offended the judge. (A drunk man holding on to a light pole, singing "starkle starkle little twink, how I wonder what you think!") The other girls giggled, but the judge arched his eyebrows. I turned red, got a lump in my throat, and began perspiring. Then I could only think of Grandma Lee's favorite cuss word, "Shitfire."

After seven weeks of dance training with Patsy Swayze and Larry Berthelot, which was intense and frustrating—for them—since they had a lot for me to learn, I did win the talent contest for my section. I was elated and very proud and I know Patsy was too. It was a very sexy dance. I wore a bathing suit covered in red sequins underneath my red cellophane hula skirt. The Houston Post has an insert in today's paper: *"Miss Johnson won the talent show with a dance that changed in tempo from an undulating hula to a torrid affair."* Undulating and torrid sounds like Ava Gardner, or Rita Hayworth.

Tonight I parade across stage, pivot, turn, smile, turn, all in my bathing suit that I realize is too fuzzy on me. It should be shiny and hold me in better.

On Sunday night, July 26, Miss Fort Worth is crowned the new Miss Texas. I am in the top ten, and I feel very left out when I am not in the top five. I keep thinking it is a mistake. After it is all over, the kids in the orchestra serenade me with the "Yellow Rose of Texas." Then they want to exchange addresses and that makes me feel better.

Patsy Swayze has offered me a part-time job keeping attendance and payment accounts at her Dance Studio on Richmond four days a week from 3:00 until 7:00 pm when her husband, Buddy, arrives. Also, I will have many paid engagements as Miss Houston, 1959. It is clear to everyone that I must enroll at University of Houston and take advantage of these opportunities and not go back to Oklahoma.

Everyone except me.

23

Among the flurry and confusion of being Miss Houston, a surprise letter from Kathy arrives with the news that she leaves for France in September. I read it over and over in disbelief, envy, and excitement. She has been hired by Miss Bluebell to work at the Lido in Paris. I am happy for her, of course, and at the same time want to ask, "Can I come too?" And to think we hadn't even met each other this time last year. She wants me to come, but that's impossible since I have no money saved, must go to school in the fall, and now I have this contest. She said she can't wait to see me and hug and "cry over all the idiotic and wonderful things we've shared and will share—and—oh everything—hurry now."

Kathy is going to be a beautiful showgirl with rhinestones and feathers and huge headdresses and learn French and have painting classes and have coffee on the Champs-Élysées before she begins work. She says I am her best friend and asks, "Why haven't we written to

Kathy Martin

each other? It seems so foolish to let such a wonderful friendship drift." And "Oh—but, Judy—so many things have changed within that I now have found a purpose for living and I feel so much better." She sent a quote, "…be not afraid of life. Believe that life is worth living and your belief will help create the fact." That's what Kathy does. She finds words that express things we feel. *Be not afraid of life.* Dream your dreams and make them happen. Kathy is going to Paris. I can go to Paris. We said these things to each other and now, in less than a year, Kathy has a job in Paris.

24
University of Houston

Oberholtzer Hall is where I pick up my mail, study, and have my meals. The place to meet a guy is around the mailboxes. Outside is a wide veranda with marble steps leading down to the walkway to my dorm, Law Hall. There are shade trees, blooming shrubbery hugging white stone walls, and wooden benches here and there that make me feel at home in this part of the campus. On the other side of Law Hall is a wide, grassy field dotted with trees, tall and friendly, stretching outward to Cullen Boulevard. It is an inviting look—the trees and branches like deep green drooping umbrellas, giving shade or a little shelter on a drizzly late night.

A year ago I was finding my way around Las Vegas. I was so taken then with the blue violet ripple of the mountains, the sandy scrabble of desert stretching beyond the Sahara Hotel. Today in front of Law Hall, on a bench facing the ancient limestone walls of OB Hall, I am touched, suspended, by the clouds of pale lavender wisteria hovering, drifting over the sharp-edged corner of the wall. The wisteria trunk is twisted, reaching, coiling up the side of OB Hall, branches gnarled and folded one into the other, spread across the roof, spilling blue, sometimes violet, sometimes light gray blossoms down the somber face of Oberholtzer.

I am snug on a bench. I watch pairs of students laughing on their way to lunch, a couple lingering near the steps, leaning, touching, oblivious to passersby. I am pretending to study the lovely lavender shawl of wisteria facing me, but I'm jealous of the boy and girl holding hands. While I decipher the significance of the wisteria, I also search for a boyfriend. Everywhere I walk, every place I go, the Student Union, OB Hall, or every classroom I enter, I am hopeful, searching.

My English teacher is Professor Hartley. If we don't answer his questions about grammar correctly, he manages to embarrass us in a humorous way. He is taking us to the library to show us how to start our research papers. If I do what I'm supposed to, I have little time to mope about not having a boyfriend.

The English building is a short walk from my dormitory, through another canopy of tall trees, and close to the Reflection Pool, which needs a lot of cleaning. Green mold grows on the bottom, and brown glops of muddy leaves float on the surface. But a few days ago, I watched a small wind guide drifting blossoms across the water, little rosy-colored wishes.

After classes I work for Patsy Swayze. There is the bus to downtown, then a ten or fifteen minute wait for the next bus, and in an hour or so I am at her dance studio out on Richmond. I collect the monthly dance fees, keep the books, and help the little dancers get their ballet shoes and leotards on or off. Usually I leave after her husband Buddy arrives from work. Patsy's studio is a family affair, meaning her own children are there, her dance students who are like her family mingle around, and then all the parents. She teaches long hours, enthusiastically, with all her heart and energy. After knowing her these few months, I know that to not try to do your very best in whatever you are doing is almost sinful in her eyes.

My bus ride is a new journey. I see students walking through Texas Southern University, which is only a few blocks from U of H. I see many unfamiliar neighborhoods. I have learned how long it takes to cross town on the busses. I contemplate the early hours one must keep to arrive at 9 a.m. for work in some lady's home, like my mother's. I am in a better place now to *imagine* how a sixty- or seventy-year-old woman feels after working eight hours, say, in my home, and then walking to a bus stop, then riding downtown, changing buses, going another twenty minutes or so, then walking home and probably starting dinner at 7:00 or 7:30 p.m.

I look out the bus window. At our changing place on Main Street I keep my head down or study the home hospital equipment in a store window. At this time of the evening, there are few pale passengers like me waiting for the Holman bus. It is good for me to travel where I've never been in Houston.

On the Beach with Ava Gardner and Gregory Peck came out during the Christmas holidays. It is a love story, an end-of-the-world story, and a story about how people decide what they will do in their very last days alive. It made me think about the play *The Diary of Anne Frank* and how they lived their hours and days never knowing what might happen to them. I have never experienced anything dreadful.

It has been fourteen years since Hiroshima and Nagasaki. We don't know if that was the end of using atomic bombs, or the beginning.

25

I have passed everything this first year at U of H. But that's because my logic professor gave a select group of poorly prepared students a second chance on several quizzes. Thank goodness, or I would be in summer school with a fair chance of a worse grade. I had chosen to spend more time with the Red Masque Players than my Logic studies. But having friends in the Drama Department saved me from bailing out of school completely and going back to Oklahoma. I think it's not only a matter of liking to be in a play; it's that I *must* be in a play.

I have made new friends, but they're gone now. We write. From my collection of letters so far this summer: One friend thought he had a job on a tug boat, but that fell through and he hasn't found another.

He is volunteering at the Democratic ward, campaigning for Senator Kennedy. His older sister is tanning in the backyard, and his dad went fishing on Father's Day. He also writes slyly that "if *he* ever has a baby daughter like *my* little sister Beth, his daughter will have to stop dancing lessons at age fifteen so she won't get a big head and have crazy ideas about "being a dancer." All in reference, I suppose, to my big head and my plan of going back to work at the Sands. He also asks, "When are you getting married?" Never, I write back.

From my dear Kathy in Paris: She says she and her friends go to an after-hours club called the "Bandtou," which is very near the Lido where they all work. She met an Italian man there. He is "tall, dark, and handsome" and works in Cairo as a petroleum engineer. She says, "He is everything I want." She went with him to northern Italy and "breath-taking Switzerland" in a little white sports car. Now he writes to her constantly. She wrote to me while she was at the hairdresser's getting ready for an appointment with a photographer later in the day. She has registered with the Dorian Leigh Modeling agency (Suzy Parker's sister) and has made a screen test for commercials to be used in France, England, and the United States. She says she is going to be "quite serious about modeling, as I believe I can be very successful (if I can be thin enough)."

From my good friend Bill in Nacogdoches: He says he was sitting around in the station and began thinking about all the fun we had this past year in drama workshops. He said for me to consider that "some people were blessed with beauty and some people were cursed with beauty and all you can do is roll with the punches." I will be happy when he gets back to school and we can have one of our long conversations to find out exactly what he means. I'm not sure whether we have the platonic relationship we think we do. But I believe we will be friends for a long time if we stay the way we are now.

My friend who is looking for a job closed with "it was really raining here...lightning lit up the sky...thunder roared through the heavens"... and his usually very brave dog sat underneath the table and shook herself to pieces. I, too, am afraid of lightning and raging winds and rising water. I also scare myself by being so erratic, telling myself one thing and then doing another. I want to be with this boyfriend night and day, yet there is that dream...of Paris. Still, we walk to the drugstore holding hands, split a grilled cheese sandwich, and I think I never want to be without him.

I am so close sometimes to falling into a kitchen, and pots and pans.

26

For weeks, we've followed the news about the Berlin Wall. We woke up a month ago and it was built during the night. Always this uncertainty and tension on the nightly news. Photos of the fighting in Algeria and the attempt to kill General de Gaulle. It is unnerving. And then Hurricane Carla disrupted our first weeks of school. Everything was closed, and I spent days at home in rain and flooding all around. Thank goodness we were safe out here in Sharpstown compared to what happened in Galveston. Oh, poor Galveston, flooded again and beaches torn up, the long-dead floated out of their coffins, and many buildings ripped and torn and spat out by an evil tornado. Bellaire Boulevard was flooded, but it never got to our house. The news coverage made me sick, and our Houston reporter Dan Rather was on national news. For three days I sat in the garage watching the rain and wind rage and act hateful.

At the beginning of every semester I meet with my advisor to make sure I am taking the right classes for graduation. This fall I have History of Philosophy, an acting class, Introduction to Comparative Government, Sociology, and Western World Literature. In Government class I have been fascinated by one of the students. She has long, curly, light brown hair, and dresses in long skirts, long sweaters, low-heeled shoes (no loafers at all) and has the look of Garbo or Marlene Dietrich. She constantly asks questions in class, and from her comments I am sure she has lived in Europe. She sits several rows in front of me. I cling to the back row in every class, except in History of Philosophy. That classroom is so small there are only two rows in it and I ended up directly in front of Dr. Tsanoff. Although you must take down notes on almost everything he says, I can't help but gaze at him when he tells us about the personal life of a philosopher of long ago. Dr. Tsanoff was born in Sofia, Bulgaria, and has retired from Rice University and I think he loves explaining these arguments and helping us find our own questions about how to think and see the world.

And what would you do if a strange and peculiar guy sat next to you in Government class, pointed his right index finger at you, then deliberately poked your right breast during the professor's lecture? Would you scream and cause a scene? I should have, but didn't. I yanked myself around and scooted my desk away from him and got red in the face with rage and tried to knock him over after class. What an asshole that guy is. And he's from my old high school too.

Because of him I moved to the middle of the room and have finally met the girl who is so interesting. We actually live close to each other in the dorm. Her name is Annette Hillman and she has lived in Paris, just as I thought. We were at Pershing Junior High at the same time. She has lived in Florida and Arizona, plays the piano and likes to paint. We are going to the Houston Museum of Fine Arts next weekend.

When she introduced herself and I began to do the same, she said in a whisper, "I know you were Miss Houston," and chuckled, like we had a secret. I liked that. It's as if she knew my conflict with that title. She asked me to come to the Political Science Club, and I have. I have met Bernie, who is quick to point out books all of us should read and certain movies that must be seen. As instructed, I am reading *The Alexandria Quartet* by Lawrence Durrell. Not just reading, but longing for Cairo and Alexandria and the intrigue of other lives. Bernie is going to loan me his copy of *The Air-Conditioned Nightmare,* a collection of short stories by Henry Miller. Everyone is reading Henry Miller. I like Miller's books because I would like to live with abandon and passion and intensity. I want to write and travel and not worry all the time about what people think and how I should act, and find friends that feel that way too. I want to be with people who like me just the way I am: lazy, reading books all the time, cussing like Grandma Lee, and sitting outside in the dark, watching stars and the moon through thin, wavering clouds.

Annette Hillman
Paris, November 1958

27

Last week we crammed into the little Hillman convertible Annette's father bought her, and drove to Galveston. It was the first time I had been there since the hurricane last year. Huddled together, we sat on the windy beach and had raw oysters out of a glass jar, French-style baguette and cheese, and terrible cheap wine. Annette makes these small gatherings with her international friends: Nebahat from Izmir, Turkey; Nadim from Tehran and Rachid from Algiers, who needs to laugh and not worry all the time about the troubles in his country. Together, we are easily silly. Nadim teases us for our *Breakfast at Tiffany's* sunglasses. Annette and I bought them together and we do look funny, but anything, anything, to be like Holly Golightly. We fancy ourselves the two drifters, "off to see the world."

Sometimes we meet outside Oberholtzer Hall, where we see the beautiful wisteria trailing down the building, and transport ourselves for a few minutes by enjoying the sun on our shoulders and good-natured teasing. We leave happier. I am introducing them to my sister Linda who is my roommate now, and everyone comments on how tall we are and how we look alike.

Annette is finished with her Political Science degree and is working on a teaching certificate. She is always telling me I need to do the same since we have to be able to support ourselves. She is right. But I have to stay with my plan. After I live in Paris, study French, and write, and live in Europe like she did, I will think about it. But not now.

I have this silly aggravating thing that is driving me crazy. My friend Tommy has asked that I play Titania to his Oberon in our spring production of *A Midsummer Night's Dream*. I was flattered, that's the problem. I said yes. But I am so afraid of Shakespeare. I do not know him. Now I am in and sunk.

In the meanwhile, I am deep into Ralph Ellison's *Invisible Man* and listening to my friend Bernie say that we are worthless shits because we aren't on a bus and going to the next march and I am agreeing wholeheartedly. With the endless sorrows in the world around us, and constant dilemmas about what we should do, I focus on the possibility of being the laughing stock on stage as Titania. It serves me right. I think I have words memorized, and then when the time comes for my entrance, my mind is blank, my eyes freeze with fear, no words croak out. I think I have the stage directions down, but each rehearsal, I frantically search the faces of Moth and Peaseblossom, Cobweb and Mustardseed for hints of where I should be. Tommy scratches out lines, cuts them to make it easier for me. He is calm but I sense his concern. He is responsible for this debacle: me.

I sit backstage with Rusty—or Puck, I should say—and marvel at the poise and grace of Helena and Hermia. If only I could be the book-holder and read the lines over and over, like I did at Central for *Oedipus Rex*, I would be able to enjoy Bottom and his group and not shake and quiver when I hear Puck say, "Fear not, my lord, your servant shall do so," which is my cue for an entrance. Oh what was wrong with me when I said yes to Tommy?

Tommy has designed many of our costumes. Mine is rose and pink and floaty and queenly. His mother is making it for me. He says that my hair will be spray painted rose and pink also. If only I could be a silent Titania and pantomime the entire performance. I will make it more of a comedy than Shakespeare intended.

Early this morning I studied my notes for our Geology quiz. But when we arrived, our professor had us put away our books and pay attention to his radio. And so we learned that John Glenn had leaped from Earth in his Mercury capsule and was viewing the planet from outer space. And it's a fact that we earth-bound geology students and many others have slipped into another chapter of history, prepared or not.

Later, I find my favorite bench by the dorm. I look up in the sky. The leaves on the trees move slightly. I watch cars stop at the red light across the grassy field. I hear voices floating from the sidewalk behind me. I remember being in a plane looking at the clouds from a window and the fantastical illusion of whirling from cloud to cloud. I remember the first time I spent the night outside with Grandma and Grandpa Johnson on the old spring bed, searching for shooting stars and being so in love with the idea and realization that I could see the Milky Way. It felt like we were floating away among stars, into space, so starstruck and warm and holding hands on a clear, cool night.

Just last Christmas Dad gave Grandma very expensive binoculars, and I remember that star-gazing, iris-loving, poem-collecting, sweet-bodied farm woman gingerly, reverently, turning them over and over in her gardener's hands, her very own instrument for closing the gap on deep space. At last, to be close to the moon, to ridges, craters, the shadowy mysteries we love in the cold crisp of winter.

I will try to reach her this week by phone. She prefers letters, though, because she gets very put out with her "party line" and sometimes doesn't answer the phone in the box on her kitchen wall. But what does she think about these strange things, humans invading space?

I have kept the book *Art and Science of Love* by Dr. Albert Ellis too long, so the library sent a notice and I felt like a brazen harlot returning it to the overdue desk. I felt the same way checking it out. But the book is liberating in a sense, with practical suggestions for innovative sex. When my new boyfriend and I scrape up enough money to check into the motel not far from here, we take *Art and Science* with us and choose some random suggestion and try it out. We end up hot and sweaty and breathless. But we end up that way no matter what we do: dancing at Cook's Hoedown all night, out in his boat waterskiing, or just having ordinary, regular sex. We drive through Houston late at night on the freeways with Ray Charles blaring and feel like we could drive forever that way.

But we are coming to an end. Graduation, next to last semester, leaving for graduate school, all in different directions. Anyway, I'm lost now in the last days of rehearsal. In these final days before the opening, my whole world shifts to back stage, between the curtains, concentrating on every single detail in the play. I feel as if we are holding our breath for hours each night. Not to say we aren't horsing around and sitting in the dark whispering and making nervous jokes. But underneath is The Play. The Dress Rehearsal. The First Afternoon Performance. If I could, I would go from one play production to another and spend my life in the theater.

Our final performances went quickly. My worst moment was being unable to rise from my "slumber" with Bottom. My flimsy diaphanous costume had wrapped around my legs and I missed my cue from Oberon. He quickly went upstage and said his next lines. I finally got upright and managed to mumble through. Tommy has been a true gentleman.

After the cast party for *A Midsummer Night's Dream,* Tommy and I walked all through University of Houston campus till early in the morning. It is full of tall trees and drooping vines and sprawling blooming bushes, and it felt as if we were still in the play, wandering through an enormous set. I told Tommy my sister Janet had come with her junior high class to see our afternoon performance and that she gave him rave reviews. She was very disappointed with me and even embarrassed that her big sister couldn't be heard. She praised my costume, though, and she liked my pink hair. I might have gotten a worse review if she had heard me.

One hopeful note on having been cast as Titania and having fairies at my command: Peaseblossom has given me the name of a woman looking for a hula dancer for a Hawaiian band. I might have a job for the summer.

28
Summer 1962
On the road

After a year and a half of various clerical jobs around campus (typing registration cards at the downtown U of H office, typing cards for a Texaco travel agent, typing a manuscript in the Political Science Department—all painful experiences, fired from the last two for excessive typos), I have a perfect job. I dance and travel to Arizona, Colorado, New Mexico, Oklahoma, Arkansas, Louisiana, Mississippi, and Texas with a Hawaiian band. Sometimes we are on the road for two weeks at a time. Usually we are gone for long weekends.

Herb, my boss, has been on the road with country-western bands since 1946, after he served in the army. He played with Bob Wills and the Texas Playboys for almost five years. Herb is tall, carefully hides his bald spot, and makes sure we stop and enjoy a mountain stream. His wife, Melba, my boss too, sings, dances, and plays cocktail drums. She is our emcee. She is small, just up to my shoulder, has dyed black hair, and has taught me how to make the roux for gumbo after we practice dance numbers.

Herb plays the steel guitar (builds them also), Lucky plays guitar and sings "Georgia on my Mind" and other solos, Dean plays the bass and sings harmony. I have a sweet dance partner, Diane, who is turning nineteen soon. She is slender, pretty face, light brown hair, but not a lot of dance background. It doesn't matter. The six of us make up the Beachcombers.

I love staring out the car window for hours on end. Then swaying on stage playing my calava sticks and listening to songs about Hawaii and old tunes like "Stardust," by Hoagy Carmichael. Or dancing to "Hawaiian War Chant" and hearing people shout and clap. I love pretending I'm a real musician on a bandstand while I try to play at the right time with my comb and scratcher. I daydream and goof up watching people dance, and Melba or Lucky says "Judy! You're off beat." I'm better with the bamboo sticks we use in one of our dance numbers. I'm okay with the feathered gourds, the uli ulis. I'm best with the smooth lava stones we click together like castanets. All these, plus the coconut candles we use in the floor show.

If we are going to play Tinker Air Force Base in Oklahoma City, we might leave from Herb and Melba's at two in the morning. Since we have to go through Ardmore, Oklahoma, where my godparents, Ab and Gertie, live, we always stop at their filling station to buy a cold drink. We go by Turner Falls, and Herb wants to stop and fish but we can't. We get to Oklahoma City and check into the motel not far from Frontier City and unpack and rest. Sometimes Grandma and Grandpa Johnson, who live just an hour down the road, drive in and pick me up and take me to the farm, even for an hour or two. Once Dean and Lucky got mad when I said Grandma had a chocolate pie ready for me, and I didn't think of bringing any for them.

In late afternoon we get ready. We three dancers do makeup, pin flowers in our hair, get into our long snug-fitting Hawaiian-print dresses with scooped and ruffled necklines that Melba sews for us, and add the silk flower leis we make ourselves. We wear our long dresses to perform as musicians with the band. For the dancing part of our show we change to hula skirts or our cloth pareus and matching bra tops that we make. We have decorated our hula skirt waist bands with beautiful shells.

We drive to the Air Force Base, or wherever we are working, and begin to unload. Everyone makes a lot of trips from the car and trailer, into the ballroom, or whatever area that's designated for the luau. All of our show costumes are in the trailer, carefully packed with the musical instruments, sound equipment, and the light bar Herb designed and made. Herb built the trailer that has traveled thousands of miles behind the blue Pontiac station wagon. Then Dean and Lucky and Herb set up the equipment. Melba and Diane and I find our dressing area, unpack our different hula skirts, the instruments we will be using, get our coconut candles and lava stones and lay them out in an orderly way. We might have time to smoke or have a Coke or snoop around and see what kind of food the place is going to have.

At 7:30 they start tuning up and Melba makes sure she has her program written out for the evening. At 8:00 Herb starts up. Lucky is a lanky cowboy type with the easiest laugh. He has a family back in Friendswood and a son who plays football. Dean is rounder and shorter than Lucky and has a grin that doesn't quit, but when he's playing bass he's serious. The six of us are the same in that we love making the music, and every audience has enjoyed it too. People can't help but dance from the very beginning.

We put on our show around 9:30. By this time the crowd has eaten and had a lot to drink, so they don't mind sitting down for a while and watching the hula dancers. My stage name is Keilani. Diane and I usually start out with "Hukilau." The three of us dance "Nani Vale" using the lava stones. We use the ulis for "Hawaiian War Chant." We go out into the audience and each of us pulls some unwilling man to come up and dance the hula with us. One huge man at the Midland Country Club stepped back on my right bare foot with his cowboy boot and twisted. He thought I was tickling his waist but I was trying desperately, with a smile, to move him off my foot. The show goes by quickly. I love it when people whistle and shout for more.

After that we change back into our long dresses, get up on the bandstand again, and I try not to mess up. Herb does his beautiful steel guitar music while Melba sings some old favorites. I watch the people getting silly. The evening flies by. Midnight and it's over. We break down, pack up, maybe get something to eat. Usually we're on the road by 1:30 and driving to the next place through a starry sky. Sometimes, if we have some nickels and dimes, Lucky talks us into playing poker. Somehow, no one ever wins but Lucky.

Most of all we talk and tell stories, and that's how we have become the best of friends. Lucky sang and played his guitar in Louisiana once, way out in the country, and Elvis was on the program too. It was long before anyone knew him, but Lucky said that everyone felt Elvis would be famous. There was just something about him that was different.

I tell them about Las Vegas and working with Frank Sinatra and Sammy and Judy Garland. It seems such a long time ago now. Four years. And pretty soon I'll be ready to work in the line again and be able to save money and get to Europe. That seems a long time from now when I'm floating through the New Mexico desert in a Pontiac station wagon with nothing to remind me of any life beyond being a hula dancer.

29
Alvin, Texas

Mom and I are sitting in the kitchen at home peeling shrimp. The phone rings. It is my old high school boyfriend, Gene. We haven't been in contact for several years. His voice is ragged and hoarse and he can barely speak. Will I come to his father's funeral the next day? I hear his grief, the terrible pain in his choked sobs. I can't believe it. How could his father die? He was too big and tall and strong and too full of laughter and how many high school basketball games had he been thrown out of for his too vocal opinions of the ref? I remember the time he caught us skipping class and thought it was funny but told us to "Get back to school!" We loved him.

At the funeral, everyone, every friend, every relative, holds Gene in their arms, even Mom. And I keep thinking over and over all day long, why does this happen? And now, Gene's mother is a widow, and these children and grandchildren don't have that growling, barrel-chested handsome man to swing them in the air and hold them tight and make them safe. And what will Gene do without him? And where does all that sweet love and mean grief go? When Gene is limp with exhaustion and mouth trembling, I see that he is a man, not the boy I knew on the beach a few short years ago.

For days now I think about loving Gene, about what love is, and how love bursts out when you don't expect it. My mother will never stop loving her brother, Jess, dead for twelve years. Grandma Lee talks about her first child, Dicema, as if that baby had lived a full life, instead of only three weeks.

I think about how Gene and I met. On my first day at his high school, I went to the library on my lunch break. I browsed the poetry section selected a volume of poems by Rupert Brooke. I read a page about a man and woman walking through a field and he told her to "Be Quiet." I liked it because that's how I feel when I walk in the pasture at the farm. I want quiet. Only grasshopper and bird talk sound right to me. I sat down at a table to read the poem over and over. And when I looked up, Gene was sitting across from me. I recognized him because every class I had walked out of that day he was there.

Weeks later, after many hours of kissing Gene, our English teacher told me that Rupert Brooke wrote about war, loss, and grief.

It's been five years since I loved Gene and we were teenagers. But the day of the funeral I loved him like before, loved his mother and sisters as though no interruption or absence had taken place. On our drive home that day, Mom and I barely spoke. I kept wondering: Once you love someone, does it go away? That feeling or emotion or longing for a time, or a person in the past?

In eighteen months, from 1950 to 1952, we lost three men from our family, all horrible accidents. My uncle Jess killed in Hawaii in a plane crash; six months later my uncle Orville died in Midland, Texas in an oil field accident. Cousin Tommy, Army Signal Corps officer candidate, was killed in a night training accident at Fort Dix, New Jersey, the following year. Our Tommy, only twenty years old and home from Korea and heavy fighting. We thought he was safe at last.

Three young men leaving behind many hearts broken, little children, my cousins left without their fathers, a fiancée without her soon-to-be husband. I know that was what mom was thinking of, and I was, too, on our drive home. I was ten when it began and with each new death we kept wondering, what next? How can this be? And how you go on, even though it seems impossible.

Tommy Abercrombie and his fiancé.

30
Last Semester

September, 1962
1400 S. McGregor Apt.

I have permission from my professors to miss class in order to travel with the Beachcombers. I have a dance class with Patsy Swayze that is full of her energy, enthusiasm, and hope. When I explained to her that I would be absent to go on the road with Herb and Melba, she said that would be no problem. Unfortunately, the two-hour PE class that I must have is golf, and Coach Andy, the teacher, wouldn't give me a break for anything. So I keep my head down and swing. I miss the ball.

President Kennedy is a brave man coming to scorching hot Houston like he did. He gave a speech at Rice Stadium, and in spite of our horrible heat and humidity, he looked handsome as ever. He said that in this decade we will go to the moon, that this goal will "measure the best of our energies and skills." We all buzzed around the campus exclaiming and feeling proud as if we had anything to do with anything.

Not that I would bring this up to my dad, who is not happy that we have a Catholic for President, but the whole event reminded me of a certain 1934 high school class motto that Dad always points to proudly when we are in Tryon: "Impossible is Un-American."

A year ago this week I was stuck at home for days while Hurricane Carla wrecked my dearest Galveston. It was a vicious hurricane: Stewart Beach was torn to bits, palm trees ravaged, homes flooded, and Marshall law was required because of looting. This weekend I will see how the famous Hotel Galvez and the Balinese Room across from it look after the year-long cleanup and restoration. Herb has a job there for the Beachcombers Saturday evening. It will be only my second time in Galveston since the disaster.

What I like about being with Herb and Melba and Dean and Lucky is that no matter how apprehensive I might be about something, when we get in the station wagon Herb or Lucky start cracking jokes and then Dean makes some silly comment, and the evening begins, and everything is right.

Terrible headlines and news: US Marshalls, the National Guard, and I think some of the Border Patrol have been moved onto the University of Mississippi campus to control the hatred of some students and citizens of the state of Mississippi. Armed troops must escort and protect a Mr. James Meredith, who is the first African American to register for classes at the university in Oxford. Riots, ugliness, and meanness have erupted around him. You would think he is a cold-blooded murderer by the way he is loathed. In newsreels, his eyes are steady and his mouth firm, but surely his heart, body, and soul pound and shake with every step.

My god, how will he be kept safe?

What did we Beachcombers know last week? We were making music, earning some money, looking out the station wagon window at dark and moonlit skies on far highways in Texas. And I come back here to campus happy with rent money, and everyone is petrified, glued to the television in Oberholtzer Hall, and waiting to see if we go to war with the Soviet Union over Russian missiles in Cuba. President Kennedy is explaining the crisis, and we hear words, but it's through a fog of disbelief and fear. And because for months we've had one violent clash after another here in the South, we do know that terrible things can come to us. But nuclear war? And the end of the world? Will this happen?

At home, Mom has my two teenage cousins, Steve and Claude, staying for a while. She is not used to having boys who want to fight all over the house. And we aren't used to this television full of insane possibilities either. I can tell how tense she is when she asks if Linda and I should get on the bus and come home. In case.

If we go home, I am going to go across the street and visit mother's friend who took me to the symphony several months ago. She is a nurse, a quiet and reflective person who loves to be outdoors. She goes on long hikes through mountains somewhere on the East Coast. She also gave me a book of poetry about a man and his beloved donkey, Platero. It is about friendship and love and celebrates small, everyday joys. The poet, Juan Ramon Jimenez, wrote, "I climb for a moment up a sunbeam to the sky." When I read any page of this book, I am back on my farm in Tryon. I would like to be there now with my grandparents. Where each morning and evening the cows are milked, chores are done, milk and eggs delivered daily, and this rage and chaos that shouts at us constantly, subsides. Chickens must be fed, hogs, cattle, horses, watered and fed. At the farm we listen to the news on an old radio with much of the story unintelligible because of static. Surely, it's better that way.

All of us need to work on staying together because soon I will be through with my classes at U of H, and my plan is to get a job at the Sands again. Annette will begin teaching soon. "You and Annette have the most interesting smiles, so full and yet absolutely looney...if only you have something which ties you together for life," our friend Nadim writes in a note. He is leaving for California and graduate school. Change comes so abruptly, even though it is what I have been dreaming of these past years.

31

We, the Beachcombers, have a two-week engagement in the lounge at the Golden Nugget in downtown Las Vegas. It seems miles from the Strip and for days I think about going to the Sands, but sleep too late each afternoon.

We work from three in the morning until 8:45 a.m. We perform for forty-five minutes, then have a fifteen-minute break. Usually, for the first two hours, from three until five, one of the headliners in the main showroom, Buck Owens, sits in the audience and claps and whistles. We like him and some of his band members, the Buckaroos, because during the week it would be dead without their catcalls and high spirits. Across the street at the Fremont the Newton brothers have an act that is very popular.

Another headliner at the Nugget is Judy Lynn and her country western band. She draws huge crowds, has great sparkly costumes, and a big band. Even though we are a Hawaiian band, I'm sure the country western people know Herb and his famous steel guitar and that he started out playing with Bob Wills and the Texas Playboys.

I manage to get down to the Sands a week before we leave. Mr. Entratter can't believe I am working at the Golden Nugget as a hula dancer. And since he hasn't heard a word from me since I left, he is amused that I am there to collect on his promise. He says not to worry; as soon as he has an opening he will give me a call.

Mr. Entratter tells me to come to any show, just slip in between the velvet curtains like before. So I go and see the Copa girls. They are beautiful, even in pill box hats and long flowing blue gowns. I have a strange shadow creep through me. That I never left the Sands. That college, the Beachcombers, and all that was a dream. Stranger than that, at the same time I feel that it wasn't me on this stage all those years ago, just someone a little like me.

A Valentine's card from Walter, a boyfriend at University of Houston, arrives in the backstage mail at the Golden Nugget. It is startling to hear from him when I am floating in the Las Vegas desert. I was crazy about him a few months ago, but now I can't think about any relationship. Even with someone as cute as he is. Especially someone who thinks they are serious about me. I am happily lonely on the road.

After the two weeks at the Golden Nugget, we pack everything, then take off for Utah and on up to Laramie, Wyoming, where we play for two nights. Then it's down through Colorado for a job near Denver, then back to Texas. The whole way I keep thinking I need to tell Melba I will be leaving when Mr. Entratter has a spot for me, but I keep putting it off. I hate to leave the band, but I have to tell them so Melba can start looking for another dancer.

We've been together nine months and that's a long time when you are in a station wagon rambling from Arkansas to Mexico, drinking Margaritas and buying silver bracelets. I feel like a traitor. But I'm not sure when Mr. Entratter will call, so I wait a while longer to tell Melba.

Almost a month goes by. It is midnight and I am at home in Houston getting ready to go to Herb and Melba's house because we are leaving for a week-long job in Safford, Arizona. The phone rings and my Mom and sisters all jump because it is so late. Mr. Entratter and Renne are calling from Las Vegas. Can I be there in two weeks? I am startled. I didn't expect this call.

Yes. Yes, I say. Somehow, yes.

In the dark, on the highway only hours before we get to Midland, I get up the nerve to tell Melba I will be leaving. I lean over to the front seat and tell her that I will be taking a job at the Sands in a few weeks. She says, "Oh, Judy, you should have told me at home. Now I have to make long distance phone calls from the motel and that costs so much."

They will be stranded with only one dancer. There are long uncomfortable silences, and there is no squirming out of the problem I have caused. For the first time we have solemn miles in the back seats, and low conversations between Herb and Melba in the front.

In Safford, Arizona we settle into our routine. Each night after the show we walk across the street from the hotel and sit in the late-night diner and play "I'm So Lonesome I Could Die," by Hank Williams on the table jukebox over and over until we run out of coins. Lucky misses his kids and family in Friendswood. Diane misses the fiddle player with the Judy Lynn show. I feel the leaving of this group in Hank Williams' voice, the words to his song. Summer, fall, and winter, we have traveled cross country, long moonlit miles. Somehow, Melba has met a young teller at the bank in Safford who wants to dance and travel, and so my departure makes room for another adventurer.

With Herb Remington and the Beachcombers

32
Las Vegas. March 1963

I trace the familiar violet mountains hugging the desert's edge. I walk from the Sands to the Desert Inn in the dark night and see stars poking out and I think of Kathy. It's with a different eye now that I study the Nalani Kele Polynesian dancers at the Stardust as they smile and call to each other in their language.

Harold Dubrow is agitated and sweetly nervous, just like four years ago. Pauline, the seamstress, measures me with maybe the same pins in her mouth as before. Al Freeman kisses me with the same sharp bite to my lower lip.

Even though the dressing room is full of cold cream and perfume bottles, faces covered in pancake makeup waiting for blush and eyelashes, small talk and low murmurs, only Charlotte's face is familiar. Gloria and Arlene and Colette are gone, and no one seems to know where. The lost feeling I had those last weeks alone here without Kathy waits for me to slip into, just like my costume.

I am surprised each night to see myself in the dressing room mirror. The startled young girl who met Judy Garland outside of this room is not there, nor the semi-serious college adventurer, nor the "on the road" happy Hawaiian band member. Instead I see an unfamiliar, standoffish sort of snob who self-consciously teases her hair to fit into a headdress with a long filmy silk scarf that flows past her shoulders. I see a stranger in tight yellow stretch pants, lime green belt, long-sleeved see-through sequined blouse and in yellow high heels, smiling and kicking across the Copa Room stage.

I prefer my red hula skirt, red bra, and flowers in my hair. I miss traveling and living in old motels and having grilled-cheese sandwiches with Diane and Lucky and Dean in a diner where we joke and talk endlessly. I'm not at home in my silent furnished apartment with Utrillo prints of Paris on the walls. I am lost without my books. I have no telephone, no one to talk to. I'm a grump. I've been trying to get here for so long, and now that I am here, I am full of everything that has happened since I left. I've got to focus on getting to Paris. Yet I can't move, can't think, and haven't the slightest idea of how to make a budget or form a plan to leave this town.

I keep having this odd sensation that I never left, never broke my wrist and missed the Nat King Cole show. That is because Nat King Cole was here for another run just a week and a half after I returned.

How can I not feel that I have slipped backstage with no time loss, that my wrist healed, and I never left and only dreamed the last four years?

Now I linger behind, slowly hanging up my costume after everyone has gone downstairs. I listen to the music from the acts on the Copa Room stage. I find my book and begin to read and listen to Nat King Cole sing "Unforgettable."

There is a strange unreality in that the incredible Nat King Cole is performing only a few steps away while I am casually listening to him as I read *The Desert of Love* by Francois Mauriac. What is believable about walking downstairs to the casino and slightly brushing against Anthony Quinn as he escorts two ladies around the blackjack table? Mr. Quinn ignores me like he did four years ago. The constant phenomenon of being admired on stage yet being invisible in the casino or the lounge or restaurant intrigues me. My new pancake makeup and shiny lip gloss and new false eyelashes erase me, and I am glad and unhappy that that is true.

During rehearsal one of the dancers steps over on one of our interminable breaks while Renne and Bob retrace their many changes in the routine and asks, "Have you really finished your degree?" We don't exchange names.

"Yes. Yes, I finished everything in January."

"And your major?"

"Political Science."

"So, you aren't going to work in your field?"

"I'm here to save money to go to Paris."

"Oh," she says, arching her eyebrows for a split second, turning on her heel, and returning upstage.

Later, I learn that Mary, the girl who asked about my degree, is from Greenwood, Mississippi. She has been taking classes at the university here in Las Vegas. I understand now that she intends to get her degree and is interested in travel herself. I have to keep reminding myself that I am serious about living in Paris, and not to get lost in Las Vegas and the life here.

My little sister Beth informs me in a letter that she has all A pluses on her report card. Also at school they are putting on a "scarf dance," and Mrs. Weatherly is making her costume. Most important, though, is she is "saving money like a dog is saving up bones." Which reminds me to try and do the same.

Marlene, who sits on my right facing our mirrors, has a little girl to support. She is trying to buy a home also. I can't imagine working

Mary Baglan from Mississippi

here, taking care of a small child, and not being half crazy. The daytime hours of a child, the nighttime hours of a mother, just that alone is difficult. There are three women in the line who have children. I don't know what they dreamed of before, but just thinking about having someone depend on me gives me the shivers. A child, boyfriend, or anyone. I keep reminding myself I am in charge of getting myself to Paris, and I can be there in the fall, if I am thrifty.

33

My sister Linda has appeared unexpectedly, like a tumbleweed. And indeed, she arrived by bus, by hitchhiking, I am horrified to say, and landed in Las Vegas, with no money, no shoes, and hungry.

Around 10:15, coming up the stairs to the dressing room to sit in the quiet and get ready for the midnight show, I hear a soft call, "Judy." There she is, disheveled, sitting outside of Pauline's room. I have no words as I listen to her story.

We find sandals for her to wear, wash her face, dab on lipstick and go downstairs, through the slot machine area, through the lounge without looking up, and into a back booth in the Garden Room. Harold Dubrow finds us. He let her in at the stage door. We order her a cheeseburger, fries, and a drink. I interrupt her story, "Do mom and dad know you are here?" "No." I leave her with Harold and call home, even though it is late. Mom is, of course, upset, glad she is here, angry, and wants to know what I will do. I don't know. We will call tomorrow. Right now I have a show to get ready for.

In a quick three days, we have found her some clothes, she interviewed for a job, and was hired by Holmes and Narver Engineering. She will live with me and pay me rent out of her salary, which is a good one. She is an excellent typist and learns quickly. My laughable "Paris savings" for six weeks is back to zero. The surprising thing, though, is the kindness and concern everyone at the Sands has shown. Harold, security guards, the Copa girls, and the casino bosses. They ask about her daily. And even more, Mr. Carl Cohen, who is boss of the casino, has stopped me every evening to find out how Linda is.

Mr. Cohen and I have slowly become friends. (I barely remembered him from 1958.) He is intrigued that my major was Political Science, yet here I am dancing in a line. But we talk about all the backstage gossip, the books I am reading, and Paris.

34

My boyfriend Alex is a dancer with a group that has second billing at the Sands now. He is from Europe. He loves working in the United States. You aren't supposed to date anyone performing here at the Sands, but he is charming and funny and will be leaving in a few weeks.

He let me know early on, though, what he didn't like about me. He laughed at my underwear. The first time I began undressing in his bedroom, he looked at me with raised eyebrows, started shaking his head no, walked over to me, kissed my shoulders and slowly pulled down my panties. I stepped out of them, and he flipped them into a trash can with a flourish. "No, no, no. You cannot wear those underwear! You must have bikini panties. No 'to-the-waist' granny underwear." I protested. He shook his head. It was a surprising start to our romance. Alex himself is so sexy that I never look at him backstage in fear that I would give myself away.

We each had a day off, so we went to Reno and behaved like ordinary tourists. He took photos of me and the main street, and his energy and outlook made me feel as if we were in some place other than a small town in Nevada.

Everything is new to Alex. He exclaims over clouds racing down the mountains, and I find a man expressing joy so easily to be irresistible. I'm explaining all these thoughts to myself each day. How nice it is to have a definite limit on a " love affair" like this, to enjoy these few hours and days together when the backdrop is separation that has nothing to do with disappointment. No time for jealousy or silly games, only our best behavior.

Although I am not the young girl I was five years ago, I do crumble, am wholly spellbound, by the sound of Nat King Cole's songs, his voice, his manner. I am especially happy to have his voice all to myself, piped into the dressing room when everyone has gone. I sit on my folding chair, holding my knees, eyes closed, listening to "Lazy, Hazy Days of Summer." It's as if he were singing to me, all alone, with no one to interfere with my reverie. Not only am I content in this quiet dressing room with a book and the presence of the mingled scent of short sprays of perfume, the lonely eyelash curlers, an unused lacy black garter belt, the discarded stocking, and dressing gowns of my Copa sisters strewn about, but I have Nat King Cole, in person, on stage, just down our steps, and his voice in this lovely room. Just imagine.

Sammy Davis will be starring here for a month and we'll have our new number and costumes for his opening. We've been rehearsing with make-believe ostrich feather fans like strippers use. Of course we will have plenty of proper cover-up because Mr. Entratter doesn't believe in any nudity or risqué costumes. Our costumes right now all look like cute outfits Betty Grable would wear in a movie.

In January, after I finished my classes and started on the road again with the Beachcombers, I missed the serious and stimulating dialogue of university life: the daily angst of our political knots, and how to better our society that is unfair to anyone not the "right" color. What authors and books was I missing? Everything my friend Bernie said we had to read became necessary to me. When I thought of Bernie, I was reminded of what a fickle friend I could be and the horrible feeling I had about letting friends down.

But gradually, after hundreds of miles of road passing by outside our Beachcomber station wagon, our rolling home carrying six musicians, dancers, friends, all of us crossing rivers and streams, mountains and plains, then landing here in Las Vegas with sand and brush sifting through my sandals, I have settled into a suspended universe that is unrelated to the other world around me. I slip into this new routine as easily as I do my makeup. I like being in the desert, sunning on a rock like a horned toad or sometimes just flying about, like a tumbleweed, with nothing to direct me but the wind. I am content to drift thoughtlessly towards Europe.

Then I see the headline that Martin Luther King was arrested in Alabama and remember the terrible ugliness seething through the South, and here I sit so carelessly listening to Nat King Cole mesmerize an audience of white people. And who stars next in our Copa Room? Another man of color.

35
Houston and Ben
Wheeler, Texas, May

Because my parents insisted, and Mr. Entratter allowed me to, I have two days off work to take part in graduation at U of H. It is costing a lot of money that I could have saved for my trip, but my parents are adamant about the whole thing.

I have a flight after the midnight show. I arrive in Houston early in the morning after being up twenty hours (since we were in rehearsal). I find Mother crying nonstop. This is because her mother, my Grandma Lee, has a broken-down car and cannot get here for the graduation ceremony. Grandma and Grandpa live in a small town, Ben Wheeler, in east Texas. Would I please return to Hobby Airport, get on a small plane with only two stops, and visit with my grandparents for several hours, then come back in the early morning? An old college boyfriend of mine, now a friend of the family, will go with me. Yes, of course I will go see Grandma Lee.

My friend and I go back to the airport, get on the small plane. I remember all the times when I was small, these grandparents could show up any time after they closed up their bar or restaurant. Early mornings or late evenings, a sleepy surprise. They are the nomads, moving often, as they did when Grandpa worked in the oil fields.

We bump up and down on small runways and arrive in Ben Wheeler in less than two hours. My grandparents, Big Jess and Cora Lee, pick us up at the airport. We all cry and laugh and hug. At their home we have steak and eggs, fresh green onions, fried potatoes, biscuits and gravy, sausage if we want, homemade jelly. We exclaim how the display of Grandma Lee's collection of salt and pepper shakers looks perfect in this small, bright kitchen, admire her flower and vegetable gardens, all the while hearing stories about the family. Later, on the porch, we rock, but I can't keep my eyes open. Probably because I have had little sleep, and this trip was unexpected, and I am full of her good food, I want to stay, forget graduation and working at the Sands, and be with my sixty-six-year-old grandmother, cruising back roads, enjoying tall trees, spying a dancing creek under an old bridge, the wind on our faces.

Back on the puddle-jumping airplane, I arrive in Houston for the second time in twenty-four hours and go home and sleep in my old room. Later, I drive to University of Houston in swelling humidity for a rehearsal on campus so we know how to walk from one point to the other. Later, in the sticky hot afternoon in our backyard, we take pictures of me in my graduation gown. There is the scent of jasmine as we get into the car. We hurry across town so I can receive my diploma. Immediately after that, I catch a plane, spend the night in Arizona, and arrive in Las Vegas in time for the eight o'clock show on Saturday.

My dad could not make the graduation that was so important for me to attend. He had a golf tournament. He wrote me a long letter. He is proud of me. He loves me. He promises to be a better dad to Janet and Beth. He has been busy working while Linda and I have been growing up, and he sees now that he needs to spend more time with his daughters. He apologizes to me for not being home for the weekend. He and Mom are bringing five couples to see the Sammy Davis Jr. show next week. He hopes I can get great seats. I will.

36

Las Vegas

Whether it is the lack of sleep, all the crying, maybe anger at the money I have had to spend, my Dad not being in Houston, the bewilderment of the hectic, sleepless schedule, I am not prepared for my reaction to the new costumes hanging on a rack outside Pauline's sewing room. The sheer, see-through, sleeveless, flesh-colored net, leotard-style costumes with sprays of rhinestones over our private parts and breasts, along with the white ostrich feather fans, give the impression, yes, even the feeling, that we are strippers. This is how Dad and his business friends will see me on stage. I feel as if I have taken off my graduation robe to reveal that underneath I am wearing only a few rhinestones scattered in the right places.

On Sunday afternoon I call home. I explain that they cannot come to the new show because of my see-through costume. Mom laughs. Dad says he will see me soon. It is nothing, he says. Are you covered? he asks.

Yes, oh yes, it just looks like we aren't. Be proud he says. You have a job.

Mr. Entratter made sure Mom and Dad and all their friends had the best seats in the Copa Room. Linda sent Mom a corsage to wear (and to apologize for the distress she caused when she hitchhiked to Las Vegas), and my parents and all their guests are mesmerized by Sammy. Mom collects several Sands place cards with Sammy's photo on the front to send to friends in Texas. Everyone admired the Copa dancers and our sparkly sheer costumes.

Since my sister Janet is afraid to fly, she and my sister Beth arrive after a two-day train ride to get to Las Vegas. Beth can't wait to tell on Janet, who was talking, maybe flirting, with a college boy who boarded the train in Arlington. Janet says a man who had had too much to drink sat with them in the observation seats looking at mountains far away. He had lost his wife and daughter in an accident and he was too sad to be taking a long train ride without someone to hear his story. Janet is thirteen, old enough to remember.

Both sisters say they never saw anything like the country outside their train window: rock formations, canyons, mountains, prairie stretching endlessly. We go to Hoover Dam with Alex and take pictures of the huge concrete wall holding back a mighty river. My sister Janet says Alex does not look at the road while he drives. But he is so happy, so pleased almost, to visit the great Hoover Dam that my sisters fall for him like I have. In my apartment, Mom cooks several meals that Alex devours and that makes her smile. Janet thinks Alex is "soooo" handsome.

My younger sisters come to rehearsal with me, and Harold takes them upstairs to the light room to watch Sammy Davis work on his music. Nine–year-old Beth shakes Sammy's hand and says to me later, "He talks to me like he knows me, Judy."

I say yes, that's how he is.

Linda has charmed our maître d', Tony. She has a ringside seat whenever one is available. She has seen our show eight or nine times since arriving in Las Vegas two months ago.

Before Janet and Beth leave for Houston, we see Mitzi Gaynor perform at the Flamingo. Miss Gaynor is tiny but fills the stage with her song and dance. Four years since *South Pacific* came out, she is sparkling on stage. My three sisters are spellbound, the perfect show for them to see. I listen to famous entertainers every night, and I am sorry she is not at the Sands, so I could hear her songs over and over, and the audience shout and clap and call for more after she tries to take her last bow.

Beth, Judy, Janet, and Linda Johnson. 1963

37

Rumors and stories have been flying around the dressing room and even backstage about a Filipino playboy who is giving fur coats and cash to dancers at the Desert Inn. Sometimes I argue with myself. Would I take money from some man for my trip? The answer is immediately yes, no matter how many times I ask. There is a big catch to that, however. How can I meet a man with money if I cannot bring myself to go downstairs after each show? I prefer being here in the dressing room, reading, listening to the music, and writing letters home.

Last week I had an unexpected letter from my friend Anne who once thought going to Paris was exactly what she wanted. With great excitement, she explained she has chosen to be a wife instead of my partner for Paris. I couldn't believe it. I can't understand why someone would choose marriage over Paris. But after I told the Copa girls my story of losing a travel companion, within a few days I had another unexpected announcement.

The girl from Mississippi, the girl I don't know at all, Mary Baglan, will go with me to Europe. I was going with or without a companion, but Mary informed me, very coolly, that she had "decided" to travel with me. She never asked, nor had we ever had a friendly chat in the several months I've been here. She calmly turned from her dressing table, called my name, and as she pulled on her mesh stockings, said she also wanted to live in Paris and this is a good opportunity for her. In the same breath she said I should move in with her since we needed to get acquainted before our departure, which will be in January 1964. She has to take an English class this fall and after that she will be ready to leave.

Because Linda is moving out to the Nevada Test Site for her new job, I see that living with Mary means more savings for me too.

Since April, Martin Luther King has spent ten or more days in prison in Birmingham; hundreds of young students have been arrested and jailed, and federal troops were needed; and right after President Kennedy addressed the nation about civil rights, a man named Medgar Evers was assassinated, shot in the back in his own yard. Yet, when Sammy and I cross paths in the casino, he says I should smile. How ridiculous of me to be hangdog for some reason when across the desert, beyond these mountains, elementary school students have water hoses and vicious dogs loosed on them.

I would never ask Sammy how he feels about these mean times, the sad hateful photos in the newspaper. Sometimes Mr. Cohen and I discuss these events but there is no talk in the dressing room about any of these crimes. Mary is from Mississippi and we never touch on these things. Instead, we put on false eyelashes and lip gloss, find our Sally Rand white feathered fans, and walk out on stage.

Image from "Viva Las Vegas," A gift from Abercrombie Clan

38

Mary and I have a lot in common because we both have big families. Mary has two brothers and four sisters. She always carries lists of clothes and gifts and toys for the younger kids and gets very upset if she can't find exactly what she is looking for.

She is an accomplished seamstress and a fussy dresser. All her outfits have matching accessories; even her underwear match. No random white bra with flesh-colored panties. Everything, even slips, half-slips, waist cinchers, or a merry widow, it's all color coordinated.

She was startled when she noticed I didn't wear a girdle. Every lady has to wear a girdle, she said. Now I have two, one white, and one black. Of course a girdle covers up my bikini panties that I bought because of Alex.

She told me about one of her boyfriends. His name is Billy, and he works for the Desert Inn and travels around the world. She said she had mentioned my plans for going to Europe to him one night, and he suggested she should go with me.

He is fairly tall, dark hair, quiet, and when he speaks, he looks right into your eyes. Mary wanted me to meet him one evening at the Desert Inn. I was uncomfortable because I'm still wearing college dresses, and I feel out of place. I am totally stumped when I'm asked what cocktail I would like. Any mixed drink makes me cough or shiver. But that night, meeting Billy and seeing Mary look natural and lively and conversational, and me feeling like a frump, has been good for me. I'm not going to stay in the dressing room and read. And I have to spend money on new clothes. Mary has seen the wealthy Filipino man at the Desert Inn and confirms that he has given lavish presents to several of the girls there. The rumors stir our imagination, and hope.

Pauline, the seamstress, pops into our dressing room and says I have a phone call on her telephone. It scares the crap out of me. She hands me the phone and says it is Mr. Entratter. I feel sick. I know I am in trouble for not coming down between shows like I'm supposed to.

"Judy?"

"Yes, sir?" (I'll never sit in the dressing room again).

"Judy, I have a friend who would like to meet you."

"Me?"

A chuckle from Mr. Entratter. "Yes, he would like you to join him at his table in the Copa Room."

"Now? For Sammy's show?"

"Yes. You don't have to, Judy. He's an old friend of mine from Tokyo and a very nice gentleman."

"Oh. Okay. Sure, Mr. Entratter. I'll be right down."

"Rudy will bring you to his table."

"Yes, sir."

I tremble my way into the crappy brown pleated dress. I rub off some rouge. Leave my eyelashes on. Blot off lip gloss.

It is awkward. I mean, I am very awkward. I am the only woman at the table of six or seven men. Rudy introduces me to Masao from Japan. He is about my height, formal, poised, gracious. I am not. I am self-conscious, red-faced, wondering what everyone around me is thinking, including the busboys, the waiters, and Rudy. Sammy's music begins. I am shaking. I get so fed up with myself. I'm such a phony and hypocrite. Isn't this what I had been fantasizing about? Some wealthy man just picking me out of the line and wanting to meet me? And what does it mean? What are my intentions? And what are his intentions? And what would I do for money to get to Paris?

I put aside my dilemma and watch Sammy. I forget about taking money to get to Paris from someone who hasn't offered it to me. At the end of the performance we clap for Sammy and stand up around the table, and I am introduced to Masao's friends. They bow slightly. I am surprised and smile, and we walk out into the casino and then into the quieter Garden Room, and Masao and I try to communicate. We make plans to meet at the Desert Inn after the second show. He laughs when we don't understand each other. He owns a nightclub. Sammy is going to Tokyo to perform there.

After much excited whispering to Mary after the second show, I take a taxi to the Desert Inn. Masao is waiting in the lounge, looking quite at ease, handsome in the way of a man who looks as if he owns the universe. He stands and arranges my chair and politely touches my elbow.

He smiles and asks me something. I know it is a question but consonants and vowels tangle. I say, "Pardon?" and he laughs. He points to his drink. Would I like something? "Coke, please." He orders for me.

We try to converse. He is very pointed. What do I want to do? Do I want to be an actress in Hollywood? No. Not at all. I am going to travel. Ahh. These exchanges are full of mistakes. We ease into laughing at our difficulties. I say "Paris...I want to go to P a r i s." He doesn't know where this is. When he understands, he laughs uncontrollably. He is so easy to like because he laughs at our ridiculous misunderstandings. We slowly have small victories and things smooth out, and he finally asks me will I come to his "loom"?

"Loom?"

"No, no. Rrrooom." He says he has something for me.

Ah. Now what? I follow him to his hotel room.

Although I am slightly apprehensive in the dimly lit room, he hands me what I think is a leather billfold, but instead, unfolded, it is his travel clock, with small jewels to mark the hours. For my travels, he says. I am surprised and begin thanking him and asking him at the same time won't he need it? He shakes his head and then hands me an envelope.

Inside is a five-hundred-dollar bill.

Now what? I look at him. He says it is for my trip also. He wants me to go to Europe. I am flushed and confused and want this money, but what comes next? He says he wants to help me and I ask why? Why is he giving me this much money? He says he likes me. Oh? He puts his arm around my shoulder, escorts me out of his suite and tells me he is leaving the next evening, but maybe he will see me after rehearsals tomorrow.

That is it. He walks me through the Desert Inn, then outside for a taxi, and I say thank you several more times and he closes the taxi door. I mumble, "Five hundred Sierra Vista Drive." I sit like a statue in the back of the car, holding my five-hundred-dollar bill and travel clock tightly. I think it will all disappear when I am inside my apartment, but it doesn't.

The next day he does meet Mary and me after rehearsals. Masao is accompanied by his assistant named Show. Show and Masao escort Mary and me out to the Sands parking lot and they both burst out laughing at Mary's old beat up '56 Pontiac. Especially when she starts it up and the car huffs and puffs and snorts smoke. We laugh too. Masao is pleased, though, to meet Mary and everything is so peculiar and comical and formal and I don't understand him, but I like him. We wave goodbye. I have his card to keep. I am to write him when Mary and I arrive in Europe. He travels constantly, he says.

39

In my excitement over the good fortune, I send Annette money for a plane ticket to Las Vegas. The second night she is here she borrows Mary's car and leaves for the night with a guy I had just met and had a date with. I am angry with myself for sending her money; angry with her, the guy, the situation, and it takes me days to stop boiling. I've never been this steamed at Annette. I don't get over it until Annette is back in Houston and writes me a letter about things to do in Europe. Finally, after two weeks, grudgingly, I get over it. Sort of. If I am honest with myself, I know the guy wasn't interested in me from the beginning. I was mad at that too.

July 10, Mother's birthday, I receive a letter from Dad. He signs off with, "Stick to your guns and firm in your ambitions. Loving you always, Your Pater." He does believe me now, that I am going to Paris. They both do.

Another philosophical letter from Annette telling me not to buy any clothes for Europe because the fashions will be different and that I should reason out "...every decision so that you can later draw wisdom from your reflections on all your past life. It's really all we have after we complete each immediate goal." She talks like that all the time. Bullshit. Nothing in her letter about running off with someone's car and possible boyfriend. One thing I know: I don't get over maddening situations easily.

Paul Anka is opening here soon, then Red Skelton.

40

From Al Freeman, Promotion Director:

On Tuesday, July 16, an MGM crew under the direction of Mr. George Sidney will start filming a picture called Viva Las Vegas. *The filming between 5 AM and 5 PM will take place in the Copa Room.*

The Copa girls must report to the Copa Room by 8 a.m. Some are furious. But if we're lucky, we might see Elvis Presley in person.

Copa girls slump in chairs, smoke, don't speak. Camera crews, light crews, assistants, people with notebooks and powder puffs swarm through the Copa Room. We are asked to get in position on stage. We walk through our number with no music, interrupted many times. Cameras, camera people, lights. Light people adjust, study, smoke, talk, and we sit back down. This goes on for most of the morning. We finally are asked to get into costumes and makeup, and we do and come back to the Copa Room and wait some more. It seems like days in a dark cave.

In walks Elvis. Just walks to the center of our Copa Room and lounges against a table. He looks around. A makeup person approaches him, and he waves her off with a friendly shake of his head. Polite. He looks sweet, like an embarrassed kid. No Copa girl moves. What do you do when Elvis Presley strolls into your living room?

I jump up and go over and introduce myself and say, "I am thrilled to meet you, Mr. Presley." He grins and he is a thousand times better looking than you think he is. I tell him that I was in a band and about Herb playing with Bob Wills, and he likes that. He laughs when I tell him about Lucky playing in the same little hole in the wall out in Louisiana with Elvis, before he was famous. I don't want him to think I am flirting with him, so I shake his hand. Tell him now I can brag to my sisters that I met The Elvis. I walk away thinking he cannot be that sweet and polite, but then, maybe he is.

Meeting Elvis Pressley was worth the long long boring day. When I was in high school, I played his records over and over for hours. Charlotte says we might not even be in the movie. That you never know until you see what makes it out of the cutting room. She's been in several of the movies filmed at the Sands. Ann-Margret plays opposite Elvis in *Viva Las Vegas*, but we never see her.

One morning, a few days after I met Elvis, Mr. Cohen sits with me at about three a.m. I tell him about meeting Masao, confess about the five hundred dollars. Now he knows how I could send Annette money for the airline ticket, and he thinks it's even funnier that she ran off with the guy. I make it a good story and entertain Mr. Cohen. I make him laugh and myself too. Laughing at myself makes everything better.

Mr. Cohen says if I like Henry Miller books so much I need to read *My Life and Loves* by Frank Harris. I've never heard of it, but he says he has a copy for me.

41

Grandma Lee received the money I sent her. She said she used it to get their TV out of the repair shop after it was ruined when lightning struck their home. She wants to buy me a US savings bond for graduation, for going to Europe on. I don't want her to do that because they always are short on money. But you wouldn't know it for all the teasing and laughing she does. She said they took my sister Janet fishing on the Big Eddy near Tyler, and Grandma caught a big catfish, but "fell down into the boat and out into the water—just bruised my hip, the water felt fine just waist deep. Lost my sunglasses but Jess found them. We had a good lunch, cold drinks, and a big ripe water melon, ice cold." Grandma Lee always says she might be getting older, but she still feels like a kid.

Dean Martin is coming, and Mr. Sinatra and Sammy and that whole group. I've seen Dean Martin lots of times the last few months, and I just smile and he looks at me funny. Like he is trying to remember who I am. He is sweet-natured and what do I say? "Hey, remember me? You gave me a ride years ago and we talked for hours and then I went to your room once." I would never do that.

I would like to say to Mr. Sinatra that I did go to college as he suggested it one night, but if I did, would he think I was flirting with him? So, if I see him, I sort of hold my breath and have a small wishy-washy smile that signals I am a Copa girl and I know who he is, but I am not flirting. I'm like everyone else working here at the Sands. A little on edge when Mr. Sinatra is here. He is a bigger star now, if that's possible, than in 1958.

I write back to Grandma Lee that Dean Martin and all the others were here, and she sent a postcard from Texas to remind me that Frank Sinatra is still an eligible bachelor, and he would be a "mighty big catch" and that Uncle Toss has been working overtime since the Shell strike hasn't been settled. She writes around the edges of every letter or card.

Linda had to fly home last month for my Aunt Ladema's wedding, so my savings went back down and I have only $255 put away and five months before Mary and I plan to leave. I will definitely need to work in Paris, so I need to screw up my courage and get over to the Stardust or the Tropicana and see if it is possible to make contacts for working in the Lido or the Folies Bergère.

Mary decides that I should register for the afternoon Shakespeare class that she is beginning. It's true that I have never taken a course like this one. And I agree that we never stop learning and just because we have strange hours doesn't mean we can't fit this into our schedule, but I don't really want to be in a class. It costs too much, it's too much work, and I feel lazy. Besides, I have books I want to read without worrying about studying. But all that doesn't matter. I'm in the class now.

There's no way I can argue with Mary. She has certain plans and ideas, and there is something about her, or something about me, that makes me agree to whatever plan she makes.

After she visits Paris, Mary says, she is moving to New York City to start her career. That has been her dream since she was a child. My plan never included New York City or working, and right now I don't even want to think about a next step because I can't be distracted from my goal of living in Paris. After I'm in Paris, I hope I can figure out how to stay there.

Mr. Cohen and I had an early morning visit, and he said I should take the class with Mary. That's what decided it for me. He and I also discussed all the news (gossip) about who the wealthy Filipino man is courting. One dancer "supposedly" got a mink coat from him, then someone else is "supposedly" getting an apartment in Los Angeles. I have seen this very tall and imposing Filipino man in our Sands lounge but haven't met him yet. Mr. Cohen delights in our dressing room drama, and I guess it is entertaining. We never touch on what might be wrong or right. Ever since I took that five-hundred-dollar bill from Masao so quickly, I have avoided any soul searching.

Having Mr. Cohen alone is the best time for me, and I actually feel a little jealous if someone else comes by and sits with us. It doesn't happen very often because I wait until everyone has left the lounge, the bartender has nothing to do but chat with the girl who has no one to sell her cigarettes to, and Mr. Cohen has seen his last customer and is about to leave the casino. He has given me another book, *Zorba the Greek* by Kazantzakis. He says this book by Kazantzakis is different from *Freedom or Death* and *The Greek Passion*. I can imagine Mr. Cohen and me having these conversations in Paris at a sidewalk café.

On Friday, September 13, I turn twenty-three. The Copa girls give me Berlitz language books in honor of my plan to go to Europe: French, Spanish, Italian, and German phrase books. My sister Linda and her friend Lynn drive in from the test site with flowers. After work, Mary and I go out for drinks at the little bar nearest our apartment. We like it there because we rarely have to buy our own drinks, yet no one bothers us. Men just buy our drinks and leave, so that's nice. Then, early in the morning, around four, I think, back at our apartment, there is banging on our door. Linda and Lynn are there, bloodied and bruised. On their way back to the test site they had stopped for hamburgers and Linda had words with a young woman over what song to play on the jukebox, and I guess they went outside to settle things and all hell broke out. So we clean her bloodied face and get an ice pack for her eye and nose and lip, and finally Linda stops crying and falls asleep.

I think she might have to go back to Houston after this. She has a very good job here, with excellent pay, but she is very young to be living in the desert in such a closed and regimented atmosphere. She can't be cooped up like that with so many rules on a government base where atomic bombs are tested and the men outnumber the women by a lot. Shitfire! as Grandma Lee would say.

On Saturday morning, Mary and I let Linda sleep while we run out to buy our notebooks for the Shakespeare class that starts Monday. We walk around the drugstore talking about Linda and how it is to have younger sisters. We both think Linda should take classes and finish her degree but see that this is impossible while she is out at the test site. I'm not certain what I should do. Linda will be twenty in December, and I'm surely not her boss. I don't want to worry Mom and Dad, but exactly what is the right thing to do? Linda and I are both in a bad situation.

Then on Sunday, after Mary and I have worried about Linda all weekend, the worst thing ever happens. A mean and horrible bombing in Birmingham, Alabama has killed four young girls—Addie Mae, Denise, Carol, and Cynthia—while they were sweetly getting ready for Sunday school. Stunning and sickening.

Yet that evening we Copa girls calmly, without speaking too much, sit facing our bright, light-bulbed mirrors and put on our pancake makeup, our eyelashes, and our red shiny lips. If ever there was a more ludicrous situation in my life, I can't remember. I walk out on stage with a foot-high headdress and shake my shoulders and hips to a Caribbean rhythm and smile when we have just had news of these tragedies.

What does all this mean? To be in Las Vegas, where every other hotel has a black entertainer starring in the main room or the lounge and crowds flock to the show, heedless of their dark skin, and then people breathing our same American air murder young school children because of color.

42

I receive Annette's letter dated September 19, 1963: of her students she says, "They are so poor and underfed yet, so over-spirted with life's simplest joys." She says they are changing her outlook on life. She is taking painting again from Herb Mears at the Houston Museum, then drops in, "Since we have no secrets, I must tell you I have gotten several letters from Dave, the boy from L.A. with a big huge fantastic philosophy, mostly about life's meaning, etc." The one she ran away with in Las Vegas. I feel a slight twinge of anger returning until she reminds me at the end of her letter that I must apply for a passport and that she is getting all the books I asked for at Marboro book store and will have them to me shortly. Mary and I agree, even though she caused an uproar for a few days, that we three have a dynamic together we can't explain. While Annette was here, the three of us talked endlessly about the dream adventure of Europe, of exploring museums and artists and writers and, of course, men, love affairs, and other silly stuff.

Notes from our first class that we contemplate: "There was great religious and political turmoil during Shakespeare's lifetime." As I write that in my notebook, I wonder if there has been a time in history without "turmoil." Last year we were worried about the Cuban Missile Crisis and whether we would be blown up, and now we are wondering if this violence we do to each other will ever end.

In English 465 we have tests every month, a midterm, final, and a term paper. Professor Crawford will give us detailed study guides for every exam. In the Copa Room we begin work on our new number for the middle of October. So classes, Monday, Wednesday, and Fridays, will be sandwiched between rehearsals and the eight o'clock show. We finish work at two in the morning, back to the Sands by ten or eleven in leotards and shorts, finish rehearsal at four-thirty, change for five o'clock class at the University, back to the dressing room at six-thirty for eight o'clock show, down in the lounge in a cocktail dress by nine in the evening. I remind myself, "Please keep in mind, Judy, you are living a superficial life, but it is your choosing. Don't feel inconvenienced because you are slightly busy. Resist your erratic, book-reading life, study and save your money."

Mr. Cohen tells me President Kennedy will be here on September 28 to speak at the Convention Center. He will be in a motorcade passing right by our apartment, so if we wake up in time we can see him. The very least I can do to show my support for our president is to walk half a block to wave at him. It would be my first time to see any president in the flesh.

Annette has sent us another five-page letter of addresses in Paris: hotels, doctors, the women's residence she lived in, the Rodin Sculpture Museum we must, must see, and, of course, the address for Lykes Lines so we can begin booking our trip across the ocean. She assures us that we can do this with no problem and little money. Annette said in her letter she misses us and "that crazy, mixed-up, shallow, soul-hungry, Henry Miller life we led" and for some reason that sentence provokes a slow stirring inside me, that *it*, Paris, is near and that I will be on a freighter within a few short months. Then I will take a bus or a train from Le Havre to Paris. I know it is possible.

I have made a budget for my last months here. Even after paying for Christmas gifts, a flight to Houston, and the trans-Atlantic crossing, I should land in Europe with five hundred dollars, maybe a little more. That should give me several months living in Paris, and maybe I can find work. It is possible that I could work at the Lido, like Kathy, if I screw up my courage and can see myself posing as an almost nude model. I know I'm tall enough for that job. That is my phantom, feeble plan for working in Paris. I will be taking French lessons and writing too. And I will walk along the Seine and find the places Annette has been before, and I will do my own exploring, and perhaps I will find out why, why have I always wanted to be in that city.

I was finally introduced to the fabulous Filipino playboy and his beautiful girlfriend Sarita (also from the Philippines). They are both elegant and formal and sweet. For some reason, that isn't what I expected.

Renne says I will not be dancing in the next show. I'll be a showgirl, walk, pause, pose. According to our seamstress, Pauline, I will be wearing a beautiful, long, red satin dress, red satin high heels, and a red tiara. She measures me for my costume while I tell her about my first crappy English test. She laughs at my complaining about the points I had taken off for poor grammar. Pauline reminds me that I have my degree and shouldn't be so upset. But if she knew I want to be a writer, she might see why I'm very irritated about the whole thing.

Dr. Crawford's comments: "Your knowledge is obvious—your writing skills (grammar and diction) and your organization keep this answer in the 'B' area. The comma splices and word omission are your major problems." Shit. Comma splices? What the hell?

I want to drop the class, but Mary won't hear of it.

43

Collette, my friend from five years ago, surprises me after the first show. She touches my elbow in the casino, I turn around, and there she is, her black hair in a bouffant, her dark blue-violet eyes sparkling, her thick black eyelashes just like I remembered. Oh, she is striking and sweet and more beautiful than ever. She has been in school in Los Angeles, and the most incredible thing! She says she met a young man in the student lounge, and during a long fascinating discussion she told him she had once worked at the Sands as a dancer. He said that was a coincidence because he had been friends with a girl in Houston who had worked at the Sands. And that is how Collette met Nadim, the Persian student I knew at the University of Houston. Nadim, our debonair and cosmopolitan friend from Teheran. What a wonderful world this is to have people you care for and they meet in faraway places and these serendipitous meetings create a mysterious meaning in our lives.

Al Freeman's news in the Sands Bulletin for November 9, 1963 says that TV ratings for the Jerry Lewis two-hour ABC network show originating from the Sands Copa Room were the highest the program had ever received. Jerry Lewis brought down his entire staff of 114 technicians from Hollywood for the show. Special guest appearances by Jimmy Durante, Bobby Darin, and many others.

44

Mary and I have been studying *A Midsummer Night's Dream, Julius Caesar, Henry IV, Romeo and Juliet, Richard III*, and *Measure for Measure* for two months. I've been thinking it's too much for me, with the term paper and getting ready to go home next month and then our Europe trip. We were up early today, rereading our class notes for our test this evening, making sure all our review questions are answered, our essays outlined, and that we know every minor character in each play.

Then the phone rings.

Mary answers. "No. Okay." Grim.

With no comment she reaches over to our old TV, fumbles, and turns it on. We never turn it on because there is no picture. Only sound. I am sitting on the floor, Mary on the sofa next to the phone, the TV on our coffee table. Our notes and review papers are strewn about. Cigarettes, ashtrays, Coke bottles. We don't move. For an hour or two, forever, we sit listening to the news and watching the flickering screen. Dallas, President Kennedy in a convertible, gun shots, Mrs. Kennedy reaching, holding, the car speeding to a hospital. Assassination. We've had an assassination.

We sit in front of our gray-screened TV watching infinitely fine dots and lines waver and shiver. The announcer, who can barely speak, says the President died this morning in Dallas.

I empty an ashtray, stack papers. Mary answers the phone again. It is Charlotte to say the show is cancelled tonight. She says probably tomorrow night, too, because word is that Sammy Davis is inconsolable. He can't dance, or sing, or make jokes. All the shows on the Strip will be dark tonight.

I go to my bedroom and began straightening my messy belongings. I throw away my hose with runs stopped by red fingernail polish. I match up the others into pairs; I find a black garter belt I thought was lost. I wash my white strapless merry widow. I keep filling up the sink, pouring in soap, swiping bubbles. Every few minutes, in between rolling up wet items in towels and hanging them up, I go back to the living room to stand in front of our faceless TV, hoping, waiting for something different, that it is all a mistake.

Mary calls home. Her mother says sadly that if he had come to Mississippi, he might have been shot there too. We have had all these terrible shootings this year. I call home. Mother says they will be at a prayer service at the church this evening. Dad says he was our President, Catholic or Democrat didn't matter. He was our President. Which makes me feel deeply how silly our arguments over Democrats and Republicans have been. All Mary and I can manage is to smoke endlessly and clean and listen to the invisible broadcaster and go to our rooms and cry for a while and then come together and try to seem sensible. As the day wears on, we know less and less about what happened. How? Why? What are we supposed to do?

Late in the afternoon, we drive to the university late to see if there will be a test. The roads are empty, probably not twenty cars from our apartment to the campus. The buildings are dark and we doubt our classroom will be open, but it is. Everyone is there, sitting quietly, stunned, like ourselves.

Dr. Crawford suggests we vote on whether to take the test. And strangely, we all vote yes.

I shift my thoughts from our murdered President to which essays I should write, which list of characters to identify. "Discuss Richard III and Cassius as comparable or incomparable political villains." The lines "beware the Ides of March" and "he thinks too much, such men are dangerous" come full-fleshed with meaning. It is a relief to be thinking of Shakespeare and answering questions that can be studied far ahead of time and that we have answers for. For two hours, I focus: writing, writing. As if the horror of the day could be suspended by writing.

One by one we leave our booklets with Professor Crawford and step outside. The night air is cold, a tender refreshing touch. I notice there are other swollen eyes, a quivering mouth.

"For the rain it raineth everyday," was from what play?

Juliet's nurse said, "O lamentable day."

45

Mary Marx has brought her radio and turned it on so we can listen to the news while we glue on our eyelashes and get ready for Sammy's eight o'clock show. Suddenly someone snaps, "Turn that off! I'm tired of listening to that crap," and it is all I can do not to slap her. Even though I know we can't stay closed another night, I can't stomach this disrespect. We were the only main hotel to be closed two nights in a row. I could have worked last night if Sammy had wanted to, but I would have been a sorry sight. But if Sammy can go on stage tonight and sing and dance and make people laugh, I can walk around in my red satin dress and pose on stage and smile.

Standing backstage in the curtains for the first show, listening to people laughing and glasses clinking and small conversations of people here on vacation three days after the assassination, makes me boil. It doesn't seem right even though I know—yes, I know—things keep going, even when a president is killed. And now we have President Johnson, and the earth keeps spinning. People come to our Copa Room and order drinks and show off their finery, and we listen for our cue from Antonio Morelli and his orchestra. I parade out with my best lip-glossed smile, stretch out my arms with my long gloves, my red glass tiara sparkling as I turn on stage, and I look to the back of the room and think, I am ready to leave Las Vegas.

My last Shakespeare class will be December 12, and I leave for Houston after the second show on December 15. I am counting each day. But I am not making any final plans for Europe. My mind is mush. I have a lump in my heart and a snarl in my stomach, and I just want to get home.

Last June, on a hopeful note, I bought a record ledger to help me keep track of expenses and to budget for my trip. It is a random, nonsensical six pages beginning somewhat efficiently on June 4 with notations that Linda owed $44 to the employment agency, and I had spent five dollars on two ashtrays for our apartment. Nothing noted in July.

One embarrassing page for August: layaway payment to I. Magnin in Reno for my black suede coat; $25 American Guild of Variety Artists dues; $15 for a girdle; $50 set aside, supposedly, for my ticket home to Houston in December.

No entries for September.

In October I made a bold suggestion, bearing down hard on my pencil:

(1) Save for boat ticket.

(2) Save for Christmas presents.

In November, I guess in desperation, I began writing in ink: $25 down payment for passage to Europe; $29 telephone bill, and so on.

For December I made fantastical projections: $5 and under gifts for 30 friends and family; $45 for "shipping all stuff home"; out of

December 9 paycheck, save $30 for passport. However, $86 went for the last payment on my very expensive hair piece (real human hair matched exactly to my hair texture and color).

In spite of myself, I have money (barely) for all tickets needed to get from here to Houston, to New York City (Mary must see her city, and so we will leave from there), to Le Havre, and finally to Paris. Where, it seems, I will arrive wearing a stylish black suede coat with glossy mink collar, a sexy loose Brigitte Bardot hair style made possible with glamorous long hair that no one will suspect is not mine. I should be carrying enough pennies in my pocket to see me through as a struggling writer and French language student for several hours.

Since our president was killed, I have used the record ledger to write about my feelings and about Las Vegas. I don't want to forget these girls because even though we have fussed, they have been my sisters. I want to remember Charlotte's stories and Rowena's too. And I have tried to write about President Kennedy and to understand why I have been emotional about his murder. I think it's a normal response to a death so violent and unexpected. We are in shock. I am in shock. And we have to get ourselves together and do the right things in our own lives. That's all we can do. Just work at doing things we think are important, that suit us.

Unbelievably, my dearest friend Kathy Martin and I meet one night backstage in between shows. She has actually been in Las Vegas for several months but only recently learned that I was back at the Sands. She is working at the Stardust in the Lido show. It is a teary meeting, both of us overcome after this long separation. We hurriedly exchange bits of history and news of our lives before we have to race to our separate shows. I learn that, yes, she has been in Paris for several years and recently was in Rome working as an extra in *Cleopatra*. We'll have little chance for long talks before I leave for Houston in two weeks, but she has promised to write since she has much to tell me about Paris.

46

I cannot take sensible notes during Crawford's lecture. It's because his words about King Lear circle in my mind. I need instruction to appreciate the phrase of "divine forgiveness." And the words I write, "cycle of creation, destruction, and reconstruction" put me in a morbid quagmire and I cannot concentrate. And this sad story of betrayal and heartache *now*? But when I randomly scribble "unknown element—world beyond this world," I stop. In my own small way, I am searching for that unknown, that world beyond this world of Las Vegas and Houston.

In forty-eight hours I will be in Houston. If all goes right, in twenty-one days I will be in New York City.

And perhaps, in less than four weeks, I will be in Paris.

47
Las Vegas to Honolulu
January 1964

Home in Houston for two weeks, I receive a call from Mary with a significant change of our plans. So incredible, in fact, that it takes a lot of bravado and all the acting skills I can call upon to explain to my parents why we are going to the Philippines instead of Paris.

To Mary's news, my initial reaction is a garbled scream and stifled multiple questions since I am standing in our kitchen with sisters walking about and my instinct is to keep the whole thing a secret. The fabulously rich Filipino playboy has changed our lives. Mary is gushing out things like "round-trip tickets to the Orient, seeing Hawaii, the Philippines, Hong Kong, Tokyo" and "all paid for, even luggage." We have many details to take care of, like shots and visas. How do you react to all this?

Mary is leaving for Greenwood to see her family for Christmas and will tell them then. She says we just tell our parents. We are going. It is the chance of a lifetime and who are we to argue with this extremely generous man? I agree with her on everything, but it will be prickly with Wayne and Wynema.

The facts are: Dan Aguinaldo, the rich playboy, has invited seven employees of the Sands Hotel to be his guests in the Philippines. He has also invited one person from the Flamingo. We receive round-trip tickets from Las Vegas to Manila. We need to immediately begin shots required for travel in the Far East and apply for visas. Another fact is, I barely know him.

It all came about this way: Only a few nights after I left Las Vegas, Mary and some of her friends were having drinks with Mr. Aguinaldo when he mentioned he enjoys traveling. In passing, Mary said that she and I were leaving for Paris in a month. He exclaimed what a wonderful plan that was, but why didn't we come to the Philippines also? From that casual cocktail banter we have this incredible development, and now I have received a lovely Christmas card from him with the sentiments, "May your 1964 travels be a thrilling one." I didn't think playboys sent Christmas cards; it seems out of character. He also arranged for a set of rose-red Samsonite luggage to be delivered to my Houston home. To my parents' raised eyebrows, I smiled weakly and kept to my story and said Mary's was a mossy green color. My ticket has arrived, so at least everyone can see I have means to get back to the United States. I am wild with dread, then excitement, then astonishment, and finally disbelief. Pain also. Yellow fever shots and more to come.

Walter, one of my boyfriends in college, has reappeared. And I enjoy, no love, every hour we spend together. Yesterday we went downtown Houston to the Majestic Theatre. He kept me laughing through the entire horror movie *Strait-Jacket* with Joan Crawford, by whispering silly remarks throughout the film. Afterward we drove directly to a motel room out on South Main and made love for hours. And I felt exactly like I did last year when we were together. I couldn't help myself then, cannot now when I am around him. When we are wrapped together, arms and legs and our bodies slick together with sweat and finished with love, I am hungry for him again.

It was hard to leave the motel and drive back to my house, as if I were late for curfew. Besides his perfect body, there is something about Walter that intrigues me. While I was still in college we had midnight walks in MacGregor Park, always in the fog, with Spanish moss moving slightly from the branches of the Live Oak trees. The effect was other-worldly and a little romantic. We talked about being children. He told me about growing up in Iowa on the Mississippi River and the adventures boys make in a small town. I told him about my grandparents' farm in Oklahoma and my walks to the big pond with my dog, Beauty, as a companion. I felt as if we were friends beyond the sex. But I know not to trust those feelings.

A few family things have been settled. I've made arrangements for Beth's dancing lessons at Patsy Swayze's for this next semester. Also, Linda's apartment on Colquitt is paid-up for two months so she can work and save for college classes this summer and not go crazy living at home. Annette has been here for the weekend, sewing me a beautiful long orange and pink-flowered dress for Hawaii. She's given me a gold-filigreed bracelet and a Metropolitan Museum calendar journal I have promised to write in each day so Mary and I will always remember our adventures.

Annette wishes she had a record of her trip to Europe in 1958. We are both very sad that she won't be coming on this great journey with me, but she is teaching and feels so responsible for her little third-graders. She is very proud of the life they have made in the classroom at Anson Jones Elementary. She is in love with every little student and she says they have filled her life to the brim, that seeing them flourish has given her a sense of well-being herself.

But we are melancholy. I tell her about Collette meeting Nadim, and we talk on and on about all of us at the university and how we are now scattered around the world. Annette has the constant longing for the next search, the next adventure. That's why we are friends. Now she is exploring making her living and managing her little students' world for hours each day.

But we always want more.

On saying goodby to my family? Grandma Lee says, "Go. Have an adventure!" Grandma Johnson asks for postcards from wherever we visit. Mom cannot smile and barely meets my eyes. I hug my Dad and hold my breath. They never questioned our plans. I have realized, in these last four weeks, that they accept all these extraordinary changes as if I am an adult, in charge of my own life. Which is exactly what I want, but it comes as a surprise.

Sitting on the plane, I am overcome by relief, away from my family. These abrupt starts and stops and changes to our plans I handle better on my own. I don't like explaining myself, feeling as if I have to hide things or smooth them over. That feeling makes me pause and wonder if this is a crazy thing, and I shouldn't be doing it. But I think Mary and I together can make things work.

I have something to do for my Grandma Lee. In a quiet moment days before I left, she asked a favor. Her eyes were moist and her chin trembled and I hugged and hugged her and said of course I would buy a lei in Honolulu and find the point where Uncle Jess's plane went down and toss the flowers there. Mother gave me money to buy Hawaiian flowered necklaces from both of them. It is now almost fourteen years since Jess died, but for Mom and Grandma Lee, at the mention of his death, always fresh tears. I know better now, since President Kennedy's dying, how those three deaths in eighteen months affected my family. Uncle Jess, Uncle Orville, and cousin Tommy. Their faces so handsome and bright.

Mary meets me at McCarran airport January 15. Do we know what we are doing? No.

48

My untyped term paper was never completed. Mary, of course, has managed to get hers in on time. We are in a mad frenzy to have the apartment cleaned, the utilities paid and disconnected, and worst of all, to pack and manage our bulging suitcases. We leave for Los Angeles tomorrow. I've wandered through the Sands feeling like a tourist. I sat in the lounge with Mr. Cohen, and even that had a different feel. Away from my home, no work and no boss, I am free to make my own mistakes and no one to answer to except myself. Mary and I determine what we do. We are in for something we don't know, our fortune tied to Mr. Daniel Aguinaldo. But so far, it all seems exotic and incredible. We are in a group, and I think, I hope, our travel adventure will go well.

Most of all, I feel I have accomplished my goal of getting to Paris, just being on my way there. Never mind that we are headed west, across the Pacific, searching for Europe.

Mary receives a call from Dan instructing us to go to the Japanese Consulate for a visa since we will be going to Tokyo before we go on to Europe. We spend over four hours getting that accomplished. There are lots of long lines, but it isn't awful. I see lots of cute guys, talk to people from Canada, a young man who speaks Japanese but was born here in California and is now traveling to visit relatives. The room buzzes with different languages, and I come away feeling as if I have been in a foreign country. It is exciting to meet someone from a faraway country and exchange stories.

My friend, Don P., a man I dated several times in Las Vegas and with whom I exchanged book lists and talked politics endlessly, entertained me at his home this evening. I carefully studied his Russian art books, scenes of old Siberian villages and farms, forests, soldiers singing, and a haunting picture of a beautiful woman, the Swan Tsarina. I kept thinking that Mary and Annette should have been here for this evening art book-trip to Russia. We listened to old forties records by Dinah Shore and Frank Sinatra and some Billie Holiday. It was the best time and we talked more about the book list (three pages long) he has made for me, and of course, the death of our president.

Don reminded me it's not the first assassination we've had in this country. He is a historian, a music and art and book lover, and a keen observer of politicians and how they conduct themselves. He says that I will find American and Filipino history full of intrigue.

Tomorrow Mary has a date with her steady boyfriend, Glen. They are making plans to meet in Hawaii. I am making a short trip to San Francisco to meet Harry, the fun fellow I've seen occasionally. He wants me to see his favorite town. It will probably be the last time I see him. I can't imagine he will be single for long, and no telling when I will ever be back in this area. Actually, I think all this dashing around keeps us from facing our departure for places unknown.

Harry and I had a whirlwind twenty-four hours that began with a walk around Fisherman's Wharf, continued with drinks at the Condor and dinner at Ninos, and then a morning drive to Sausalito for breakfast and a stroll through little art galleries. (The whole time we were together I never had time to take off my false eyelashes, so I worried that one might peel off and the other stay on. Luckily that didn't happen. Same for my new hair piece. I kept my false pony tail and long curling strands of hair flowing around my face Brigitte Bardot style and prayed it would all hold together until I got back to L.A.) I wouldn't cry over Harry since we've never had a serious relationship, just a good time. But when I waved goodbye to him and San Francisco, I did have a little lump in my throat.

Back in Los Angeles, Mary and I check out of the Hilton, take a taxi to the airport, fumble and struggle with our six pieces of luggage, and check in for the eight o'clock Pan Am flight for Honolulu.

As we board, feeling nervous and excited, we are jostled and bumped by other passengers as we find our way down the aisle. Ever so fortunately, I fall against a tall, beautiful young man and our eyes and lips come too close together. I want to let go of my purse and makeup kit and magazines and throw my arms around his neck. Without saying a word, we manage to find seats together in the back of the plane. We kiss several times, then introduce ourselves.

"I'm Judy," I mumble. What has come over me, to take one look at a stranger and feel a heat throughout my body and have no control at all?

"Gerard," he says. "I'm Gerard." Then we kiss, three, four, five more times. I'm sorry we don't have a private room. Even for me, this is unusual. We spend the entire flight enjoying the dark, each other. He is from Australia. We talk, laugh, wonder about our intense, instant attraction, sail across the Pacific lost in and exhilarated by each other's stories, plans, histories. Anyone who sees us must assume we are long-separated lovers, and who knows, maybe that's true. It is an intense six-hour affair. I'll always think of it as perfect in every way.

Honolulu's airport is small, or it seems that way in the dark. Heat and humidity dampen our arrival, or is it the letdown from the sexual excitement of the flight? We collect our too many, and way too heavy, pieces of luggage, get a taxi, and find our hotel. We walk through a dimly lit bar on our way to register for our room. An aquarium full of fantastic fish illuminates our passage, and delights us. Their colors are bright, the shapes of the fish mysterious. We can sit and drink and watch the fish and envy their watery, undulating world. We can walk right out on the beach from the hotel too. Wherever we look, we see beautiful palm trees and sweet-smelling flowers and shrubs: jasmine and gardenias and carnations, heavy with scent.

We are going to be here for a week, but maybe we should have planned to stay longer. I see a notice for hula lessons, and I start tomorrow two hotels from here.

I keep imagining Mitzi Gaynor popping out from behind palm trees and singing, "I'm Gonna Wash that Man Right Outta My Hair," or Bloody Mary appearing on the beach in the evening and telling us, "You have to be carefully taught." *South Pacific* and the newsreels and movies about the attack on Pearl Harbor formed my impression of Hawaii. I know nothing about the goddess Pele or Queen Liliuokalani, or why Hawaii became a state. Why do we have a state out in the Pacific? I've never understood that.

49

We have been Mary, Jerry, Judy, and Joe at a bar listening to Arthur Lyman, strolling in the early evening down the boulevard to meander through a pink mirage—the Royal Hawaiian Hotel. Mary and I separate from our new friends we met on the beach while we enjoy steam baths, massages, naps, and solitary walks to admire the Pacific. I didn't know what to expect of Hawaii. There are fellow tourists everywhere, men in luau shirts and ladies with flowers pinned behind their ears, and many carry colorful drinks with paper umbrellas stuck in them that make a sip difficult. Jerry and Joe have been here for days and steer us to the best hotels and bars on the beach.

You can try to imagine the mystery of Diamond Head when you roll your oily, sun-drenched, lethargic body up off a beach towel, shade your eyes, find that famous shape in the distance, and think to yourself, My god, I am really on the beach at Waikiki. And while you are lazily intoxicated with the music of drumming waves, the constant shriek and chatter of unseen and unknown birds, and the fragrance of pikake and plumeria, you realize these sounds and aromas belong to *the* Hawaii.

Blossom is my hula teacher. She greets our class with a sweet, patient smile, explaining that she is Hawaiian and married to a man in the Navy. We are excited tourists, eager to learn to shake our hips, make signs with our hands to the words of the music, and after several days, and several hours, know a hula dance.

Blossom surprised us. She is young, beautiful—a more graceful dancer I have never seen—yet she is large, fully rounded. I'm sure most of us thought our teacher would be small-waisted, like the picture postcards, a grass skirt, smiling, maybe bossy and sassy looking. Instead, we have quiet Blossom, thoughtful, sincere, and thorough.

She gives us a short history lesson as she performs to music and we follow her motions. The hula was, is, a sacred dance. But one that was forbidden by the missionaries in the early years. Teachers and elders and the keepers of ancient customs went underground. We learn this tale of suppression as we warm up to rhythm, to the ebb and flow of a sad history told to us by a gentle, dancing, full-bodied woman. For me, the hour lasts a suspended moment or two.

After our first class, I ask Blossom if she gives private lessons. She does and we spend a half hour talking and dancing. She listens with wide eyes to my stories, how the hula found me, my uncle stationed here in Hawaii, my aunt Jo teaching me steps and hand movements to "Little Brown Gal." And that I hoped she could smile on me for thinking I knew anything about her dance, its history, and the meanness that has happened to Hawaiians. She does laugh about my travels with the Beachcombers, about Dean and Lucky and playing cards in the back of the station wagon all hunched over. I like it when she laughs. I ham it up.

She wants me to come with her to eat the food she knows and grew up with. And she likes it when I say no dances—no Lovely Hula Hands, or no Hawaiian War Chant—only technique. Let me watch you, Blossom. How do your hands and arms and body and hips move like a ripple through the surface of still water? Or a wave tumbling and falling through the deep ocean?

Mary is busy. She has flown to Kauai to meet her boyfriend. And she is staying with her "Quit-Smoking-with-Vitamin C" regime. She feels Hawaii is perfect for her to quit cigarettes, since we are served fresh fruit with every meal. Then there is sightseeing to keep her occupied if we are not on the beach, so she stays busy until she falls asleep. I should quit smoking, too, but I haven't thought about it yet.

I am alone since our friends Jerry and Joe have left Hawaii, though Joe says he will see us in Rome.

Blossom tries to tell me how native Hawaiians on these islands live. Yesterday, we walked to a small café five or six blocks from our hotel. But in those few short blocks we left the commercial hotels and beach shops for a quiet, rundown neighborhood. No "Hawaiian" shirts. I saw no cameras or leis, and no one was smiling or laughing or speaking loudly.

The café was silent. There were five square tables with mismatched chairs, cracked and chipped cups and saucers stacked on the counter. There was a black-and-white faded photo of Queen Liliuokalani hanging on the wall. Blossom explained that she was Hawaii's last monarch, deposed in 1893 by men with no authority except for their blatant greed and total disregard for the native population.

Seated next to us, in the center of the café, was a very husky Hawaiian man who glared at me as I looked around the room. He gave Blossom a disgusted nod and turned his chair away from us. The man and woman sitting in the back of the room raised their eyebrows. Blossom said not to bother. They weren't used to having tourists like me in the café. Some Hawaiians—*some,* she said—don't like tourists at all. They resent tourists and their ignorance of the shameful history of the Hawaiian people. She said she was glad to have her teaching job, but it's difficult for native Hawaiians to make a living. They are surrounded by people who come to their island to visit and spend money, but disregard Hawaiian traditions. Unfortunately, I fit that category.

The "poi" arrived at our table. Blossom wanted to know what I thought of it.

"Sticky mashed potatoes," I replied. The raw fish was my favorite, spicy and tangy. We ate and talked about the old hulas and her former teachers. I told her about dancing at the Sands and about the Leilani Kelly dance troupe at the Stardust that I admired for so long.

Later that evening I had an umbrella drink. It gave me a headache and I walked through the shell shops and lei shops and shirt shops and my head got worse. I remembered an old photo of Uncle Jess under a huge banyan tree and wandered around thinking I could find the tree. No one I asked knew of a gigantic banyan tree. I thought of sitting with Blossom in the little café, and the guy who snarled at me. Tourists usually don't really know where they are. They want a vacation in a place that is a change of scenery. They want to feel happy and don't want to know about other people's troubles.

Drinking makes me depressed, whereas everyone else was drinking and being happy, and for some reason that got on my nerves. I think what's wrong with me is that I know I understand nothing about Hawaii, and that makes me dislike myself for being like every other person visiting here.

50

We've been in Hawaii three days and I have gained four or five pounds eating and drinking while Mary has lost as much on her fruit diet. When Mary says she is going to do something, she does it. That's an irritating thing about her because it's hard for me to stick to any resolution having to do with a diet. These were the things I was thinking of today, driving around the coast looking for Kaʻena Point. I had no idea how far I had to drive, or how lost I would feel, but I promised Mom and Grandma Lee that I would come here, bring the leis for Uncle Jess.

I hadn't counted on this heat and sticky humidity. I drive with my map blowing around in the car and my hair slicked together, plastered across my forehead, strands slapping across my eyes, stinging. My fat is uncomfortable, sweat-sticky globules mucking behind my knees, underneath my arms, between my breasts.

I pass deserted beaches, curving into endless, uninterrupted scenes of the Pacific with enormous waves rolling menacingly in the distance. How friendly my Galveston is, the warm and child-sized waves of the Gulf compared to this cold immense Pacific. And how ferocious these islands are, bursting through the ocean floor, holding fast, surrounded by an endless assault of marauding waves. I curse my sweat, my fat, my bad humor, my silly little fear, and only for a few moments do I manage to think tender things and remember Jess—Jess who was one of six DC-3 pilots handpicked by Admiral Byrd for his expedition to the Antarctic, to explore "the hitherto unknown," as Jess's famous commander had written. I remember how we passed around the October 1947 *National Geographic* when it arrived and were amazed to see our uncle posed nonchalantly with his fellow pilots, smiling handsomely out of his fur-lined parka, snowy, icy mountains in the background. Operation High Jump. I remember Jess's gray-green eyes.

Finally a sign. Kaʻena Point, the northwestern point of Oahu, named, according to Blossom, for one of Goddess Pele's brothers, or maybe a cousin. I pull my rental car off the highway. In the distance, a cliff rises high above the road; waves burst and heave against rocks. I park and lean over for the leis. A breeze finds them and stirs their fragrances.

I think of Jess's wife, my aunt Jo, and how we waited until late afternoon for the heat in Houston to let go so that we could practice our cartwheels and splits and somersaults in the little shade. Jo was the best, still a kid, it seemed, at twenty-four. And beautiful. That's when she taught me to hula. Bend your knees, back straight, step sideways one, two three, touch, step and go the other way. The song "Little Brown Gal," played by Alfred Apaka. The words, "I wanna go back to my little grass shack in Kealakekua, Hawaii." We had a hedge of gardenias in the back yard, carnations of all colors in the beds out front. At Christmastime, upside-down in a cartwheel, I would catch fragrant bursts of ginger.

Jo and my cousins Kandy, Jessie, and baby Nancy lived with us for half a year after their dad, our Jess, was killed. For months, Mom washed dishes with tears running down her face.

I walk slowly, closer to the ocean. One newspaper account told of the fisherman who had watched Jess's plane. The fisherman must have seen plenty of the P2V Neptune patrol bombers firing rockets at their fixed targets. But that day, Jess's starboard wing tore off as he began pulling the plane out of its dive. The fiery explosion was handled efficiently by the deep Pacific. The fisherman and several others rushed to the site where mangled debris slid quickly into dark water. A rescue boat from Pearl Harbor came. It wasn't needed, nor were rescue helicopters, the Navy strike rescue seaplane, the navy destroyer. Eighteen Navy divers, going down two at a time, two submarines, the Caiman and the Cabezon, underwater floodlights for work through the night—all of that, and only scattered bits of plane wreckage and human remnants were found. Heavy seas hampered salvage operations.

Grandma Lee's "sun," Jess was.

I sit down. I fiddle with the flowers. They are heavy. I dig my toes under the sand, toss pebbles. I try to think of a prayer, remember our

Navy pilot. I wonder instead if the fisherman who saw Jess go down is still alive, and what fish did he catch that Monday, November 27, 1950? What watery, darting sea creatures were startled by the writhing dying plane? But then, these waters and its creatures moved and lived with angry volcanic eruptions, ancient feuds, fire shooting from endless crevasses in the earth, then plunging into great green ocean depths.

My only prayer is Grandma Lee's cuss word, "shitfire." SHITFIRE! SHITFIRE!

And why in the hell did that right wing fall off? Jess had three little kids. And who knows about all the other little kids and wives and sisters and brothers and mothers and fathers who were left behind that day. "Death was immediate and merciful," his friend wrote. That is good for the pilot we loved. But I don't think for Grandma or Jo or my mom or anyone else in the family was death immediate. Jess keeps dying, all this time.

I jump up and walk to where the waves disappear, cautiously, only my feet and toes and ankles cooled by water. I start throwing the leis—hard, as far as I can throw, which isn't far at all. As fast as I throw them, they float right back to me. Kiss my ass. They don't want to float out deep, maybe a mile away, drop down 120 feet and rest, undulating on the ocean floor, marking our lost singer, our pilot. I inch out farther, water above my knees. I throw the goddamn leis over and over. I can't go out much farther; I am afraid. At last, the pikake lei slips over a wave, journeys off on its own, a fragrant circle out to sea. The plumeria follows, humors me. The Pacific thunders against the cliff, swirls, pushes against my thighs.

One letter to Grandma Lee said, "It is with greatest regret that I must inform you that there is no possibility of Jess being alive." It is a fine letter, praising Jess. It is almost fourteen years old now. The letter.

And Jess's dying.

Over and over, Mom dreams she sees Jess, her lost brother. She walks across a fine white sandy beach, walks as far as she can until the water reaches to her shoulders, then she dives into the sea and swims down into the deepest part. Jess lives there. He waits at his door for her visit. He is happy. They go inside his bright blue watery home. She sits down at the piano and begins to play. They sing, harmonize, like old times. They sing "The Gypsy," "The Whiffenpoof Song." Or "On the *rue de la Paix*, there was once a cabaret, and MiMi." They laugh and laugh and sing and tell stories like they always did when they were kids. He leans on the piano, his head tilted to the side. Sometimes he is in his uniform, other times he's in his khakis and T-shirt. Much later, but too soon, she has to leave. They hold each other. He waves goodbye.

"Hurry back, Wy."

"Love you, Jess. We wish you would come home."

"It's better like this, Sis," he tells her.

She swims, gliding upward through sunbeams, light shafts piercing the green-silver sea, millions of bubbles swimming with her to the surface. She breaks through the dream's edge, eyes wet.

Jesse and Wynema Linn

51
February 1964
Guam

Mary and I have too much luggage. We pay a lot of money for its being overweight. We knew there was a forty-pound limit, but we didn't have an understanding of "forty." My two pieces are almost double that. And my makeup kit alone probably weighs forty pounds, but I managed to lug it aboard the plane with my bag full of books and my purse. At least Pan American didn't charge me personally for weighing five more pounds than I did in Los Angeles.

I can't sleep. The plane is crowded. I am making notes to myself. Exactly how long is this flight from Honolulu to Manila? I must ask the stewardess when she comes by, except I am in the middle seat and Mary is dozing in the aisle seat, and I don't want to wake her. We are worn out from vacationing in Hawaii and snappy to each other and both know we have to solve our luggage problem. And I have my own uncontrollable self to deal with. Why can't I send half of my dinner back uneaten like Mary does? I eat every roll, with all the butter; every scrap served to me vanishes. But not Mary. She is happy with a few bites, while I secretly want to pick off of her tray and am already wondering if we will get a little snack served to us. When we get to Manila, I will begin a diet.

I can see that it doesn't matter if the shades on the windows are open or closed because outside, from my seat, there is no sign of morning, no light at all. And where are we right now, five or so hours after leaving Honolulu? I can barely place in my mind where Manila is on a map.

I wonder if we fly over the island Eniwetok, where my uncle Orville was stationed as a Seabee. The last time I saw him was in Midland, striding through the front door after work, opening up a cold can of beer, sitting down in the living room and teasing us kids. I remember staring at his dark blue eyes and thick black eyelashes. At age ten I knew he was handsome like Gregory Peck, and now I wonder why he was so unselfconscious about his eyes, his face. He was tall, too, and no matter how many times we sat at a kitchen table with him laughing and drinking, we had to remember not to stare, or act stagestruck when he smiled. He grew up on a farm in Kansas and could fix any tractor or small motor or any farm implement. In high school he won a prize for his woodwork and was on the track team. He and my aunt were married, he enlisted in the Navy, went to the Pacific. He was like all the other guys, but to us kids he was our movie star.

He died on a grimy hot day in a Texas desert. A power line fell across a truck in an oil field, and Orville was electrocuted trying to help a young man to safety.

Sitting now in the dark on a Pan Am flight across the Pacific, it is the story of him as a Navy Seabee stationed on Eniwetok in 1944 that I try to remember. They were there to build a fueling station for airplanes, my uncle Toss told me. Toss remembers the chocolate bars Orville sent to him from the far Pacific. A package stamped first in Pennsylvania arrived in Eniwetok, then traveled back to Oklahoma to Toss's great delight. Somehow, in the evenings, Orville knotted and braided parachute strings together to fashion the silk hula skirt that became mine.

The stewardess said we have crossed the International Date Line and so our Sunday, February 2, has slipped away, leaving an empty square in my 1964 Metropolitan Museum journal.

Uncle Orville and Aunt Ladema, Steve and Claude. Uncle Toss, 1949, Cora Lee Linn

52
Philippines

Sights on leaving the Manila airport with our hosts, Dan, the generous Filipino playboy and his girlfriend, Sarita: Farmers in loose white shorts, some wearing cone-shaped straw hats, bare-chested, bare feet, following water buffalos with plows; tall towering trees framing each scene; long swinging vines, beautiful bunches of wild bougainvillea, dazzling white, some a deep magenta; children playing, smiling, running past small huts with thatched palm-leaf roofs; rushes of color, palms everywhere, hens scratching for feed—is that a barnyard?—and amazing watery fields planted with crops I don't know. I hang my head out the window like a child.

An enormous banner strung between tall trees: MABUHAY! "Welcome" in Tagalog, the native Filipino language. Dan and Sarita giggle and laugh with each question we have. They think it is funny that I am starry-eyed over the water buffalo, or caribou. I can't help it. Why am I struck by shirtless farmers? Their skin glistens and the watery fields glisten, and I act like the fool. Even the stray, brown-spotted dog trotting so happily down the highway and every shy smiling child waving to us as we speed by seem exotic. I am beside myself. I wave back.

Dan and Sarita have changed. He is neither a tall, haughty man dressed in a suit or the playboy who seemed to be courting multiple chorus girls. She is not the small, beautiful, cool, and remote woman dressed in a cocktail dress and fur coat like she was in Las Vegas. Now he is tall, friendly, dressed in a beautiful white embroidered shirt that is loose and comfortable. She is smiling in a sundress and sandals, greeting us as sisters.

When we last met, four months ago in the Sands casino, I never dreamed, never expected, to see them again. Now I have the full realization of what that chance meeting has meant. I am in a foreign country surrounded by beautiful faces, glorious blooming trees, a wondrous countryside, and I am delirious with the newness, the unexpectedness of this feeling. I am free of everything that has ever happened before, as if I am starting life all over again right now, in the back seat of this car, gazing out the window at all new human beings.

The traffic jam in Manila is thrilling, outrageous, full of clutter and clanging. Houston traffic jams are in black and white, but this Manila one is in full spectacular color. There are no traffic lanes, no rules, red lights mean nothing. Only the honking of horns, the ringing of bells, and loud music are respected. And this traffic jam is made more colorful by the many "jeepneys," painted in every design and color imaginable, decorated with plastic flowers, fringe, polka-dotted umbrellas and people jammed and crammed and hanging out with their dangling packages. Will they fall? Mayhem. Whoever honks and bullies the loudest earns the right of way. Here there is no open space. No time to contemplate. With great finesse and a minor miracle, we arrive at our hotel. We check in, go to our room, unpack, and dress for lunch at a country club.

Again we plunge into traffic, emerge near a harbor crowded with yachts, medium-size fishing boats, smaller boats with a single fisherman all rocking against each other in their own traffic jam. The bluest sky makes me tremble. We weave, we hurtle along towards a green space with a gigantic golf ball on a gigantic tee announcing the Manila Country Club. Palm trees frame the long winding drive to the club house. I lean back against the car seat. My eyes won't stay open, and I feel like a nap. I can barely make sense of where I am and how I came to be here. What casual and careless plans we have made, Mary and I, to take this long detour to our destination.

Dan and Sarita have friends waiting to meet us for an afternoon drink and hors d'oeuvres on the wide veranda. Curved rustling palm trees and whirling overhead fans give the illusion of a breeze, but the humidity sucks every ounce of energy from us. We exchange names, pleasantries. I might pass out if not for ice and lemonade. I press the cold glass against my cheek.

Unbelievably, as dripping in sweat and faint as I was, we do not go back to the hotel, but drive again through clanging streets to the Manila Jai Alai Building. We are amazed at the rounded glass front structure, the light-filled noisy entrance, the intensity of the betting inside, and then the rapid fire of a hurtling ball that is impossible to follow. Dan explains something we can't hear. Sarita tries also, but all words are a blur. One of Dan's guests, a physician I think, tells us that this building survived the Battle of Manila, which actually began nineteen years ago today. We smile and don't know about this battle but he says, offhand, with a shake of his head, that one hundred thousand Filipinos died in the month-long battle to recapture Manila. That this bouncing city full of crazily decorated jeepneys was methodically destroyed by the retreating Japanese. That is the cold water I needed to throw off my lethargy. Now I look around me and look at these wildly excited jai alai fans anew. We are cheering life in this fine Art Deco survivor.

In three brief hours I see Dan as a completely different man from the one I thought he was. He has our itinerary planned: a tour of the city, a visit to the World War Two Memorial, a flyover of the Bataan Death March in his private plane. Tonight we have dinner and then drinks later on his yacht. And in four or five days we leave Manila for Davao and his Pearl Farm. Also Sarita will take us to her beauty parlor for hairdos and manicures and a visit to her home to meet her mother.

We have no time to entertain fatigue. We are stuffed full of new sights, new clothes, new sounds, new music, many languages at once, and warnings: Only take a certain taxi, never another. There have been incidents. Do not give to beggars on the street. It is their business and a profitable one. And watch for pickpockets when you are surrounded by a crowd. All this as we barrel through streets, traffic, crowds, marveling that we move at all, and intrigued by how this chaos works, how it came to be. We stop so faithfully at red lights at home. It is unimaginable that there is a place where red lights have no authority and collisions are avoided magically and with great gesturing and flair. I am amazed that traffic has such personality. I will never understand how life dropped me off at a country club in Manila today on my way to Paris.

53
Pearl Farm

Imagine this first evening in an exotic country. We sail out of a harbor on a sleek yacht. Cocktails on the deck. Twinkling lights from the mainland and all around the vessel. These mysterious lights are from the gently rocking, lolling lanterns in the small invisible boats of invisible fishermen scattered as far as the eye can see. This can only be compared to cruising through the heavens with stars blinking and nodding.

Early morning we meet Sarita's mother at their home, have too many cookies and soft drinks, inspect her Storybook doll collection from around the world, then have a four-hour appointment for manicures, pedicures, VIP hairdos like Elizabeth Taylor's. In the evening, an hour or more at another jai alai game, then on to dinner at a Chinese restaurant with many people, some who are polo players, and finally to our hotel at four a.m.

We don't wake up until noon. We head to Tesoro's gift shop where we buy presents for everyone. We are happy with our souvenirs and postcards until we walk outside and have a terrible scene with a woman beggar, so pitifully thrusting her tiny baby wrapped in rags at us. When we resist her request for money, both of us thinking of Sarita and Dan's warnings, she begins calling us names. It is very embarrassing. Then, as we are squirming our way out of the crowd, feeling heartless, a flashy black car screeches to a halt in front of us, a young man hops out of the passenger side holding yet another baby in grungy blankets, and what happens? He quickly makes his way to the woman's side, they exchange babies with not a word, and he jumps back into his car with off-duty baby and speeds away.

We hurry off, too, but not before I make eye contact with the professional beggar and return her disgusted look. We disappear into the nearby bookstore, where I wander aimlessly until I collect myself. I buy two slender volumes of Oriental History for high school students. Back at our hotel we spend several hours wrapping gifts and then deciding what to take to the Pearl Farm. We will fly to the city of Davao in Dan's private plane, then transfer to a boat to take us the rest of the way.

We have dinner tonight at Dan's home. His son Victor and some of his other friends are there. The evening is an exciting blur. Foods I've never heard of, too many handsome men, too much to drink, and stories and history that I won't be able to half remember. I learn the President of the Philippines, Diosdado Macapagal, is the son of tenant farmers and wants to reform the land codes. These codes keep poor people from owning their own farms. This situation was handed down from the Spanish colonizers. I am reminded of Blossom and the history of the native Hawaiians who lost their lands to Christians and pineapple plantation owners. No one at the table seems to think the reforms will work. There is trouble from the communists, who want land reform also, so something must be done somewhere. The president would like to eliminate corruption, but perhaps that will be more difficult to address than land reform. After much discussion, food, and drink, the problems remain. The conversations are rapid-fire in Spanish, English, maybe some Tagalog, and change directions and topics from one end of the table to the other. I keep thinking I have a lot of reading to do.

But one thing is amazing. Dan's grandfather is Emilio Aguinaldo, a person I never heard of until late in the dinner. He is alive, very old and feeble, and led the fight for independence from Spain—and then the United States. There is more Spanish spoken at the table at this point, so I think this part of their history is what I need to read about.

Three conclusions from the dinner table: I cannot learn history when I drink three or four glasses of wine. During World War II, Manila was decimated and everyone at the table was terrified and involved in the fighting, which went from neighborhood to neighborhood. Filipino resistance groups were formidable, with few or no resources. Heroes.

I also think that the issue of land reform was being discussed by the land owners. We were with educated, worldly, wealthy Filipinos who have a background totally unlike my own.

And, while I was trying to concentrate on the themes of war, destiny, and the personal history of the Aguinaldo family, I couldn't help noticing that Mary was definitely flirting with the handsome man next to her. And it was obvious he was fascinated with Mary. I struggle with the fact that Mary is my dearest friend, yet I am jealous of her. She has so much fun when we are out but the more drinks I have the more I feel sullen, tired, and jealous.

We leave for the Pearl Farm at 4:00 a.m.

Main House front view Pearl Farm

54

We flew low yesterday, skimming over hundreds of small islands in the Pacific. It didn't seem real, but even now I can feel my forehead pressed against the plane window. I was hypnotized by the colors, the ever-changing shapes of the islands, their beaches edged by a white froth of waves and faint emerald green waters, with deep blue and purple shadows leaping from one islet to another. It was lush and dreamlike and no one spoke. We floated on a cloud far above palm trees curved from the winds. And yes, those were small canoes, or fishing boats, between islands, mysterious dots on the green waters. Where did they come from? An exclusive showing of the Pacific and its treasure of islands we were privileged to view.

Now I am on our beach, my ever-growing stomach sticking out over my bikini, and tiny Mary next to me in her beach chair with no fat at all, just sweat beads decorating her perfect body. But today it hardly matters, fat or no fat. It is too beautiful here at the Pearl Farm to be silly and shallow over how I look, when what is important is that I know I am the most fortunate person to be here with Mary, on this beach, in the shade of palm trees, and reading *Noli me Tangere* by José Rizal. It seems at first to be a love story, but actually its purpose is to expose the brutality of the Catholic priests and the unfair practices of the Spanish government. After studying in Europe for ten years and obtaining degrees in Spain, France, and Germany, Rizal returned to his homeland and was executed by firing squad for his words attacking the Catholic Church. His death incited revolution. All this from my new friends, who encouraged me to read this beloved, brilliant author, José Rizal.

Behind us is our lovely beach home surrounded by a forest of palm trees and green foliage. This island is a forty-minute boat ride from the dock at Davao, and we are going to be here for ten days or so. Tomorrow we will walk down the beach and Dan is showing us the lab where they are culturing pearls.

Fishing boats, called "bancas," line our beach. Mary and I are going to learn how to use them. Dan says we can row over to a small island we see from our beach and explore it. We are also going to go scuba diving. Dan's pearl divers will teach us, and later we will go to a coral reef and explore underwater worlds.

Today, though, Dan is working at his lumber business. Sarita too. So Mary and I are sunning, dripping sweat and suntan lotion, shading our eyes from sun and white-sand glare, and feeling stunned by the force of the faraway blue sky, the nearness of the green jungle, and the deep sparkling mystery of our being here.

"Someday there will be sudden miracles," writes Carlos A. Angeles. This small book of poems by six Filipino poets—my unknown friends and guides to these islands.

Our bedroom at the Pearl Farm is dark and cool. We try to organize our clothes, suitcases, books, magazines, writing materials, and soggy bathing suits and towels. We have our own cosmetic store too: suntan lotions, olive oil for our hair, Cover Girl base makeup in at least three different shades, Max Factor pancake makeup, and every shade of eye shadow a girl could want. Of course, we also have combs, brushes, curlers, hairspray, lipsticks, lip gloss, compacts, eyelash curlers, and mascara, and, in case they are needed, eyelashes and glue. They seemed so necessary once. But here we are like untended children with no rules and free to run wild between the water and our room. Be ready for the afternoon tea and dessert. Later dinner on the dock.

I have been seduced by food. Lush, abundant fleshy mangos are served all day, sliced or whole, sexy and delicious. After naptime, we are offered bananas—flamed, sauced, mouthwatering—and served by bashful houseboys. I am feeding myself, grooming myself, with hours to daydream on the beach, read under palm or coconut trees that cover me with shade and shadows, sun and light brushing up and down my glistening, oily skin.

I am transfixed. Underneath lacy palm fronds, shading my eyes, staring at small waves as they inch their way over the sand, seductively disappearing into the skin of the beach, I find I am thinking of Walter's body that last night in Houston, making love again and again. And my old memories of a deserted beach, all those years ago with hot sweat curling down my arms, Gene and I marveling at our own sixteen-year-old bodies in hot and humid sandy Galveston.

55

Mary and I are like Odysseus on the island of the Lotus-eaters: drugged by food, sleep, sun, snorkeling, swimming, dancing on the pier, the sound of waves disappearing. We are waited on at tea time at four in the afternoon, offered cookies, unfamiliar desserts.

How do Mary and I repay our hosts? We have no responsibility except to contribute to our group's well-being, and I think we have been successful. We provide comic relief. What we are trying to do is master the banca, the transportation to the nearby small islands we can see from our beach. I feel, I don't know if it's true, that Dan and Sarita and all the men (the chef, the houseboys, the cleaning crew) pull up chairs in the main house to watch and laugh as Mary and I try to get a boat in the water, stumbling, falling, pushing, and not moving a thing. Mary tells me what to do; I yell back that I am indeed doing that. Of course, we are laughing too. Probably the funniest thing is when we do get the banca into the water. Jumping in head first, or slithering my whale-like body awkwardly aboard after struggling to reach floatable depth, I am exhausted and not ready to synchronize our paddling. We go in a full circle first before heading in the direction we intend. We are slowly improving.

We have to give ourselves credit that, awkward as we are, we have launched each day, made it to our destination and returned on our own. Snorkeling is new to me, but habit-forming. I like spying on the watery world beneath me, scaring up every color and shape of fish that I can imagine. The swirl of blue fish who thrust and turn like hundreds of swimming starlets is hypnotic. Then always the yellow-jeweled star of the show flashes by for a teaser.

56

Mary and I are living on the beach and learning to breathe underwater with the Aqua-Lung. Dan has commanded that we do this, as we are going to explore deeper water at a nearby coral reef. It is a watery life but we are adjusting well.

We were stranded for four hours on Tuesday on the small deserted island we see plainly from our shore. No one came looking for us either because I'm sure everyone could see us from the main house. We had paddled ashore and very carefully lugged our banca out of the water so our transportation would not float out to sea. After an hour of exploring through tall palms, rolling coconuts around, and casually inspecting small pools of water for darting creatures, we strolled back to our boat, which was very safe and very far from water. Yards from the sea. Beached. We are not strong enough to pull or push our vessel over sand.

No books, no paper or pencils or pens, only sand, shells, and graceful palm trees, pebbles, scattered palm leaves, and our private thoughts. We stretched out, found our own little watery pools to study, and wondered if these small creatures that looked like baby octopuses could really be octopuses? I would like to have a book that told me the names of the plants and animals that are around me. In the stories I am reading, the author N.V.M. Gonzalez mentions a "soursop tree." What is that? What if I have passed by a soursop tree and cannot tell my Grandma Lee how this tree is different from others?

Mary and I are learning the samba, the mambo, and the rhumba. Dan and Sarita are teaching us on the pier each evening. Dan brings his tape recorder out after dinner and we become dance students. He and Sarita are like professional ballroom dancers. We are the amateurs, but improving.

While waiting for the tide to come in that day, I stirred my baby octopus and watched its graceful body furl and unravel and thought of Mom and Dad and the summer of 1951. It was their thirteenth wedding anniversary, and to celebrate they took dance lessons. After each lesson they came home and we put on records and danced the samba, the mambo, the rhumba, and the tango. I wonder now if Dad, who has a birthday today, took lessons to humor Mom because her brother Jess had died.

Several years ago I came home from college and Mom was in bed in the middle of the day with the shades drawn. She had tears rolling down her face. I asked her what was wrong and she said she didn't know.

"Sometimes I just want to go dancing…and have fun," she said. What I heard was something I hadn't expected…her ache and longing for the joy of music and dance. She was more than a wife and homemaker and busy mom to four daughters.

Wynema, like her name, was musical. She needed music, singing and dancing. When her brother, my Uncle Jess, came for a visit, they could easily spend a day at the piano, singing and visiting, dad mixing their drinks. That's what she was longing for that day. In a very direct way, I am in the Philippines today because of my mother and our love of dance. She was the one that took me to the Shamrock Hotel, in August 1958, to audition for a chorus line at the Sands Hotel.

I have finished *Noli me Tangere* by José Rizal. It was banned by the Catholic Church and government officials when it was published in 1844. It is a novel, a love story, and a sad history of the injustices endured by the Filipino people under foreign rule.

Dan's friends encouraged me to read it. Now that I have, I understand how much is left unsaid during our dinner conversations about the history of the Spanish presence in the Philippines.

In *Six Filipino Poets,* edited by Leonard Casper and published in 1955 by the Benipayo Press, Mr. Casper explains in his introduction that these poems are "between war poems," exploring "What are the possibilities of humaneness in an age of slaughter?" I know so little history about these islands, the light and dark of them.

57

I spend every day sightseeing as the guest of Dan Aguinaldo: one day lunch at the lovely Manila Hotel, then enjoying a performance at the University of the Philippines. We were entranced by a program of native Filipino dancers dressed in colorful pastel dresses.

Another day we have a flight over the route of the Bataan Death March in Dan's private plane. He explains in a low, subdued voice how the already malnourished and exhausted troops endured further heat, brutality, and dehydration until they couldn't. Thousands died. After the war, Japanese officers were convicted for these war crimes and were executed. I hear the dates, 1942, 1945, 1947. I was safe in Oklahoma, two years old, four years old. Dan points out the outlines of destroyed houses, buildings, below us.

Sarita takes us to the World War II Memorial, where the American fallen are at rest. We spend a long time among the names and home towns, the particulars you find on white engraved marble walls held in place by white marble columns on top of a green grassy rise. Dan is insistent that we know what happened here barely twenty years ago.

On several evenings when we dine on the yacht, and we are a small group, I learn more about Dan's grandfather, Emilio Aguinaldo, the first president of the Philippines. Dan has sad stories of the wars inflicted on Filipinos. He ends an anecdote with a chuckle, and a certain detachment, then casually orders fireworks to entertain us during our after-dinner drinks. We ooh and aah over the show as thousands of pieces of light arc against the sky, then break and fall into the dark waters of Manila Bay.

I will be sorry I haven't taken notes on all this. What I will remember is the time spent on educating us in all things Filipino. And the wonder of how we came to Manila. And if ever we are dependent on the kindness of strangers, this is the prime example. Every single day we are honored guests of Dan and Sarita. Their laughter, the silly hours of learning to samba and mambo, the history, the cold facts of war, and seeing the life on the streets. Each new day ....

Out of naïve curiosity, Mary and I take a taxi on a Sunday morning to see the cockfights. We walk into the barn-like building with circular seats winding up and around the cockpit. Men are shouting and waving their hands and the place is a roaring frenzy. A man in charge of accepting the bets walks around the arena pointing at whoever catches his eye, and somehow, miraculously, that means the wager is agreed upon. When that is over, the two roosters are brought in by their handlers, shoved at each other and finally freed, and then all hell breaks loose. They attack, glossy feathers flying, wings beating, heads ferociously hammering against one another amid loose feathers fluttering in all directions, again charging up in the air, the spurs attached to their heels flashing in the light. Then, a break, then a charge again, until one or the other cock weakens, and sits, breathing hard, and then the handlers thrust them once more to make sure there is no fight left in the loser.

Mary and I are horrified, spellbound, and mystified by the whole process. Even though the gentleman sitting next to us tries to explain how the roosters are trained and cared for, we last less than an hour,

our curiosity more than satisfied. As we get up to leave, our neighbor on the bleachers asks if we are in the Peace Corps. We say no. We are only tourists. We don't say "extremely privileged tourists," but we know that we are. And during the day I am clearheaded and tell myself constantly that we are being spoiled.

We are fortunate to outrun the street children looking for handouts, jump into a safe taxi, and ride through the jaunty streets of Manila, with a deep feeling of gratitude for our quiet hotel room. There is no doubt that Mary and I have seen enough of thrashing roosters, blood spurting. We realize we were out of place since we were the only women in the crowd and should have been escorted by one of the men in our group. Between the cockfight and our trip too far out to sea in the banca when Dan's security guards had to come rescue us, we have had enough of beating-heart misadventures that we alone created.

When I reread my journal, instead of gratitude I find grumbling. I complain and whine, written proof of the scowl I am becoming. The day up in the plane learning about the Death March, I say it was hot. Then I can't stay awake for the nightly entertainment: a jai alai game, followed by drinks at a club, dancing even, then dinner at midnight and home at four a.m. to our hotel room. We sleep until noon and I wake grouchy and groggy. The long evenings out kill me, and I grump and snap. Any conversation in a noisy club makes me pout; too much to drink, and I become surly and am afraid I will stomp my feet and be put in a corner. I am a guest, so I must be agreeable until the evening is over. Dan is ever the gracious host, and I hope he has so many people around him each night that he doesn't notice the spoilsport I become, usually before midnight.

I am at my very best on Dan's yacht for a quiet dinner, like this

Sunday evening. There are few guests, the night wind is cool and balmy, the yacht rocks comfortably at the dock, candles flicker, and Fred (a friend of Dan's) and I sit together in quiet, enjoying the sky, some small clouds as they sail across the moon, stars appearing one by one. I could stretch out and stay there easily until four in the morning.

How can I complain about a strenuous "nightlife" when Dan keeps on and on, changing our lives during the day? He exclaims roughly, "You can't just fly from here to Paris. Don't you want to see some of the world? You must go to Thailand, and India, and Iran. A 'Grand Tour'." Mary and I glance at each other.

"Of course we do. Why, yes," Mary and I reply, stumbling and thinking of money, but what do you say when someone asks if you want to see more of the world?

You say yes. Yes, we do.

"I'll have Mr. Zodas meet with you tomorrow," he commands. Mr. Zodas is his travel agent and will design our itinerary, which will begin after we see Hong Kong and Tokyo and other cities in Japan. We are postponing Paris to see Bangkok and Calcutta and Tehran and Baghdad and even Cairo. No argument there. Dan is educating us, day by day. His world is wide, and we do not know why, but he is sharing it with us.

I would go back and scratch out all complaints I have made, but I won't. They will remain to remind me of my audacity, my small, bitchy nature, and what a lump and spoilsport I am, because now Dan has truly astonished us. Upon hearing that between us we barely have eight hundred dollars, and most of that is Mary's, he marches us to his bank and gives us each fifteen hundred dollars. A staggering fortune. We stand at the bank counter like chastised children and sign one American Express traveler's check after another until all is done. We thank Dan humbly. He has given us each a leather folder with our initials engraved in gold.

It is for our passport, our shot cards, our traveler's checks, and our plane ticket. And what have I given him? Nothing but feeble conversations on a yacht, on a private beach, or in his home while having dinner with his many friends. He is a strange "playboy," a complete mystery to me. Mary and I, no matter how we try, will never know how all this has happened. Thank you, Mr. Aguinaldo.

My passport holder is rose red, which matches my luggage.

58
Hong Kong

No doubt that, because Mary has a dashing boyfriend who escorts her endlessly around Manila, I am feeling sorry for myself. The long evenings pass quickly for her, but drag on and on for me as I constantly scan the room or club or bar for someone suitable. Or I eat, pout, and lose sight of what is really happening: that we, for no other reason than being on stage at the Sands, and sitting in a lounge with our fellow Copa girls, find ourselves traveling around the world.

Soon we leave for *Hong Kong*.

As a last minute afterthought, we take a taxi to the Manila American Express office, never expecting much, and good grief, we discover letters from family and friends, and I've a telegram from Masao, the man who gave me a clock and a five-hundred-dollar bill. He says he received my letter from Honolulu, that he can meet us in either Hong Kong or Tokyo and to let him know our schedule as soon as possible. I did write him a card in Hawaii, but I haven't thought about seeing him. It's been almost a year since we first met, and I only wrote him on a whim. And in pencil. I hardly expected it to arrive. But it did.

As if we don't have enough men in our lives right now, Mary is taken with this man in Manila. She even wore her hair down, loose and sexy, the other night when they met for dinner, and looked—how should I put this— quite fulfilled, yet eager. When they are together I just turn green with jealousy and try not to squint up my eyes and curl my lip and reveal how mean I feel. Dearest friend or not, it drives me crazy to see her so romantically involved, and I stew like some forlorn goose. Our four weeks in the Philippines have been full of handsome and fascinating men, and I've managed to become the large platonic friend to all of them. And when I am with Mary, I feel larger by the minute.

Arriving in Hong Kong, we receive a terrible shock. Dan and Sarita, for a brief moment, appear at a loss. Mary, oh, poor Mary. We go through the airport customs and her shot card isn't on the proper form, so she has to take all the shots over, today and tomorrow, in order to stay in Hong Kong. It's terrible. At first I am afraid she will have to stay at the airport and take every required shot at once, but Dan knows someone very important and somehow Mary is let through and we go on to Kowloon, President Hotel, Rm.1404.

The bellboy helps us with our bags and then tries to explain the water schedule for the hotel. Hot water during certain hours, no water at all for bathing on other hours or certain days, and we listen, sort of, in a trance. We don't care about water. We only want to be in this quiet room and get warm and find something to wear that looks right for Hong Kong. It is so cold here. It's not at all like Manila. Women are dressed in fashionable suits, dark and sophisticated, with gloves and shoes and handbags that look like ads in *Vogue*. Jackie Kennedy-kind-of suits.

The first evening we have dinner at the Hong Kong Hilton with Ralph and Julie Tung, who are friends and employees of Dan. They are very interested in what we are doing in Hong Kong. Why are we here? I have a long answer that doesn't make a lot of sense (planned to go to Paris, Dan was interested in a dancer at our hotel, chance meeting, etc.). It is all true, but I have a hard time believing it myself. I understand when people raise their eyebrows and smile politely and nod when they meet these young women from the Sands Hotel in Las Vegas, Nevada.

The next morning we are a party of nine for breakfast in our hotel, and all the noise and plans for shopping are overwhelming. I walk and shop with them for an hour or so. When we come upon a bookstore, I excuse myself from the group and browse quietly and buy a few books and then begin to feel sick and dizzy with a painful sore throat. I make my way back to the hotel and call for the hotel doctor. He arrives, looks at my throat, takes my temperature, and then gives me a shot and says to stay in bed.

Mary drags in from the clinic where she endured as many cholera and yellow fever shots as she could. Any mean thoughts I had of her totally disappear and leave me sick and ashamed for feeling jealous and silly about my friend. Later in the day, Mrs. Tung—Julie—comes to check on us. We feel like small children as she tucks us in bed, so we stay there for the evening, writing postcards and letters.

I did notice in myself a certain anxiety today as we were walking outside our hotel. Here in Hong Kong there is a prickly feeling of not knowing what is ahead, or around a corner, or what is behind a closed shop window. It could be my imagination, or being feverish, or walking by myself, but I had a slight sensation of being totally unprepared, of not knowing anything at all about Hong Kong, and that made me aware of how "foreign" I am.

Hong Kong has been leased by the English since 1898, and eventually it will belong to mainland China again. It is Chinese, but must be English for ninety-nine years and then will become something unknown, a capitalist city returned to its communist parents. So maybe, because of this odd situation, there is an uncertainty that hovers in the air.

Dan bought us dresses. And perfume! We have had a shopping spree. I am a happy child until I model my dress. When I tried on a cheongsam in Sarita's favorite shop, Dan took one look at me and burst out laughing. "Judy's fat! Judy's fat!"

It's true. I've gained six or more pounds in one month of travel. If I gain two or three pounds each new place we visit, I could weigh twenty-five pounds extra by the time we get to Paris.

But I can't stop eating and tasting all this new food. The Hoover Sky Restaurant Dan took us to the other evening was like a circus. It was noisy and aromatic, circular in design, with tables winding up floor after floor. I thought each serving was surely the last, but it wasn't. And I ate everything: shark's fin and chicken, abalone soup, barbecued Peking duck, prawns with chili sauce, and much more. We kept the menu for a souvenir.

During the noisy evening, Ralph and Julie told us about their long and difficult trek through mainland China to get to Hong Kong and have a freer life. I tried to follow their story, but the towns and places they mentioned were unfamiliar, and I have no geography of China that would help me. But I know that they are earnest and wise and learned, and their story with its many hardships has intrigued me. It would help if we had a map of China so I could picture their journey. And in a quiet place.

After dinner we walked, and this time Mary and I were bundled up and enjoyed the cold night air and the shops and sights of the city.

We ended at the harbor, where the bobbing Chinese junks with their jaunty sails were silhouetted by the lights coming from passing boats, from nearby hotel and shop windows. Then there was the light reflected from the water, the wake of ferries and motorboats. All in all, the haze of the last week, the poetry and exotic look of this harbor, the fullness of good stories, and the serious admonitions of the Tungs have me spinning. Whether I am tired and can't get rid of this sore throat or what, I have this pull, this urge, to stop traveling, to stay for a while here in Hong Kong and memorize these neighborhoods, visit more with Ralph and Julie. They want me to register for classes at the American University here. To begin writing now, here in Hong Kong.

But I keep thinking that I am going to Paris, or that was the plan.

Ralph says that I am a hypocrite. He says it in a kind way and what he means is that I can't say I am going to be a writer if I don't slow down and begin writing daily. And being in Hong Kong for four or five days means nothing, and I can't begin to know about a place unless I live there, here, for a decent amount of time and study customs and history and try to learn the language. I agree with everything he says, yet I am not writing every day except in my journal, and I can tell I am not the best tourist since I spend a lot of my free time reading and sleeping in my hotel room. I am wondering, though, why I have it in my head to begin "writing" in Paris, instead of now, in Hong Kong. I do write letters and postcards each day, keep up my journal, so somewhere I should scribble some facts down. When Ralph and Julie hid in a forest and were out of food, where were they?

Mary and I find gifts for our brothers and sisters. Delicate Chinese dolls in ancient dress and hairdos for the girls and elaborate cloth Chinese toy "junks" for the boys. I send Annette's third-graders at Anson Jones Elementary some, too, so she can show them on the map where Hong Kong is.

Photo of Julie and Ralph Tung with Lee.

59
March 6, 1964
Tokyo

On our flight to Tokyo we celebrate Mary's twenty-fifth birthday with champagne and many toasts. It is such a generous birthday party given by Dan and Sarita as we fly over the China Sea.

Our taxi ride into Tokyo is gray and drizzly with endless turns and head-pounding stops. Out the window, tiny twisting streets are slick with rain, and drab, with no apparent street signs. I am grateful and amazed that we arrive at an imposing hotel that appears from nowhere after heroic and harrowing efforts by our driver. The chaos of traffic here makes Manila seem tame.

When the bellboy opens our hotel room door, Mary and I both gasp. There are two enormous flower arrangements, two delicious fruit baskets, and presents for both of us spread around the room. All from my friend, Masao. Why, it is exactly like a movie scene.

We unpack and admire our new cocktail dresses from Hong Kong. I think my black bugle-beaded clutch and my custom-made black beaded high-heeled shoes, both sprinkled with Le De Givenchy perfume, are my favorite things.

Eleven nights in Tokyo. Eight nights we've been in the Latin Quarter or the Copa nightclub until three or four in the morning. We have been sick, to the doctor's office twice, and barely leave our hotel during the day. We don't wake up until the afternoon. We visit our Okura beauty salon or the hotel bookstore where I was able to purchase all of Henry Miller's *Rosy Crucifixion* for Bernie and Stella, my friends from the University of Houston. We have entertained the idea of joining the Ikebana flower design class the hotel provides, but after days of contemplation we have not made a firm commitment.

We have a masseuse come to our room for massages at four in the morning. We begin writing letters and postcards at 5:30. We think we will take a train to Nara. It is recommended that we see Kyoto. Mary always worries about her family. They are a team, and she is missing, she says. I am buying too many books and I eat too much. On occasion we exclaim, "Can you believe this? Tokyo?" A year ago Mary and I hadn't met. We sleep until one or two in the afternoon.

What drags us out of bed? We must go check for our mail. It's a decision each day. Do we chance the wild crazy taxi ride hurtling through tiny streets to get to American Express? Or the American Embassy? And will we have time to have our nails or hair done also? There might be a dinner to attend before we arrive at our designated nightclub and join our party of nine or ten for dancing and drinking. We have been entertained by Earl Grant one evening, singing "Ebb Tide" and playing the piano. One night we might have seen Claudia Cardinale, the young

Italian actress.

My surprise and dismay has been Masao. After our fourth day here, and many sweet gifts arriving daily for both of us, and two dates with him, he is no longer speaking or communicating with me. It's certainly possible that after our several evenings together at the New Latin Quarter, he has discovered I am a shallow and fickle person and not worthy of his attentions. That hurts. Or maybe it's that every time Mary and I go to the bar at the Okura, we meet some interesting person and have a drink with him and maybe Masao doesn't like that. Or that I am seen in the company of a French playboy, Georges, having lunch at the Imperial Hotel, or afternoon drinks here in our hotel. And of course I am with Dan and the large group that Dan has escorted from the Philippines to Hong Kong to Tokyo.

All of this misunderstanding has made me cross, and I'm worse when I have drinks each evening. I wear Mary out with my agonizing. Now I am putting it all behind me, because Masao is not the only attractive man in Tokyo.

Tonight we join Dan and Sarita for dinner here in the hotel. I like having dinner here because it is a polite restaurant where you can converse and actually follow a conversation. Sarita is leaving in the morning to return to Manila. She has attended to us for six weeks with a smile and good humor. She has coached us in what to wear, taken us to the beauty parlor, helped us shop for ourselves and our families. She has been our mother hen and our older sister, and we will miss her beautiful smile and sweet ways.

Dan has lent me his typewriter. I have written long, three- and four-page, single-spaced letters to Annette, trying to describe Tokyo and our shopping sprees our dilemma over whether to go to Hiroshima/Nagasaki or not. I am not in favor of going because I think Americans would not be welcome. Or do I just think that because I am afraid of going?

I told Annette about the twenty-four-hour-a-day preparation for the Olympics that is taking place everywhere in Tokyo. I know that it is twenty-four hours a day because we are out at all hours of the morning and there are huge lamps illuminating work sites, the workers wearing miners' hats with lights on them. You can't go from one nightclub to another without being dumbstruck by the constant pace that men keep. On a date with a Lt. Huston, we went to Manos, a popular all-night coffee shop, and sat until almost dawn watching the construction on the street in front of us.

I spent 450 yen ($1.50) for *The Sound of Waves* by Yukio Mishima and carry it with me everywhere. I have also bought *The Poetry of Living Japan.* After my nightlife I enter my secret world of books and tell myself I am discovering Japan through stories and poems.

Goodbye Mrs. Tung, Sarita, and Lee in Hong Kong

60
March 1964
Okura Hotel

At 4:00 a.m. when Mary and I sleepily return to the Okura after hours of dancing, we check the hotel desk for mail and find that I have a letter from Linda. I open it in the elevator, race through all the family news and her gossip about her office and her boyfriend, and then crap: another of my former boyfriends has gotten married. The fourth one in two years.

I see us, face to face, sitting in an old car, my full skirt covering us and our lovemaking. I was grateful for his love and sex and tender feelings. My arms around his neck, our bodies tight together, holding on forever, it seemed. Yet I knew, he knew, that it wouldn't be forever.

I was unfaithful, and he went on and I did too, and now here I am, years later in Tokyo, on my way to Paris.

In my last week of college we came face to face in Oberholtzer Hall. I was sitting on a sofa reading. We had been careful not to cross paths for two years. Even after all this time, it still felt too soon to be near him. What do you say? I wish it hadn't ended like it did? I still think of you? I'm sorry?

"Your new girlfriend is beautiful, Joe." I meant it. I meant to be light. To be happy. His tender look, his sweet, forgiving words were unexpected. Then he kept walking. My self-confidence, my plans, everything I thought I was sure of that day, followed him down Oberholtzer Hall. Every feeling I had for him came rushing forward, the memory of touching his face, hanging over his shoulders, hugging him, his arm around me, sitting next to him trying to study. The yearning, the aching for him. But always there was the plan for Europe keeping me cautious. That day, everything was in doubt. But I stayed on the sofa. I didn't call his name.

61

Upon entering the Ryoanji Temple, we are given a small note card. One side has a line drawing of the Temple grounds and writing in Japanese. On the other side are instructions in English, from the Abbot of Ryoanji, Joei Matsukura. He "invites us to sit down quietly and contemplate this garden of sand and stones." Following the slow-moving wave of fellow tourists, we make our way to the world-famous Zen Garden. Lamenting the long wait, I pray that I will appreciate the symbolism of carefully placed stones, artfully sculpted sand.

When a tourist near me rises from his viewing point across from the sand and stone garden, I move quickly to claim his place. I work at a serene expression in order not to appear complicated and unappreciative of the "spirit of the garden masterpiece by the famous artist, Soami." However, I am twice as large as most of the other tourists, and I feel awkward and unprepared for this experience. I am grateful for the notecard to cling to, to lose myself in reading and rereading in order to follow instructions from the abbot. I search my heart and mind, hurriedly, for the key to simplicity.

I observe the movement of the carefully arranged sand and stone composition and am brushed constantly by the many reverent, solemn, crowded sightseers winding beside me, awaiting their anxious turn to sit, to wonder, to meditate. I keep telling myself: memorize this scene, remember this garden, keep it for another time. Ignore the crowd, the uneasy feeling I have because I am a foreigner and have no knowledge of Zen, or meditation, or this place. I know nothing about the essence of these gardens, temples. So remember the light on sand, on stones that the abbot says may be viewed as a "great ocean surrounding mountainous islands, or as mountaintops rising above a sea of clouds."

The abbot hopes for us that "…we are filled with serene wonder as we intuit Absolute Self, and our stained minds are purified." For several minutes, I create my own garden: the sand becomes small, rolling hills, and stones shift into worn farmhouses and barns, and I discreetly place Papa's fishponds in the landscape and add grasshoppers sizzling through dry brush. My true and deep meditation spot has always been on the banks of the big fishing pond in the pasture. I know my Grandmother Johnson would agree in spirit that "In Zen, everything, even a leaf of grass, expresses ultimate Reality." I happily remember listening to cicadas in the cedar tree of Grandma Johnson's front yard, wind blowing hot out in the garden, hummingbirds hovering near the honeysuckled gate leading to the barnyard.

It is possible to walk here in Kyoto, in this famous Zen garden with Mary, and see Grandma's iris garden, rows of deep dark plum and blue-black-purple blossoms open to the sky; yellow rows too, planted in red dusty soil behind the row of cedars, but in sight of the barn and the pig pen. I think the Zen Garden must be full of other scenes, like mine, that tourists remember as their own ancient meditation places. No telling what dreams and places we walk through as we concentrate and follow the abbot's instructions.

We are making final plans to leave Tokyo, fly to Bangkok and begin our trip through many exotic places, but we have too many distractions that have detained us. Mary might meet her old boyfriend from the Desert Inn in Manila. We can't decide what clothes to send home, and what do I do with all these books?

A strange turn of events for me after weeks of wringing my hands and coming to the conclusion that I would never know why I was dropped from Masao's list of friends: Because of a chance encounter with one of

Masao's assistants, I have received a call from Masao, and we agreed to meet in Hong Kong in three days.

62

On this day I am grateful for many things. One, that I am half way around the world, far from my parents, and will never have to explain this life Mary and I are leading. I have exhausted myself on this constant merry-go-round of dates, appointments, meetings, drinks, flirtations, a brief, light and merry affair with Georges T., and then the angst over Masao. I wondered constantly that I was too unworldly, or too large, or had somehow offended his nature.

Then I puzzled over why I was wasting so much valuable time being disturbed by him when I was not lacking for company. Not only that, but Mary and I have been so well taken care of by Dan, and we have more than enough money to have a successful trip to Paris, so why did I so readily agree to meet Masao? When he has hurt my feelings and caused me great anxiety?

Is it because I remember the five hundred dollars he gave me in Las Vegas last year? I would like to think I agreed to the meeting to repair a friendship, that I was curious about what had happened to make him act so coldly. Men, boyfriends, have dropped me before, but I always knew why. I knew I was responsible for the break. I wasn't sure about Masao.

But I know now. Because he was a well-known resident at the Okura Hotel, he felt that people in the hotel would know that he had sent daily gifts to our room, so I made him feel uncomfortable by being seen in conversation with different men at the bar or restaurant. Not such a mystery after all.

Masao and I were together for hours today. He laughed, explaining how he felt I had caused him some embarrassment. After dinner with friends of his, the two of us went back to his suite for drinks. We talked about his travels to Indonesia, his observations on Sukarno, and my hotel reservations for Bangkok with Mary. He says it is a good hotel for us.

In the evening I forgot that at one time I had felt self-conscious and unsure about my body when I thought he disliked me. All those thoughts are gone now, and we had a romantic evening and night together and I regret that we had the misunderstanding in Tokyo.

The next morning he readied for a trip to Djakarta, and I accompanied him to the airport. There, in his limousine, he presented me with a gold watch. He also explained that several other gifts would arrive later in the day, including two thousand dollars that I must go to the bank to sign for. He wished Mary and me a "Bon Voyage," and he hoped to see me in Paris in the fall. He was lighthearted, and although we were with one of his assistants who was accompanying him, he kissed me sweetly and was out of the car, into the airport, while I sat with little expression because I felt awkward and only managed a weak "thank you" and "have a good trip" and then I was whisked back to the hotel in the empty limousine. I am bewildered. I stare at my new watch. I like it. It is more like a bracelet than a watch.

63
March 31, 1964
Bangkok

Leaving Hong Kong the second time makes us think that we might leave Hong Kong a third or fourth time. We arrive in Bangkok, Mary and I. No one greets us or eases our way through customs. We handle our own luggage. We wait for a taxi outside the airport. We gasp at the heat and humidity. We check into the hotel on our own. We manage to tip the bellboy in our new Thai currency. After a change of clothes, we collapse on our beds. Eventually, Mary goes downstairs to see what time the evening performance of Thai dancing begins.

I am in bed with my books, journal, and postcards. I admire my string of pearls, the diamond ring Masao had made for me. I take out my passport billfold, count the travelers cheques Masao has given me. It's strange. A boyfriend who gives me these beautiful things and then says he will see me, maybe, in six months.

The next morning, Mary and I book a tour. The brown Chao Phraya River escorts us through canals, floating markets, houses on stilts lining the river bank. Amazed tourists don't deter morning bathers, children brushing their teeth, babies feeding. I take picture after picture: women washing clothes in the dark river, unknown vegetables and fruits piled high on sampans, a dancing, darting life without land. It seems people wake up and jump into the river, like Americans wake and stumble down to prepare coffee.

As a child visiting my grandparents in Oklahoma, any time we crossed a river in the car my Grandmother Lee always shook me awake, "Look, Judy! It's the river!" In Oklahoma, I have seen homes built along the river, not far from a creek. But here, in the Chao Phraya, houses on stilts are built *in* the river, and these homes and their people must rise and fall and sway with the movement of water. Watching from my tour boat, I feel wooden, awkward, remote from the dance and color of this enticing river spectacle. I wonder if the sampan, or the roof of every house and temple sitting near the water, was designed to honor the shape of waves on the river.

At a silk factory we float in colors of pink, rose, blue, ivory flecked with silver. We buy long dreamy scarves for our mothers and grandmothers, pastel bandanas for aunts and sisters and ourselves. The silk slipping through our hands, brushing our arms, is seductive. Hot, very hot, skin-sweaty slow moments. Shopping is interrupted when one of the king's barges cuts through the river, glistening royally, competing brilliantly with the silk and gems sliding through our arms and eyes.

Two young U.S. Army dentists, stationed in Vietnam, are on the river cruise, shopping for gems, mostly. They ask us to join them for dinner. Bud says there are lots of soldiers in Vietnam and is surprised when I say I didn't realize there were so many.

That evening I have a good time. The hotel showroom is packed with American soldiers. We, the audience, are mesmerized by the performers. The Thai dancers are stoic delicate flowers, balancing golden temples on their heads, their finger cymbals and bells hushing the audience. Their hypnotic gazes slide over the crowd, every movement a slight ripple from the river.

Afterwards, in a piano bar, after a drink or two, my new friends try to explain about being in Vietnam, about the war going on. I remember about the French having been there, the "Angel of Dien Bien Phu." The next morning I awake wondering exactly how many American soldiers in Vietnam number "more than I know."

On our second full day in Bangkok we hire a Buddhist guide from Merryland Tours. He is solemn, determined that we see hundreds of temples and palaces in one hot sticky morning. Driving the car, he explains diplomatically that he is a communist, and we listen politely to his intense overview of Thai history, struggle, and politics. Between the Army dentists talking about Vietnam and this earnest communist discussing the Western powers that interfere, and remembering Ralph and Julie's stories of their long journey to Hong Kong, I feel shallow, blundering, and confused. My desire to live and write in Paris has taken a strange turn, and why? I know I should be writing each story down, like Ralph and Julie said. Also, I know that I will regret not writing these vignettes as I hear them. I have already forgotten many of the stories from the Philippines.

After lunch, we drive to a rural area, a small village an hour outside of Bangkok. There in an open space, sun battling through the dense leafy canopy, an exquisite child dances on a small platform for no one, for the splashes of sun that filter through tall trees. Delicate, moving to the music of her finger cymbals and to the sounds of the tropical interior, she seems trained in light and poetry, her tall headdress a thousand tiny mirrors. We are just in time for this solitary pageant, shattered sunlight, a hush in the heat. Our guide gives me a worn and smoothly rounded Buddha, small enough to slip into my coin purse.

I buy sugarcane from a small, irresistible salesman on the side of the road. He smiles and waves as we head on to Bangkok.

Mary and I have a Thai dinner in our room. We barely have energy to pack. Another pleasant surprise: We have made friends with a beautiful lady from New York City. Her name is Rose Rosenthal. She is staying here in our hotel and has much the same itinerary as ours. We will be in New Delhi at the same time. She is delighted that Mary wants to work and live in New York, and says she will be Mary's point of contact there. We keep meeting these extraordinary people, like Rose, who seem to be, in a very short time, old friends.

Mary and I both have feelings that this whole trip is a dream.

64
April 4, 1964
Calcutta

Outside Calcutta's Dum-Dum Airport we follow directions and find a taxi. On the highway we strain to see outside. It is a shadowy dark evening. We pass streams of people headed somewhere along the road. We are astonished to see a cow, illuminated by car lights, meander through traffic. Maybe we see huts and a chair and a gas station, but in the dark we can't be sure. Then there are flickering lights, intriguing, stretching far away in the apparently flat fields on both sides of our road. It reminds me of being on Dan's yacht in Manila Bay and watching the night fishermen in their boats, their small lanterns rocking and bobbing in the darkness.

It is fascinating, thousands of tiny fires surrounding us as far as we can see.

I ask the taxi driver, "What are all those little fires?"

"Ah. People are making their dinners now."

"What do you mean?"

He explains that people live in the fields beside our road.

"In tents?" I ask.

"No." Nothing covers them except the night.

Although we could only imagine what was beside the highway during the dark drive from the airport, once we arrive in Calcutta we find the streets lit by the combustion of all humanity, and nothing is left to our imagination. From every direction people and traffic flow around us. We are terrified by street beggars who press against the taxi window when we slow in traffic. We hold our breath: Rickshaws propelled by men riding bicycles squeeze between trucks and cars and ancient wooden carts pulled by a struggling human, yet no one is crushed or mangled. On the narrow sidewalk, small grimy carpets, or towels, or mats are lined up against buildings, some with a pan or a teapot and a few utensils laid out. A woman and child sit on one mat, several children on another, while a man lies curled up, resting, with his face hidden, on another. Our driver explains that each mat, towel, and carpet represents home to an individual or family. Hundreds of pedestrians are walking over and among them each second.

There is a bewildering collision of sounds and sights: honking horns, tinkling bells, belching, hissing, shouting; a cow wanders here, there, among the thousands of people seemingly converged at this point, then the next, and the next point. Even if someone had described it to me, I never could have imagined this city. It is like a boiling, seething, roiling, explosion of people, decrepit buildings, wooden shacks, animals and plants that appear, disappear, assemble, dissolve before our eyes and nothing seems possible, but it is.

We arrive, hearts pounding and eyes bulging, at the Great Eastern Hotel, 3 Old Court House Street. We inch two feet or so to our hotel door. Startling bodies are crowded on either side of the door, packed with wretchedly frail humans who live on mats that define their household, a teapot or a glass representing their possessions. We twist and slowly open the doors. Inside I am startled to find, within the hotel vestibule, another family residing on carpets, tucked up against the walls, and we edge by, dragging our luggage, careful not to brush against the small child in its mother's arms. We go through a second set of doors, no more than two or three feet from the first, to arrive in the lobby. We have traveled from the taxi to the lobby of our hotel, a matter of five to seven feet, a short but unforgettable journey. Our Fodor's 1962 *Guide Book to India* has nothing to say about this entranceway or how to navigate through cloth homes on a sidewalk.

We are told in the guide book that the Great Eastern Hotel has the "atmosphere of a good English commercial or an American convention hotel" and that its Maxim's restaurant has nightly dancing and a floorshow. How can that attraction begin to compete with the dance of life and drama we have just encountered?

I learn about Calcutta while safely in bed. Rabindranath Tagore, "the flower of the nineteenth century Bengali revival in all the arts," died here in 1941. Calcutta is home to writers and filmmakers. They are inspired by "the ferment of Calcutta." On page 585 of *Fodor's Guide to India*, Fodor's writer encourages us to visit the birthplace of Tagore before we leave, "for Calcutta has been able to produce far more than jute and slums and the palaces of merchant princes. Even in its darkest days, the flame of its spiritual and creative life has never sputtered out. This flame will still burn in the new Calcutta India is trying to build."

I will keep this foremost in my thoughts when I venture out into this "ferment." Just the sheer number of people lying on the sidewalk outside our hotel has been seared into my brain. For all of Manila's wild jostle, and the occasional beggar, there were no people lying asleep, curled up, living on a main thoroughfare. And if we were aghast in Tokyo when officials helped stack more people into a train, here in Calcutta that would have been futile. We have much to learn. And I must keep in mind that this subcontinent won its independence the year I turned seven. Mary and I are learning to live independently, and independence is a struggle, whether for a country or a human being.

Until this moment, I have been on my way to Paris, willy-nilly. But three hours in Calcutta has jolted me to the core. I have looked into some deep corner of humanity tonight, and I have to search and study my reaction because no one can come face to face with this scene and not wonder why: Why isn't this me on the sidewalk? Don't I know that my hopes and dreams are the same as this frail woman curled on her mat? To live and to have means to live and survive? I mean, surely it is impossible to be the same person after Calcutta pierces you. Will I make a turn? Will I always remember this feeling? Fear and wonder and shock and disbelief? Not only from how life is being lived in Calcutta's streets, on sidewalks, in wide and dark and spreading fields in the night, but how I live, and have always lived, and expect to live.

Mary has no fear of these Calcutta streets. I believe she has lost her heart, or given it away to a small boy who lives on the sidewalk with his family. He has followed her for these two days. He took her to meet his family. She is too tender-hearted and what can she do? It's not like she can take him or find shelter for them. I mean, what do we do when hundreds of ragged and desperate children crowd us with tiny dirt-encrusted hands thrust forward? With eyes infected, teeth missing, sores covering them? Mary is not the same. She wanders around our hotel and finds the lovely Amber restaurant for us to try. Later that evening, when we walk on the semi-darkened streets and I am fearful until we are safe inside the restaurant, Mary only worries about her shadow. She orders her little boy a dinner and takes it outside for him to share with his family. We leave tomorrow for Benares, but Calcutta will never leave Mary. Or me.

65
April 6, 1964
Benares Ganges River

Today Mary and I are pressed and jostled, slowly separated from each other by the thousands of pilgrims wending their way toward the Ganges, eager to step into the holy river and rejoice. The crush of joyful bodies, heat and flies, flashing smiles, kohl-rimmed eyes, the musical arms with jangling bracelets flashing in the sunlight, clouds of bodies draped in diaphanous materials (why, why, why can't I live in the gauze and light and color I felt this morning?) sweep us along, as if we are a rushing human river ourselves.

The Ganges doesn't look that clean, or clean enough, to fulfill so many dreams, to warrant so mighty an army of worshipers. But for millions of Hindus it is restorative, life-giving. I want to know why. I want to stay a few more weeks, months, to read and write, to speak with strangers, to walk daily with new pilgrims until I know...*what*?

Which holy man, sitting cross-legged on a cement slab at river's edge, gazing at the Ganges with closed eyes, divines what the river is thinking? Do sins leap away when a trembling eager worshiper first enters its rippling water? Does the mighty river itself want to race on, free of expectation? Years from now, will I regret not trying harder to ask better questions of myself here in Benares?

Whether because of the heat or the fatigue of rushing from place to place, I want to stay in Benares, to find a place to live for a while and think about why I am here, to understand my purpose. I have been on my way to Paris for years to begin my life as I have dreamed it. But maybe I should listen to this voice that says to stay put, to explore the mystery I feel here in Benares—to ride a bicycle to the girls' school at the convent, stand under the spreading tree there and listen to children's voices, birds calling to each other in the morning sun. There is something in Benares that I feel; it flashes in the sun and disappears ahead of me. I am behind it in the crowd, reaching. I feel it swelling in my throat, a longing. I want to understand what I cannot explain about myself, to be a person I can admire.

Tomorrow, Mary and I are going on to Sarnath, to contemplate the spot where Buddha gave his first sermon, then on to Agra, to gaze on infinite variations of filigree within the love story called Taj Mahal. I am afraid not to see these many famous places, but I think I am also afraid to stop and wander too long in my thoughts.

India

66

We enjoy our room at the Clarks Shiraz Hotel so much that we don't jump up early in the morning to see the Taj Mahal at sunrise. We repack, pull out the sundresses we wore in the Philippines, and I clean out my purse. We slow down. It's extremely hot, and we should have been out earlier, but we chose to enjoy the quiet cool of our room.

Guess what the Taj Mahal looks like? Exactly, precisely, like every picture I've ever seen of it. While Mary and I and many other visitors wait inside the Taj Mahal, we are able to see the many variations of the tiles that compose this famous structure. Face-to-face with whatever section you are near, you are lost in intricate filigree, an endless spiral of beauty and story.

We are beguiled by the clever children, so handsome and smiling, each trying to convince us that he is the best guide in all of Agra. "Come, Missy, I can tell you everything." Then an older official guide with his official badge shoos them away, which is a futile gesture. We stagger among the blooming lavender trees, heat-drugged, hoping to land in shade. Hours fade and we keep on. This is our short time in Agra, this suspense, the constant surprise of India.

Along a dusty path I pose with snake charmers and a heavy long boa constrictor they drape across my shoulders.

Several hours later, Mary and I have dust and sweat along our arms as we collect our things and go to the airport for the evening plane to New Delhi. At the ticket counter I search through my straightened out purse, and I find no plane ticket. We race back to the hotel; Mary rummages through the many piles of trash from cleaned rooms. I stumble around in disbelief and hopelessness and say to her it is a sign I am to stay in Agra. Mary replies with something like "Bullshit." She finds the ticket in a remaining bag, hustles me to the taxi, and we race to the airport. I am worthless in the emergency, "my head up my ass," one of the Copa girls might say.

That evening we arrive at the Janpath Hotel in New Delhi. There is a large crowd checking in. I am delirious with stomach cramps, a weakness coming over me. I can barely fill out the many forms, in duplicate, that each hotel requires in India.

We follow an attendant through the night to our room. It is large and spacious with unmade beds and dirty sheets and towels on the floor.

Our phone is ringing: "Miss Johnson has not filled out all necessary forms."

Miss Mary Baglan snaps, "Miss Johnson cannot fill out another form until we have toilet paper in our room and clean sheets."

These necessary things are a long time coming, and even when they do, we have many doubts about the room. We sleep fitfully, listening for unknown creatures who may or may not be beside us in the dark.

Next morning we huffily move to the Ashoka Hotel and rest and reunite with Rose, the New Yorker friend we met in Bangkok. I read about New Delhi sitting in my bed or in the bathroom for most of four days. Although each day I think I am better, I stay the same. Mary says we are waiting until the mountain pass clears and then we are going to Srinagar and renting a house boat and resting in Nepal. It's fine with me. I can't recover from, or reconcile with, what I have felt in Calcutta, or the holy search at the Ganges, and all the heat and splendor of India.

I have written to Annette to tell her she must buy any books by Rabindranath Tagore. Why haven't I known about him? He won the Nobel Prize and he founded a university where he wanted students from all over the world to come to study life, not in a strictly academic manner, nor in a monastic setting either, but in a practical search, a "day-to-day aspiration towards truth together," I read on page 594 of Fodor's. "Classes are held outdoors in the mango groves to increase the students' awareness of Nature." And best of all, "...the ultimate aim is to create in young minds a hunger for the unseen and the eternal."

67
Karachi to Persia

Mary has had a beautiful day sightseeing in Karachi. She is energized by the bustle of the city, the splash of blooming trees and flowers along the streets. And how could she not enjoy the sun and fresh air and the joy of being in a new and unexplored place?

For me, I have explored our new bathroom and find it much the same as the one in New Delhi. I spend yet another day in our hotel room, writhing with stomach pain, racing to the bathroom, crawling back to bed, and rolling up in a ball like a slug. It is five days now of sipping tea and nibbling crackers and cookies. I am prisoner of the toilet, but I think I am getting better.

I chance a few hours at our hotel pool. Mary is right: the shrubbery and flowers are a beautiful sight and give me hope. And then there are German boys making everyone laugh, including me, with their silliness and diving antics. I stay just long enough to get sunburned shoulders and to be humiliated by the tanned and smoothly muscled Lufthansa stewardesses in their bikinis.

With very little pride, I rush back to my room, arriving at the toilet just in time. We leave for Tehran tomorrow and I hope for better days.

On our flight to Tehran, Mary and I meet a journalist, Hans. He works for a German news magazine. He tells us of his assignment in India to investigate the claim that children are sold in a bazaar somewhere. I don't believe him at all, and he just replies, with a shake of his head, that it's true. He laughs at me. He asks me what I think we did with the African slaves brought to our country? In spite of his blond, handsome appearance and his confident, easy smiles, I don't like him. But he keeps talking, and his stories of this area of the world intrigue us, and by the time the plane lands, we have made plans to meet later in the afternoon.

In the bazaar we receive harsh looks from some of the tall, somber-faced men passing by. Even though Mary and I are dressed in skirts, sweaters, hose, heels, gloves, and jackets, our uncovered heads and faces are unwelcome.

Hans has ongoing commentary about the recent Status of Forces bill that the Shah wants to enact, granting diplomatic immunity to U.S. military personnel serving here in Iran. It has caused a lot of hard feelings, and people here criticize the Shah for being too close to the United States and trying to westernize Iran. They also don't understand how U.S. politicians can say democracy is the best form of government but support a monarchy in Iran. But Hans says the whole thing is about the oil: Who gets the money from Iran's oil, or at least how do the western powers divide it among themselves with enough to let the Iranians have some? Didn't we know that in 1953 the newly elected Premier lost his position because he wanted a bigger share of the oil money for Iranians? No. I knew nothing about that. And that he was replaced by the current Shah, with help from western powers? No, I didn't.

We would be lost without Hans in the bazaar. The shops are crowded and the twists and turns of the many paths crisscrossing the bazaar are made more impossible to recall because of the many shoppers hurrying by. There are women in full-length black chadors, the traditional full body cloak, with small slits for their eyes; women in suits and gloves and heels just like we are; women with scarves covering their hair, and men in thin dark suits with piercing dark eyes and heavy eyebrows. I never pause to browse or shop because I am afraid to take my eyes off Mary or Hans. I don't want to be left behind. And then any stern face among the shoppers frightens me today. If looks could kill, I keep thinking.

However, back in our Hotel Sina, the friendly clerks, Iraj and Laleh, greet us like friends. They have mail for us and present it to us happily, as if they had brought it from the U.S.A. themselves.

The next morning Hans and I sit outside the hotel in the sun and talk. He can't believe our story of Dan and the Sands Hotel, the places we have seen. Mary is upset with me, I know, spending this time with him, and not going on the city tour, but I don't want to leave the sun on my face. She leaves for a tour by herself.

We are tired of being together night and day. I am over having to run to the bathroom, but I have a headache and my moods are up and down. I am tired and wishy-washy, liking Hans one minute, disliking him the next. If Mary gets disgusted with me, I do too. Thank goodness I have had letters at this hotel from Annette and two from my sister Linda. As far away as we are, and as carefree and unattached, Mary and I are both beside ourselves when we have letters from friends and family.

In an evening conversation, our friendly clerks convince us that we shouldn't leave Iran until we see the Blue Mosques in Isfahan. Mary and I are intrigued and decide to go on the early morning bus.

We find our way through the crowded bus station and buy tickets for Isfahan from a surprised cashier. There is a line to board the small, worn bus taking us on a six-hour drive. And in spite of our efforts to dress conservatively, we can't disguise the fact that we are two young, unaccompanied female tourists. Unlike the women on the bus, we are not wearing a chador. The men in their dark suits, sweaters, heavy boots, and grim demeanor are unsettled by our Western dress. During a long traffic stop in the city, while an endless caravan of limousines passes by, we try to disappear in our seats.

The Elburz Mountains framing Tehran are snow-covered. Ahead, the road vanishes, lost in the endless desert plateau. From our window we see mountains, boulders, sometimes a lone person beside the road, waiting. I search for signs of homes or villages. There are none. We meet few vehicles.

Our fellow passengers seem as distant as the landscape. The men fit the mountains, handsome and severe. Several women remove their head covering but keep their eyes straight ahead. It is a silent ride, except for the whistling of the wind through the windows, the rattling of our slow-moving rickety bus, and the moaning of the clutch with each shift of the gears.

With every passing mile, the bus is colder. Mary and I huddle together. Her distress becomes noticeable, and I do my best to shield her from the wind. She says the bouncing and shaking of the bus makes her shiver too. We are the only passengers without shawls, or heavy coats or turtleneck sweaters to keep off the cold. We are hungry too. We packed no snacks.

Mid-morning the bus slows, pulls off the road and stops. All I can see out the window are a few scrubby plants and hard flat land stretching to the mountains. Nevertheless, the men file out of the back of the bus to relieve themselves, and smoke and chat.

After the last man exits, a woman across from us rises and begins speaking to us. She is holding a large, heavy wool blanket and offers it to us. I take it and she begins pantomiming, pointing back at the men. She points to the blanket, motioning "no" and pointing at the men outside. Finally, after much shaking of her head, taking back the blanket, then "no, no, no," returning it to us, we understand. We think. We hope. We are not to return the blanket until the men are off the bus. Give the blanket back, but not when the men are present. We smile, we nod, we say "thank you," over and over, hoping she will understand if we repeat and smile enough. She smiles. She nods. Should, could, I hug her? I want to.

Mary and I wrap up together in the rough, heavy blanket. The wind blowing through our window is no problem. To the lady who shared her blanket, we thank you. Thank you for the warm tender gesture.

When blue-gray clouds settle into the horizon, we stop for lunch. Even though the roadside inn is small and plain, it is a warm and joyous break. Mary and I have a small table to ourselves while everyone else crowds around the remaining ones with noisy laughter. There are baskets of bread on the tables, with small menus written in the beautiful script we love but cannot read.

A young man walks to our table, nods with a smile and introduces himself in English. He is a schoolteacher in Isfahan. Could he help us select a meal?

Oh, yes. Please.

There is a short hush in the boisterous room.

He suggests that we have the plate with yoghurt, diced onions, rice, and hot tea.

We are thankful. We are hungry.

He says, "Thank you. I like to try my English." We assure him his English is perfect and sounds wonderful to us. We relish the round delicious freshly made bread, enjoy the rice and onions and yoghurt. We eat with gusto, and feel, as never before, "the mercy of strangers." On this deserted road between two ancient cities of Persia, Mary and I have been well cared for.

Upon arrival at the bus station, we follow our plan. Wait for the men to file off the bus, fold our merciful blanket, present it to our unknown friend across the aisle, hold hands briefly, and say, "Thank you, thank you." How do you say in Farsi, that lyrical language, "You are brave and kind and I will always remember you?" One long look into her beautiful eyes and sweet face and then we are rushed along with curious smiles, and jostled by the eager ladies with full baskets and bundles leaving the bus and swept into the streets of Isfahan.

Iraj was right. Not to have seen this famous Blue Mosque, the Masjid-i-shah, would have been a sad loss. I follow the late afternoon light as it moves through green unfurling leaves then crosses over the blue-tiled grace of columns. I follow the maze of starry mosaics tracing their way over the dome, shadows revealing the mysteries of arches, of calligraphy, the deep blue statements of faith. Is there a way to memorize this afternoon and the feeling that we have, for at least today, stopped time? We are speeding through each country, and I have blurred images of faces, stories, encounters like today, and how do I keep them?

We walk into a small tourist bureau where a helpful clerk maintains that we must go on to Shiraz, and then to Persepolis! We smile weakly. She is so earnest.

Tomorrow we are scheduled to visit the ruins of a fire temple, Atashgah, which is believed to be an ancient Zoroastrian site. I purchase a newly published guidebook, *Historical Monuments of Isfahan*. I read this advice, "take time to walk along the river bank, and from the romantic and lovely Khaju bridge…listen to enchanted lovers singing from the woods, or from the blue mosaic alcoves." This bridge has thirty-three arches over the Zayanderud River. We saw them from our car, and it is impressive.

Our last stop before returning to our hotel in Isfahan is a bookstore where I find *Hafiz of Shiraz,* who lived centuries ago. I haven't heard of this writer, but two scholars have translated these poems into English. The bookseller assures me that poetry is a passion in this country. And also, there is a living Iranian female poet that is well known, and I should find her books in English. The poet (I don't remember her name) is controversial and writes about women's feelings.

Mary is sick. We started out for our tour this morning, and she began shaking and had to find a restroom, so we went flying back to the hotel by taxi. I was holding Mary, trying to get her to our room when we meet Art and Rita Harris from California. They are leaving for Tehran and see immediately how weak Mary is and offer their help. They have a large rental car and driver waiting outside and insist we pack and leave with them. Mary should be in a larger city. Mary says yes, yes, please, so in a flash, we gather our things, Mary visits the toilet, and we hurry to the car.

We stop multiple times for Mary. Our stoic driver escorts her through dark fields with his flashlight to use Iranian outhouses, much like the one on my Grandma Johnson's farm except no board to sit on, just a hole to balance over in the dark. But at least we can stop when she needs to, and by nine o'clock we are back at the Hotel Sina in Tehran. Iraj and Lelah immediately come to her aid, and she is now resting, covers piled high and, mercifully, not needing the toilet every half hour. Art and Rita saved us. The whirlwind race in the hired car made us travel partners. They will be waiting for us in Baghdad in two days.

On our last day in Tehran, Mary rests. Iraj recommends a driver for me who will take me to a tea house or *chaikhaneh*. Inadvertently, I leave two essentials in the hotel room, my camera and the new book of poems by Hafiz.

The pleasant driver parks at the foot of a mountain outside of the city. He indicates a path nearby. He will wait, and I am to take my time and enjoy the afternoon. I wind through low shrubbery and small boulders to find the tea house.

A leafy canopy marks the entrance. Persian carpets are spread up the incline, the path dotted with a meandering placement of small tables and chairs winding up the mountainside with a wildly exuberant stream falling so close to the celebrants that if you lean just a little, you might catch a spray of water.

Waiters are balancing trays of teapots and beautiful small painted glasses, cups and saucers and cubes of sugar; friends are laughing and enjoying fresh air and the fine mist on their faces. Sweet almond cookies, journals, music, and books. It is divine. I've never known of such a place, and now how will I live without it? Who dreamed here first, enjoying wildflowers, mist and clouds?

The joyous falling water quiets me. I, too, am a mountain stream, rushing wildly by, guided by serendipity. Today I have wandered into a sacred tea house. This is where I rest and listen and give thanks for the Good Samaritans who have placed me here. My hope is that they, too, have guardians hovering nearby, as I have had, on this brief journey we share.

From my new book of poems by *Hafiz of Shiraz*, "Celebration of Spring":

The rose has come into the garden, from Nothing into Being,
And the violet bends low at its feet in adoration.

Hafiz lived around 1320–1389, about the time of Chaucer. In Persia it was a time of "turbulence and social disruption." This from the introduction by John Heath Stubbs and Peter Avery. They translated the poetry from Persian to English, for which I am grateful.

Blue Mosque, Isfahan

68
April 20, 1964
Baghdad

After threading our way through the noisy and crowded airport, finding our gate and struggling with luggage, I settle in my window seat and take a photo of the Elburz Mountains, my last snowy sight of Persia. I am angry at myself for not having the camera with me yesterday, to have proof of where I was because no one will believe me when I describe the tea shop. There can't be another one like it. But without a picture, will I believe it myself? That I leaned out from the small round table to feel the spray of a mountain stream?

We land in Baghdad to several surprises: heat, after the cool of Tehran, and armed soldiers everywhere. We have been in seven different countries and seen many exotic sights, but men holding guns, or guns slung over their shoulders, or guns hanging from a strap over their shoulders, are unexpected. And they are not just at the airport either, but standing on every street corner, walking up and down a tree-lined boulevard, and patrolling outside our hotel. Can I remember a particular building or the Tigris River that runs through the city or any remarkable sight observed as we came in from the airport? No, only soldiers and guns and bright sunlight and a rather grim feeling.

Midnight, April 20, or 21. Has my watch stopped? What day is this? Mary is trying to sleep, and I am counting days in my Metropolitan Museum journal. I have traveled ninety-five days since leaving Houston. Tonight we were in a nightclub with Art and Rita and their guide, a young lively man who said he would be afraid to visit the United States because of the gangsters in Chicago, the ones he has seen in the movies.

We chided him that this was long ago, but he was firm. America is wild, he said. Look at what happened to our assassinated President. And he is sorry for us and our country because he liked President Kennedy very much. And am I part of President Johnson's family from Texas? No, I reply.

At the nightclub we watched the belly dancers; they watched us. Everyone is watching one another in Baghdad. Last year there were two political upheavals in this country; thus, armed soldiers watch for any suspicious activity. We are suspect because our country and Great Britain try to keep control of the oil production, and no one here likes this interference. All this from Art. The cautious young guide was reluctant to say anything, but would agree with Art's comments with a nod, a noticeably deep swallow and a glance around the room.

Now, at midnight, I am thinking it is ridiculous to travel like this, knowing nothing about anything, and trying to soak up information from a casually exhausted stroll through a dark and mystifying museum. The only thing I am sure of is that with each new adventure, my ignorance grows leaps and bounds. What is revealed to me? That I am fortunate, that I know nothing, that I am stumbling through deserts and unknown places, lost on my way to Paris. That I have a coin purse full of pesos, Hong Kong dollars, yen, rupees, rials and they are jumbled and tossed about like I have been. And without Mary I would still be in Hong Kong, or Benares, and why am I so whiney tonight? I have my postcards ready to mail to Texas and Oklahoma and have written in my journal. I hope my birthday card to my sister Beth, sent from Tehran, arrives in time. This week she will be ten.

Mary and I have a solitary day sightseeing. We take a taxi to the ruins of Babylon, follow our somber guide through the hot and dusty remnants of this long-ago city. Although we have been many places in these several months, we both feel the ancient sand on our feet and are transported. There are no other tourists, and I am free to imagine that I am brushing against lively ghosts, the worshippers of Ishtar, goddess of love.

In the Hanging Gardens of Babylon there is nothing to do but surrender to the heat and desert and imagine the fantasy of this green oasis built for a queen who longed for the childhood memories of her lush and blooming homeland. It is a story that I add to my vast vault of "to find out about later." Mary and the guide wait in the shade while I walk to the Tigris. I scoop water into my hands, send Grandma Lee a message on the wind: *This is for you, Cora Lee. I have knelt on the banks of the Tigris, and sent you a greeting.*

Well, today, after being turned away at the airport, all seats taken, "try tomorrow," and storming back to our rooms pouting, we are immediately grateful for the inconvenience because of the two incredibly handsome Italian men having lunch at the hotel. They smile at our distress and ask so seductively in their beautiful accents have we been to see the Arch of Ctesiphon and can they take us for an archaeological tour?

With little hesitation, we drive into the heat and dust of the desert. Not until it is written on paper can I understand the name, Arch of Ctesiphon. A remnant of a royal palace, from the Persian Empire, now absent its blue ceiling and painted stars. Another mystery to investigate. Because there is barely a road, only obscure signals to guide taxi drivers to the way here, this mirage of a long-ago kingdom has no guides, no small stand of postcards, nothing. We are its only admirers today.

No luck again. It's because of the many Iraqi students returning to their universities. Fathers, sons, uncles, brothers, saying their goodbyes in such an emotional way it brings tears to my eyes even while I am grumpy for the delay.

Mary is out with the very nice Iraqi gentleman who insisted she come with him to a small local restaurant on the banks of the Tigris. I have time to write and organize my postcards. It is midnight in Baghdad. I'm not sure, but I think we must be half way to Paris.

Arch of Ctesiphon
Cover of *From an Antique Land* by Julian Huxley

69
April 24, 1964
Beirut, Lebanon

We are near *the* sea. Yes, the blue-green, ever-changing mesmerizing *Mediterranean* Sea is a short walk from our Hotel Excelsior here in Beirut.

Light comes through the windows in our comfortable room. There's space for our luggage and even an extra chair. We put away our things and go downstairs to the small bar to have "Coca-Cola with ice," and we fall into conversation with the only other people there in the early afternoon. Joe had been on our flight from Baghdad and recognizes us from the plane ride. His friends, Kamil and Gabi, were at the hotel to greet him. They insist that Mary and I take a walk with them so we will know how to find our way around the shopping area.

Our first afternoon in Beirut.

Strolling casually, I love the same stirring female voice singing to us from every car radio and shop we pass. According to Joe, her name is Fairouz, and she grew up near Beirut and now is famous for her unique style of combining pop, love songs, and Arabic folk music. Her voice and music remind me a little of Amalia Rodriguez from Portugal and the "fado" songs of love and hurt.

Joe is probably forty with some gray streaks in his hair, showing off his suntanned, handsome face. Both he and Kamil are Iraqi, while Gabi, who is married to Kamil, is French. Enjoying the warm sun, listening to a verse of a song by Fairouz, I feel a melancholy ache for this unknown place. Why? At the same time I am intrigued by a faded blue house with peeling paint, white shutters, and lace curtains gently flowing in a sea breeze. A moment later I am delighted to be in front of a bustling bookstore full of English books. I know already I will not be leaving Beirut in two days.

Joe says the buildings and homes are arranged to catch the breeze from the ocean and withstand the setting sun in the afternoon. We pass green-shuttered, arched windows and balconies with small palm trees settled in worn clay pots, or white blooming flowers growing wildly round the wrought iron railings. Most homes and shops are plain, square and fifties-modern with louvered glass windows. They are not as interesting as the old, faded wooden buildings with maybe someone standing in the shadows behind the windows that reach to the floor.

With a constant tease of the sea in the distance, little shops with their doors wide open, and the voice of Fairouz calling to us, Beirut is irresistible. Yes, I was—I am—right to dream of faraway places. To want to travel for the rest of my life, to be in unknown countries and to meet strangers and exchange stories as bright sun and cool shadows play across our faces.

I return to the bookstore the next morning. I have to, because yesterday I didn't have time to look carefully at each shelf, every display. But I am interrupted in the best way. Joe is there too. And when I see him, I can't think of anyone I'd rather browse with in a bookstore. Last night we all attended a party and I found out that Joe has been to Houston several times because he does business with Brown and Root, the large construction and engineering company. When I told him my father worked for Houston Natural Gas, he had heard of it. Joe, who travels constantly, works for a family from Abu Dhabi, which is in the Trucial States, an area I need to see on a map. His wife works in Geneva with the Red Cross, and so the two of them are constantly moving between here and Europe.

Joe's friends are all meeting at the Hotel St. George for lunch and would we join him, as well? We find Mary at the hotel, and then mingle with the many other Saturday strollers on the Corniche, the walkway above the shore of the Mediterranean. How fortunate are we? Rich or poor, native or tourist, young or old, lovers or would-be lovers, we gaze at the sea and know we are all rich in this moment. A blue sky, puffy white clouds, small fishing boats, yachts, water-skiers, bikini-clad sunbathers, wind ruffling up towels and sails—a fine show, with everyone happy to have their part this Saturday morning. Do we walk like this back home, to enjoy a pleasant day?

Most of the people we met last evening arrive for lunch on the veranda of the St. George. I find out that, in a few months, there will be an incredible summer arts festival that Fairouz often sings at and, my god, Rudolf Nureyev will also be performing this year. Gabi explains that it takes place at Baalbek, a Roman ruin not far from Beirut. Several others stress that it is an event not to be missed. After a glass of wine, I feel the same. Not to see Rudolf Nureyev and Margot Fonteyn dance among Roman Ruins, or not to hear Fairouz sing a ballad while we are seated under the stars and night sky of Lebanon would be a sad thing.

After lunch, we leave the sunny veranda for a quick look at the neighborhood from our Excelsior hotel rooftop. Down below us, the view of our swimming pool and garden full of green, deep flowering shrubs with light bouncing off the water seems a friendly invitation to rest and chat more. Joe and I sit in the light and shade of the garden and I tell stories about Mary and me and our life at the Sands, our travels, our future plans. Joe says I might be on my way to Paris, but he thinks I will be home shortly and marry one of my boyfriends. I laugh and tell him the only boyfriend I have left in Houston is too young to marry and I don't plan to settle down for years anyway. He chuckles and shakes his head.

Since I have mentioned my grandmothers several times today, he says it sounds like I have a touch of "homesickness." I imagine Grandma Johnson in her sunbonnet and gloves working in her iris garden, the water trough in the middle of Papa's barnyard. We stop our conversation while Joe peels his orange from beginning to end in one curling mesmerizing motion. We listen to birds calling each other. Men and women in bikinis glisten and sunbathe and sleep in the sun around the pool. We enjoy the murmur of the garden while Joe carefully separates the orange, so fragrant and juicy.

We water-ski in the Mediterranean sea. I have bought a red-and-black bikini which would look better on me if I still had my tan from the Pearl Farm. So, to bikini or not to bikini, that is the question. It's better to enjoy this life in Beirut instead of waiting until I am less lumpy. I don't have to be slim like Ava; I can be a busty Anita Ekberg. I just avoid sunbathing next to flawless Mary.

The cute Italian man from Baghdad has sent me roses here in Beirut. Then Gabi has insisted we shop at the Pharmacie because I am frowning and squinting too much and must have a tube of Lancaster masque for nighttime to hold back lines in my forehead. I don't argue; maybe it will help. I marvel at Gabi: her superb bearing, flawless complexion, petite figure, and of course her French accent. Most of all, I like to hear her comments about life and art and dance. I like how she is at ease being quiet in a group, without being withdrawn.

We have been introduced to an architect from Chicago and his wife, then Arkan Abadi, a political writer from Iraq, who has autographed his book for me with the hope that we will discuss it one day after I learn to read Arabic. Kabil, Gabi, and Joe have intense discussions with their friends, in French, Arabic, sometimes English. Conversations are not always on art or dance or history and nearby archaeological sites. Most often they are speaking of local politics and what is happening in Lebanon: the turmoil of the Palestinians, hostilities among the feuding factions throughout the country, border disputes with Israel, the heavy hand of Syria. There are many opinions about what will happen in the near future, and what they most agree on is that they are fearful for this beautiful life.

I understand very little. I don't want to ask for an English translation for each conversation. I know, though, that in spite of our lively dinners, or an hour or two of dancing at Cave du Roi, everyone is deeply concerned about the troubles here, and each day they work and walk and gather and discuss these problems, but always try to enjoy life today. Many are here in Beirut because they left Iraq after the 1958 revolution. They know personally how abruptly a sunny day can bring rubble or death or prison.

I do remember my professor warning us many times in his Comparative Government class that this Israeli-Palestinian situation must be resolved. As if it were up to us personally to see that a fair solution comes about. Also, he said to work at the United Nations if possible, read all the Don books by Sholokhov, and listen to Shostakovich symphonies. If only I could call him for an update.

Which city have we been in that has escaped turmoil in the past twenty-some years?

Not one.

Byblos, Phoenician Harbour

70
Baalbek

I am with Kamil and Gabi for a Sunday outing. We drive through small towns, up and over the mountains and down into Bekaa valley. With every bend in the road, we are happy to be in the country, to admire the trees and small roadside stands decorated with blooming potted flowers. I tell them that one of my mother's favorite books is *The Prophet* by Kahlil Gibran and that as a child I was intrigued by the drawings: the eye in the palm of a hand with angel wings like clouds around it and the many nude drawings. I browsed through it many times, read a page or two, and found it mysterious. In the bookstore several days ago I read a few of the chapters. His ideas seem similar to those of Tagore, the philosopher and educator I learned about from my India guide book. Gibran says simply, "Your daily life is your temple and your religion."

At Baalbek we take photos of each other among the ruins. Our photos will be like the ones I've seen of tourists at the trunk of a giant redwood, tiny figures dwarfed by wondrous columns reaching for the sky. Kamil says it is the largest of the Roman temples. And to make the pillars appear even taller, everything was built on top of an enormous man-made platform, so the entire complex rises from the valley floor. To help one absorb the grandeur of this ancient place, there are tiny red and yellow wildflowers peeking from beneath massive blocks of fallen stone. I see why a festival is celebrated here each year: to honor an ancient place of worship with prayers of dance and song and friendship.

We drive to Aley to visit the artist Mouazzez Rawdeh, a friend of Kamil's. We have lunch in her garden. A sculptor, she works outside in the summertime. She says she usually is able to complete maybe ten pieces in four months. In the winter she returns to Beirut to sculpt in

wood and to paint. All her words are translated for me. I apologize that
I have no French. They speak in Arabic, French, and sometimes English.
I am happy to be with them and am transfixed by the sound of their
languages, the light and beauty of Mouazzez's garden, and by someone
who lives in her art, her work. I want to live like this—to write and be
with friends and live outdoors as much as possible and be happy in any
country, wherever life sends me.

Light slips through slender branches while we enjoy tea, surrounded
by shadow and movement. I recognize the moment. It is exactly like
being under the cedar tree with my grandparents when a breeze finds
us. Mouazzez offers me an orange.

Leaving Aley, we see the metallic blue-green Mediterranean catch
fire, watch the sun, water, sky, fold one into the other: a silver cloud, a
golden sea, rose crystal shards of sun erupting across the horizon. Kamil
pulls off the winding mountain road and we three stand silently beside
the car. Except for small singing insects, we are alone facing the sea in
the cool evening air.

I have spent three days traveling to Damascus (by taxi) and
visiting my friend Carol. We last met two years ago, outside Law Hall
at University of Houston. Since then she has married and now has a small
baby boy. Her Syrian family hosted a luncheon for me, and I enjoyed
the home-cooked exotic foods. We went sightseeing in Damascus and
saw the beautiful and ancient Great Mosque that I must learn about.

From Damascus to Beirut I share a taxi with a young Syrian
teenager. We each gaze out our windows in a pleasant silence. I am a
practiced car-window gazer, and profound thoughts bubble up. I can
never be married. Just like I have always known, a child is a lot of work.
I'm not suited for it. And a husband to cook for and all that.

Watching the desert fly by, I keep thinking, *this* is what I am suited for. Travel. Living in hotels, discovering new cities, discovering more and more and more of what I do not know.

This can't be my last night in Beirut. I won't think like that. I'll be back for the Baalbek festival later this year.

Touring Baalbek. May 3, 1964
My guides in Lebanon

71
May 9, 1964
Cairo, Egypt

I leave Beirut by plane, on my way to Africa. Before we land, I barely have time to recall bits and pieces of *The Alexandria Quartet* by Lawrence Durrell. Alone in the taxi to Cairo, I note that there are few cars on the road. I see jaunty red flags placed low to the ground waving brightly along the highway. There seem to be hundreds of them, and finally I notice the hammer and sickle and realize they signal the USSR. I ask the taxi driver about them. Yes, he replies. The Soviet Union and Premier Khrushchev are being honored because the Premier is visiting this week to celebrate the Aswan Dam project. Everything is topsy-turvy with journalists and television coverage by many countries. Main streets are closed and so are many tourist sites.

Still, I am not prepared for the chaos at the hotel. Though we had confirmed our reservations only a few days ago, I am told there is no room available. Mary isn't there, but has left me a note. She thinks we have a room now at the Semiramis. I take a taxi there, only to find another note, followed by another ride through hot, noisy, crowded streets. In the taxi I feel an absurd resentment toward Khrushchev, find no delight in tall palms or red flowering shrubs, and feel my eyes squint in a hateful look as I grind my teeth. I blame my attitude on being up so early and leaving Beirut and my friends there. Just when I am comfortable in a place and feel at home, we move on.

Mary greets me with an excited hug and immediately begins to tell me how delighted she is with exotic Cairo, the beautiful Nile, and, most of all, the interesting man she has met. The happier she appears, the more unsettled I become. Gnawing envy returns. Also, she says so merrily, I am to quickly go through my luggage and find a bathing suit and sundress and go with her in yet another taxi ride to the Cairo Hilton. We are meeting her new friend to sunbathe and have drinks at the pool. I curse silently and wonder why not drinks at a bar with overhead fans and sitting fully clothed. Does Mary have any idea at all that I do not like to be beside her in our bikinis?

The Hilton is packed. Mary and I have arrived in Cairo in the middle of a huge historic event, and I guess that to have a hotel room at all is something. I remember seeing pictures of the Aswan Dam being built, and articles about the raising of the famous statues at Abu Simbel. We scoot in between newspaper writers and dignitaries gathered from all over the world for important events here in Cairo. We nod and listen to multiple learned conversations while sunbathing, drinking, and dangling legs in the swimming pool.

Mary's friend is dashing and a great storyteller. I listen to all the talk, half covered up with my towel, my arm across my face, baby oil seeping into my eyes, and feeling warm and sleepy. It's always the same. No matter my petty jealousies with my friend, I'm so much better off being with Mary.

Tonight, sitting at the bar at the Hilton, I am able to make out the silhouette of a pyramid. Then I find out from my new friend, Frank, a journalist with NBC, that for the next few days, that's the only view I will have of the famous Egyptian pyramids, since everything will be closed to everyday tourists like me. Khrushchev will be touring all those famous sites without the annoying crowds. In the chaos of arrival I understood from the taxi driver that tourist sites would be closed *today*, not for days. I order a Black Russian.

Mary met her friend early this morning. When I wake up at noon I order a sandwich and stay in bed all day reading *The Ginger Man* and *One Hundred Dollar Misunderstanding*, writing letters and postcards, pouting because I am fat. By some miracle, I have received a telegram from Annette, announcing she has decided to come to Europe and to send her money as quickly as possible, like I promised I would. I will happily do that, but I also find out that it is impossible to send money to the United States from Cairo.

I tell Mary I must leave for Athens in order to send money to

Annette. She gives me a strange look. I realize that Mary is completely infatuated with this guy she has met. It seems as if she has lost her senses. But she has sense enough to remind me, more than remind me even, that in Europe it is five dollars a day. No over spending. Cheap hotels, no food, no beauty appointments, and no books. We do our own hair from this day on. Nails too. No more trinkets and gifts for the family.

At the airport I buy an ancient-looking silver necklace with a scarab. Fifty-cent special in a glass bowl at the ticket counter. My treasure. Frank, the journalist who lives in Paris, has given us telephone numbers and says he will be happy to meet us there. Oh yes, I think to myself. I *am* on my way to Paris.

Mary's photos in Egypt

72
Athens, Greece

Upon my arrival, I select a moderately priced hotel, Nikis 13, unpack and walk to American Express on Constitution Square, where I have letters from my mom and two high school buddies.

I stop on the hot, busy, crowded street and buy ten postcards of the Acropolis. As I began winding back to the hotel, I am delighted to see the real thing: There, in plain sight, up on a hill, is *the* Acropolis. I walk slowly, peeking through empty spaces, watching the famous, glowing, gold-and-dusty-pink apparition appear, disappear, appear.

In my room I write letters to Annette and Charlotte, and postcards to the family. I scribble entries for May 10 through 12. I brood too. When I'm with Mary, I'm jealous. I am fussy with her when she reminds me we are on a budget. We've been companions now for 118 days. I counted them. She is aggravating because I am overweight, and she is not. She is aggravating because she has a boyfriend in Cairo, and I do not. The most aggravating thing of all is when I am not with her, I miss her.

The next day, Wednesday morning, I go back to American Express and send Annette five hundred dollars for her trip to France. That alone should take care of my budget and overspending.

I find a tourist office, information on how to get to Crete, and discover a young man, Jody, from College Station, Texas. Even with my back turned to him, I instantly recognize this stranger's Texas drawl. "Yes, ma'am. No ma'am," to the clerk behind the counter. I don't grab his arm and tell him we are going to be friends and he has no say in the matter, but almost. He is nineteen, in the Army on leave and trying to see Athens. He is tall, with close-cut hair, the cutest face and friendliest smile ever. We eat lunch at the Hilton, spend the afternoon wandering the Acropolis until I feel faint in the heat. We meet later for the Sound and Light show featuring the one and only, the Acropolis. In the cool night, we stumble around and wind our way through the outdoor cafés and crowds until we luck upon a tiny table and two chairs hemmed in by hundreds of other excited tourists. We eat and talk and I am so happy he doesn't mind that I am bossy. I make him promise he will let me follow him around another day.

Sunday, Jody and I go see *A Midsummer Night's Dream* with Sir Ralph Richardson. Isn't that amazing? To be in Athens, a stone's throw from the Theatre of Dionysos, where Sophocles had his plays performed, and here we are seeing Shakespeare? I remember a few of Titania's lines. "Not for thy fairy kingdom. Fairies away!" Jody and I have too many Black Russians at the Hilton after the play.

Before Jody heads back to Germany, we try the Acropolis early in the morning. We listen in on some English tour guides. We take photos. We exchange addresses and look across the city and meander through a museum.

Do you ever meet these people again in life? These fine companions, like Rose and Art and Rita, Joe and Kamil and Gabi, who step in to usher you through a few days on your journey? Maybe I will see Jody again in Texas. But in this fifth month of travel, I feel sometimes that these goodbyes and be-sure-to-writes are our last words.

73

I shiver in the sea salt evening air and celebrate that I am alone and going to Crete because I want to see the island that Kazantzakis has written about. I lean over the railing and marvel at the moon following this ferry, see Athens fade from view. Smile to think of Mary in Cairo posing as a photographer covering Khrushchev's visit with her new friend, and I am not jealous, just now.

I regret that first hot day at the Acropolis when I tried to be still, to listen to Athena, to imagine stars decorating her blue ceilings, to feel the business of devotions. Instead, I was hot and sweaty, stumbling and tripping. I was anxious about being suffocated by the sun. I will be a different tourist in Crete. I will take my time; I don't have to rush and dash and "see" everything. I will write and study.

While boarding the ferry, I meet a young doctor who tells me a little about Crete. Tomorrow, May 21, is a holiday. There will be memorials remembering the Battle of Crete. The Allies—Australians, New Zealanders, and U.S. troops—retreated from mainland Greece to Crete. The Germans wanted the airfield that is very near to Chania, where I will be. German paratroopers were dropped into Crete expecting to overrun the Allied forces quickly, but that didn't happen. Instead, the battle went on for ten days, and thousands lost their lives. The doctor and I are at the same table for the evening meal, and he continues his stories in English and Greek. He is serious and helpful and has written down the hotel I should stay in and says that if I am a fan of the writer Kazantzakis, I must go to Iraklion and see the ruins of Knossos. I will also find Kazantzakis's grave there. He says the bus stops in front of my hotel, and I shouldn't miss Knossos. But I might.

If I had a phone, I would call Mr. Cohen at the Sands to tell him about Chania and my small hotel and how I enjoy my room with its window overlooking the square, where I watch from behind the curtains as people come and go, wait on the bus, visit quietly. I would tell him that if I had the copy of *Zorba* he gave me, I would anoint it in olive oil from the escargot I had last evening at a small café in old Chania.

Chania itself is a quiet place, with the sea a gentle pulse in the harbor, a few tables set outside a deserted café. It is an ancient Phoenician harbor, like Byblos in Lebanon. It is also a perfect place to remember the harbor in Hong Kong, its strange beauty created by the slender sails. I think of Isfahan and the mystery of the Blue Mosque. These places linger together now that I have time to remember them.

The U.S. Navy has landed at Souda Bay. I was having breakfast early yesterday morning when five boisterous young men came in and sat at the table next to me. As with Jody, I had instant friends. They were from Texas, New Jersey, West Virginia. When you are in a foreign country and meet someone who speaks your language, there are no barriers to friendship. I cast myself as the older sister and had good companions. They brought bicycles to my hotel and we spent a long day at the beach and I know the way now. We went to the harbor and had beer in the quiet, empty, ancient site and took turns telling funny stories about home. They miss their girlfriends and their local hangouts (a Dairy Queen for one), and one boy misses his hunting dog, Chief. They are so cocksure, blustery, and I've only sisters, but I would have any of them as a brother.

I have brought many books along with me so far, but not *Zorba the Greek*. And no doubt I should have it here in Chania to note that on this day, with a blue quivering sky overhead, a remarkable, unbelievable, and I-could-never-ever-have-made-this-up coincidence, has happened.

Earlier this morning, sitting outside in my little *plaka* at my favorite wobbly table with its delicate twisted wire legs and its worn, round, wooden top so small a cup of coffee and my journal wrestled for space, I sat thinking of many things. That I must write Mr. Cohen about being in Crete. And wondering why do I get down about gaining weight when I am proud to be here alone in Chania? That I have this privilege to travel, explore, and now time to try and make sense of what all this means. Moments like this help me see that I feel happy when I am alone in a new place and can do exactly as I please. I couldn't have done any of the earlier traveling without Mary, but now that we are in Europe, I have more confidence in myself. And just as I was pondering these pleasant questions, a young, brown-haired man emerged from around a corner and walked straight towards me. He asked me a question in French. Of course I had to say, in English, that I didn't speak French. Slowly, with that mesmerizing accent, he explained, in English, that he was with a movie crew. I thought surely he had to be kidding when he said that they are filming *Zorba the Greek* here on the beaches and villages around Chania.

He asked if I would be an extra in the movie. What a come-on when he didn't need it at all! Then he asked that I come to dinner tonight to meet Mr. Cacoyannis, the director. Lila Kedrova will be there too. She plays Bouboulina. He tells me Anthony Quinn plays Zorba. My disbelief fades, and now I am struck dumb by this coincidence. And how beautiful this man is, and he is not making eyes at me, only needs an extra in a crowd. I accept. Yes. Yes, I would love it. Be an extra. Come to dinner. I never mumble that I am sitting here in this somber sunlit square because I love to read books by Nikos Kazantzakis. I can't express my surprise at this serendipitous encounter about Zorba just as I was thinking of writing Mr. Cohen and was enjoying the sun on my face. This man thought I was Greek. He asked me to be a Greek villager in their film.

A day later a car arrives early in the morning outside my hotel. The silent driver nods after I say, "Zorba?" I get in and we begin a slow drive through Chania on poor roads lined with short, crooked, twisted silver-leafed trees. At times, as we curve up into the countryside, there are glimpses of the sea. We pass a small village, one man sitting outside a small whitewashed café, smoking. And all along the drive, there are wildflowers.

When we arrive in our village, a small friendly crowd gathers, amazed at the unknown car, and the tall surprised passenger, me. I am a curiosity, and apologetic, trying to respond to the enthusiastic greetings. It is apparent immediately, however, that it doesn't matter what language I speak, I am welcome.

The attractive, sexy young man who asked me to be an extra appears and steers me to a makeshift dressing room. I won't be in a crowd, like I thought. I have a scene. I walk down a path, with the sea in the distance. But not alone. No, I lead a goat behind me.

In the changing room I am transformed by a long skirt, white blouse, a short embroidered vest, a necklace of small coins. I have a scarf arranged carefully around my head and face, with strands of hair placed just so to look casually loose. No conversation, just friendly nods, a tuck here, there. Eight months ago, Pauline was fitting my red satin dress, with little conversation.

How do I feel? Is this happening? Have I walked into a village from Kazantzakis's *Freedom or Death*? I am slightly in disbelief, in love with my costume, but cannot express such a childish emotion (didn't I feel like this on Halloween once, dressed as a gypsy?). No, I must stifle this impulse to jump for joy, and instead go outside calmly and make friends with an adorable white goat, my costar. The goat isn't self-conscious, hesitant, or curious about his surroundings.

This movie location is not like our smoky Copa Room filming of *Viva Las Vegas*. We are in a small village with curious bystanders walking about, and small children sitting quietly, watching the proceedings. And the process goes quickly, no long hours waiting for our scene to be shot. Here is the path, here are your directions, and, and... Begin! It's not that hard to walk on a path, leading a goat who takes to the camera so quickly and never gets out of character. He trots nimbly behind me, with solemn Garbo-like eyes, very long eyelashes that I am sure will steal the scene if we aren't left on the cutting room floor.

When our scene is completed, I wish I had a bigger part, and I wander around for hours, happily escorted by the hospitable residents of the village. I am invited into every home and can't believe that some of the "sofas" or "beds" are carved from the mountainside.

During my adventure through the village, a young girl with long wavy brown hair, a bright confident manner, and lively eyes approaches me with no hesitation and speaks English so expressively I am captivated instantly.

"You are American?"

"Yes, yes, I am," I say, happy to have English.

"I knew it!" she shouts.

She turns to my escorts, translates for them that I am from Texas, and conveys my gratitude for their attention and acts of kindness.

In no time, Lisy and I are in deep conversation, as if it is imperative to know everything about each other in the fewest of breaths. I try to tell her of my decision to come to Crete, how it came about, the books I read, the stories, but she interrupts too many times, exclaiming, "Kazantzakis! How you know his writing?" And with every answer I attempt, she interrupts with another question. I tell her I am enjoying Chania, that I have been in Athens, and before that Cairo. She interrupts with "Where do you go next?" She says she wants to go to Spain and France and study in Paris. I am spellbound by her energy. When she asks me to dinner for the following evening, I accept quickly. She shows me pictures of her family. Her mother is beautiful, like Irene Pappas, the Greek movie actress who has a leading part in this film. Lisy's family has made friends with their new neighbors, cast members of the movie. She admires the actor Alan Bates, who plays the young writer, and she is starstruck, having famous actors coming and going in the home next to hers.

Screen shot from the film, Zorba the Greek

74

Lisy and her parents moved me out of my hotel and into their home. I am free to wander while Lisy is in school. One day I accompany her mother to her club where she likes to meet friends and play cards. After many introductions, I find a comfortable nook and read. We walk and talk and cook in her kitchen. She speaks only Greek; I reply in English. We laugh and shrug and pantomime and pass the hours. She is a great beauty, and her daughter Lisy is her look-alike.

In the evenings we listen to Chopin piano recordings and Lisy's father tells me more about the war here in Chania. I look at the framed family photos in their parlor and notice a signature, Helen Kazantzakis, Nikos's widow. Oh yes! She was a houseguest six months ago. They have a lively, warm, and close family. They are interested in my travels and must have reservations about a young American woman traveler, former dancer at a casino, yet they embrace me. I emphasize my traditional education, try to hide my ignorance of European politics and geography.

Lisy and I talk late into the night, sitting on her twin beds. In a low voice she says, "I want to be free, have the whole world for my home." I agree. It is good to have a sense of the world and to roam at will. She goes on. "There are so many things to do in life! Life is wonderful: to make trips, to see people and places, to work, to dance with all the young boys and girls in the world, to speak about your problems." She is not free to speak to boys in the street, to nod, to call out their names. It would be much too forward.

"You understand, Judy? You understand how difficult everything here? The customs of my country are stupid! It's a crime to speak with a boy and if you speak with many, is a greatest crime because they will say that you are in love with all of them. Such a trolley heart!"

I can barely meet her eyes, considering my own trolley heart. But I see she has such a deep respect and love for her parents that I don't know that she could ever displease them, or hurt them in any way. Lisy has long dark hair, determined eyebrows, lively, intelligent eyes. Her nose and mouth are perfect. She wants to go to Paris, to study at the University and live away from her family.

She continues, "The bad with me, you know what it is?" I cannot imagine any bad in Lisy. "That I got the sense of life, and now I revolt against these customs and that way of life." That way of life? She doesn't want her parents to find her a husband. What does the freest of American girls reply to that complaint? And not offend my host and hostess, yet remain a confidante to this passionate young girl?

"No, Judy. It's impossible, not only the husband, but the way I want to live. You know, Judy, how many days and hours and beautiful moments we lose living like that? Few girls understand it here. They find natural the way they live."

Living like that? Lisy cannot "be closed to a house, make children, make the dishes, and all these." She doesn't find it natural. I listen to her, shake my head, nod, agree.

"Oh Judy, I want to see, to meet, every beautiful thing in life, then I will see about marriage and all these things. Now my heart is so far from marriage, firstly because I am in love with no one, and I am REALLY happy that I can see the sun, the sea, the moon free! Free!"

My young friend Lisy

234

75

The sea is so near Chania, with wildflowers beckoning along the road. I want to leave the path and climb up the hillside, make a comfortable nest, and sit down next to pink and wine buttercups and read my book. But I don't. I go on to the shore and fancy dancing whitecaps instead, study watercolored rocks and admire the sky. I use the book for a pillow and listen as sapphire-colored waves somersault into the sand. I remember my dream of living in Paris in a small hotel and writing each day, sipping coffee at a sidewalk café. I never thought once about the small hotel being in Crete, or writing on a beach with yellow flowers nodding, peering from behind rocks.

Not too many miles from here is the Maleme airfield and several military cemeteries. Red poppies and other sympathetic wildflowers race pell-mell up and down the hillsides, bringing life and offering a timely memorial for those who died too young and were buried here after the invasion.

According to Lisy's father, the Allies retreated from Greece to Crete, their bodies, ammunition, supplies, communications depleted. Cretans— men, women, and children—fought with farm instruments, branches, walking sticks, canes, broken furniture. And this ethereal beach (which is sea or sky? Cloud or fields of buttercups?) was the scene of vicious fighting. There were thousands of deaths: Cretans, New Zealanders, Australians, Welsh, Maori, British. German paratroopers dropped from the sky. These flowered hillsides, the quiet Chania, covered with dead. Lisy's father speaks plainly and slowly so I can remember these stories. Now, with any and all town citizens I pass in their solemn dark dress, I wonder: Did this grandpa use his cane as a weapon? Did this grim, wrinkled grandma gather her children and fade into the landscape, the impossible terrain of the White Mountains? Did she live in a hidden cave, resist the occupation, give shelter to a Cretan resistance fighter?

I want to wander through Chania, street by scarred street, figuring out which building has been reconstructed, which one survived. This quiet town was in flames, rubble, twenty-three years ago, bombed relentlessly. Many homes near the old Venetian harbor are still without electricity. I want to stroll about and find where women go for bread each morning. I want to buy scarlet and purple flowers, and write in my journal. And I should see the ruins of Knossos, the leaping dolphin frescoes, learn about the Minoans. I know I should.

But it is hard to leave a wildflowered path to the sea.

Oh, those Navy guys fooled me! At times during the few days they are here, I wonder why none of them seem interested in me. I tell myself I am overweight, or that they enjoy having a "sister" around, since I am a few years older than they are. But I know better now.

While I am in my hotel, they take me to dinner. Laughing and teasing, we walk behind the hotel, through several neighborhood streets, then the edge of town, on a moonlit path through an olive tree grove. Talking and jostling and walking backwards, they tell stories about each other as we angle away from the harbor and to a part of town I have never seen. Then one boy asks, "Do you know where we are going?" They all giggle and give out great hoots of laughter.

"No," I say.

"We're going to Boystown!" Now they double over with laughter. I am speechless. I'm not sure what they mean. I think I do. I always think I know so much.

We stroll on down this lane in Chania, Crete. The night air is frisky too. I listen to their stories about girlfriends, basketball teams, last port, a beautiful girl. In the background are insect sounds, night-calling birds. I tell them I have a sister their age at the University of Houston. I tell them about being a dancer at the Sands (seems so long ago). They love that, pretending to be showgirls, hands on hips, swaying superbly, silly. Our stomachs hurt from laughing.

We walk into one short block with a make-believe hotel, like doll houses, with one or two beautiful young girls leaning over each of the window sills, laughing, smiling, beckoning, calling to the boys. The girls have on camisoles, frilly off-the-shoulder blouses, thin nightgowns.

"Hallo."

"Come see me, boys."

My brothers laugh and wave and say, "Hello" back.

The girls' sweet faces, their friendly calls, the make-believe English, make me smile back and wave.

I feel at home and enjoy the cool night, bright lights, wine and good spirits. Who would ever know that our tiny porch, our table with a worn, clean, white-starched tablecloth and a little carafe of wildflowers, our quaint street, is a walk on the wild side? This is sanctioned prostitution. Legal sex for sale. A weekly checkup by a physician.

The tiny wrinkled madam brings us plates of food, then joins us. She leans across the table and strokes my face. I am sure she thinks I would fit in easily with her ladies. I've never thought of what girls selling sex should look like. Like Jane Fonda in *Walk on the Wild Side*, like Melina Mercouri in *Never on Sunday*. But those were stories, and sad ones too. I want to know how these fifteen, sixteen, girls across the street became prostitutes? On what day, what hour, did the girl on the second floor, corner room, directly across from my table, begin having sex for this madam? That is what I am wondering about on this cool moonlit night, far away from home and family, on my five-month long inventive way to Paris, courtesy of men who gave me money, plane tickets, friendship, and independence.

76
June 1964
To Spain

Twenty-some letters waited for me at the Athens American Express: thank you notes from Annette's third graders at Anson Jones Elementary. Their Chinese dolls and little ships arrived safely from Hong Kong.

Gloria Flores writes to me, *You are a nice girl.*

I like you Judy. Thank you for the dolls you sent us. Your Friend, Alice Garcia.

We hope you are well. Your friend, Genaro V.

Judy, we hope you visit us sometime. Thank you for the ships. Arthur Z.

We are collecting the stamps from your letters. Manuel Sotelo.

In the next few days, I unfold and hold and caress these letters many times.

Since the taxi drivers are on strike and Athens is hot and busy, I've walked and complained all over this city. But it is always worth it to arrive at American Express. I have greetings from Masao, asking how our trip has been so far and saying he has received my postcards. Also from Carol across the street, wishing she could be with us for the "rest of the way." I will write a postcard, saying that her gift, *Platero and I* has been my companion these many months, always reminding me of our friendship. I also have word from Bernie and Stella, my friends from University of Houston. They have had several of their letters returned recently and wrote again to Athens after they received my postcard from

Chania. Sitting in the shade of the Parthenon, reading Stella's words for me to "love every moment of your trip," I feel shame for being bothered by idle taxis when I am lazily lounging around yet another Hilton pool. Bernie and Stella have been married a year now and have a new baby to take care of.

This blazing sun and a poster of "ruins of Liban" prompt me to step inside an air-conditioned Olympia Air office and buy a round-trip ticket from Athens to Beirut for the festival at Baalbek. I do not want to miss it.

Mary and I meet in Athens. For the preceding twenty-three days we had traveled separately. While I was in Crete, she stayed in Cairo and then traveled to Jerusalem. She was exhausted when she came from Israel, and then felt she had to go on to Crete, where she expected me to be, only to find out that she had just missed me, and I was back in Athens. Not just in Athens. But at the Hilton (not a five-dollar-a-day place). Not only at the Hilton, but when she arrived, hot and dusty from the ferry, I was in the beauty parlor having a manicure and my hair dyed blond. I had spent at least half my money for June in two days. She was completely exasperated with me. I was too.

We book passage on a small freighter from Piraeus to Marseille. Our space on the ship is so small, we have to sleep with our luggage crowded around us. The tension between us grows. Mary stays in the room most of the time. I sit in the dining room and eat nonstop. Who can stand being with me when I can't budget and eat like a pig?

I meet an interesting guy, Richard, from New York City, and we spend a lot of time talking about the countries we've been in and our plans for the summer. Richard also tells me that there is a famous philosopher on this little vessel who attracts a small crowd whenever he speaks. His message is something like this: If we cannot get along with our family and friends and neighbors, how can we expect our countries and governments to get along? If you and I don't make peace among ourselves, how can we expect our countries to do so?

I am intrigued by how this big question relates to the tension between Mary and me, yet no way can that conversation squeeze into our tiny room, crowded with gloom and a maze of luggage we must jiggle around in order to open and close our door.

To add to our travel fatigue and great surprise, we have a stop in Naples to wander (stagger) around, and later find ourselves in Pompeii. I have no guide book, no English pamphlets. Something is bearing down on me besides the heat and tension. I can barely comprehend the objects, the sad forms of men and women, small children, encased in lava, kept in place for centuries by volcanic eruption. Oddly preserved, but tenderly, achingly, human. It's as if one might stumble on a distant relative, a beloved friend. It is lovingly poignant. All of us, at one time or another, sit frozen in time.

On arrival in Marseille, after four days of being cramped, feeling crappy, acting surly, Mary and I decide to split up. We are sick and tired of each other. Mary stands in one line leaving our boat, I stand in another. She exits to the left; I exit to the right. I watch her pull her luggage down the gangway. Many thoughts fly through my head and I feel sick. Why are we fussing? Before we left Athens we did catch up on our separate adventures and to think she stood right next to Mrs. Khrushchev and saw the City of Alexandria. She had a thrilling time in Cairo and I know she is a little heartsick leaving that fine fellow who spun her head around. Really, why are we so crabby with each other?

We have been traveling for 146 days.

Fortunately for me, there is one taxi left at the port in Marseilles. After frowning at each other at the taxi stand for a long second or two, Mary and I shrug and struggle into the taxi. At the train station, we wait for something going to Barcelona. All day we act as if nothing has happened, and I will never agree to separate from Mary again. Nothing could be better, as far as I am concerned, than to be grimy and dirty with Mary at a train station, with no place to sit or stretch out except on top of our luggage, drinking cheap wine and getting tipsy, then meeting three American schoolgirls and agreeing to share their apartment on the train leaving Marseilles after midnight.

The next morning we arrive in Barcelona (on five dollars a day) and spend nine hours again in a train station. After our thirteen-hour ride to Madrid and having accumulated even more grime and broken fingernails, we take a taxi to American Express. We are overjoyed to receive many, many letters from family and friends, and even though we find a very cheap hotel and check in, we don't stay there long. Mary calls the Plaza Hotel to see if her friend from the Philippines is there, and he is, and now we are at the excellent Plaza Hotel too. He insisted.

My eyes, my feet, my legs are swollen. It's from being cramped on the boat, the heat, the long train rides, cheap wine. It doesn't matter, though. Mary is sightseeing with her Manila boyfriend, I have our room to myself, and I am grateful we are together. I walked down the Avenida Jose Antonio and went to see *West Side Story* alone, came home and composed a respectful letter to Masao and asked, could he send me more money? It is a brazen thing to do, but it's done and I hope for the best. And if he doesn't, that's okay. Mary says she is going home to the States sooner than she expected, and I might too. Annette will arrive in Paris in less than a month, and I will have a little money to share with her, like I promised, and then I will go home when Mary does.

Mary's boyfriend has a red sports car convertible, a two seater. He drives, petite Mary is in the middle, I sit forward on the seat, hang out the window. Through mountains and fields of Spain, I daydream, look for Don Quixote and Sancho Panza, try to remember a line from *Platero and I* by Juan Ramon Jimenez. Why didn't I rummage through my book bag and bring that with me today? Crowded or not, we each have room for our thoughts.

Through hours of clouds and blue sky, I have time to think about being in Pompeii and Naples last week. I feel free and happy that I don't know where I am at the moment. With the wind rushing us through the miles, we enjoy the comfortable privacy you have when it's useless to make conversation. All of us are content with the road and driving endlessly in no hurry to anywhere, as our thoughts trail out and around us.

Back on the Mediterranean, away from busy Madrid. I order breakfast for one to the patio outside our room. Afterward, the hotel has a pool, or I can walk to the sea. Later, we snack on tuna and sardines, drink wine, and a friend of Mary's boyfriend joins us. He and I walk through town, to the sea, and later have dinner under the stars. The second day the men drive to Gibraltar, and Mary and I stay at the pool. Last week I was morbid and weepy; today I am cloud-like. Mary and I have been friends for a year. Last June, at this time, we moved in together and were making plans to take a freighter to Paris. We never knew about a village in Spain and swimming in the Mediterranean. We have been on a journey for months, and now we are making plans, still, to go to Paris. But first we will see Grenada and visit the Alhambra, then drive on to Madrid tomorrow evening. Mary says she is eager to begin her real life in New York City.

I have spent the last three weeks reading *Crime and Punishment* until two and three in the morning. During the day I am exploring the dark rooms at the Prado with Mary, searching out somber portraits by Ribera. We stand and study the blue in a gown the Virgin Mary wears, as painted by El Greco. We drive to the Valley of the Fallen, see El Cordobes in the bullring in Toledo. We try not to shudder or gasp at spurting blood, a plunging knife, an animal heaving, laboring on its knees. We try to understand this spectacle of color and horses and costume and "bravo" shouted by the thousands. In the early morning hours I am once again lost in St. Petersburg, repulsed and fascinated by Raskolnikov.

77

Mary's boyfriend has left, and we have moved many blocks down the street to a ninth-floor room that costs one dollar a day for each of us. We can climb out our window to the rooftop and see up and down Avenida Jose Antonio. Mary is not happy. We discuss her situation endlessly. She has boyfriends that live halfway around the world, and it is useless to be heartbroken over men you are not with. And when we travel, attractive, fascinating, well-educated, adventurous men keep popping up. At first, a love affair in an exotic place is wonderful. Later, we are annoyed when we can't decide whether we want to travel and attract many fascinating, educated adventurous men, or find one and settle down. I think that I must always travel, keep memories of love affairs tucked away somewhere, but stay true to faraway places.

Again and again we walk to the Prado Museum. One afternoon we discover a place where people are sitting at tables drinking pitchers of fruit juice (or so we thought) with sliced oranges. We point at their table and order. I pour us each a glass, and with that we are introduced to sangria. Later, we walk slowly back to our hotel in the afternoon heat and feel heavy and full of El Greco and Ribera and free and silly. We go to our room, put on bikinis, and sunbathe on our exclusive rooftop.

One day while having lunch at the crowded cafeteria in the fine Plaza Hotel, we meet Jorge P., who invites us to his apartment at the Plaza for drinks later in the evening. We see immediately that Jorge is a lover of life, of women too, I suppose, handsome and irresistible. We accept. When we arrive that night, we find the apartment full of handsome men and beautiful women eating and drinking. Some are with a bullfighter named Curro Giron. Much later all of us are at a hole-in-the-wall place, packed around tables as we watch the flamenco. Early morning, many of us drive outside of the city for more singing and dancing.

Jorge is from Mexico but has a business in Madrid. His friends in Spain go from one bullfight to another. For seven days Mary and I follow along. We drink and see bullfights in Segovia. We drink and go to flamenco each night in Madrid. We celebrate his friend Iva's birthday by drinking at La Estrella. We are a large group: Gabrielle, Don, Johnny, Pancho, Ehemio, several of Jorge's former girlfriends, other people's girlfriends. Curro, from Venezuela, joins us when he is recovered from a bullfight.

On July 1, Mary receives the Eurail Pass she has been waiting for. The next day, I receive a money gift from Masao, and we celebrate with martinis. I will see her in France in seven or eight days. We are silent in the taxi to the train station. Annette and Mary will use their train passes to see Scandinavia, maybe Germany, who knows? But I can't miss out on next week.

I stay in Madrid because in a few days Jorge and his merry crew and I leave for Pamplona and the running of the bulls.

One night at a Mexican restaurant, where the food is spicy hot and all the tables are outside under drooping tree branches, the young woman sitting nearby leans over to ask if I am American. Yes, a very drunken one too. She says she has a friend from Houston, Texas. Ahh, that is where I am from, I tell her. Really? Her friend has a television show here in Madrid for little children. Her name is Judye S. My God! Judye S. is my friend from high school who gave me my prized turquoise necklace and earrings made in Iran. Once, Judye got me a part in a children's show at the Alley Theatre while I was at the University of Houston, and every Saturday morning after our performance, we signed autographs for tiny theater-goers. I ask if this woman will get a message to Judye to meet me on Avenida Jose Antonio the next day. "Yes. Of course." The following day, at the appointed time I go to see if Judye might be at a certain street corner at a certain time. And she is.

We walk through Retiro Park. Judye says in no uncertain terms I look ridiculous as a blond, so we make an appointment for the next day to turn me back to a brunette. She tells me about her boyfriends, her disappointments, living with her parents in southern Spain after her work at the theater in Houston. She loves sewing by hand, designing her clothes, even making some of her own sandals. She speaks fluent Spanish and might go back to Houston in a few years. She is in touch with another one of our compatriots from our Bellaire High School drama department. Tejas Englesmith is in London, working at a museum and studying art history, and shouldn't we all meet there for Christmas? So many possibilities open up because I sat under a tree drinking in Madrid.

Jorge and I get ready to leave for Pamplona. Although we rush to the train station and buy our tickets and run and run to our platform, the train is already pulling out. Breathless, we go quietly back to his apartment. Then a former girlfriend appears who thinks she is going to Pamplona with Jorge. They walk downstairs and sort things out. I shower and fix my new long, tangled, curly, brown hair. I now have my luggage in Jorge's apartment, which is like a train station too, with people arriving and leaving and searching for clothing left behind a couch or in a closet. I am not a flamenco dancer, but maybe I have become a gypsy. That night we leave early for the last train out for Pamplona. We arrive the next morning.

From our fifth-floor pensione, we lean out our window and see bulls raging and plunging through the street below us. Later, I sleep through much noise, and then we go out and drink wine and have red scarves for our necks, and somehow wind through the streets to the bullfight. After Curro's fight, we go back to the dancing in the streets. I sleep all the next day and try to forget the men I flirted with, the drunken conversations I had, the stumbling through streets. Right before midnight, we make the last train to Madrid. Now I have been to the Basque country and danced and had wine and made a spectacle of myself.

I wait all afternoon in Jorge's apartment for quiet and the exact time to call and wish my mother, "Happy Birthday," chat with Janet and Beth, and hope and pray that I sound like a sister and daughter and not the drunken person I have been for the last ten days. I am holding my newest letter from home while I speak cheerily into the phone and hope I sound like I should.

My little sister, Beth, sends me a page of 423 carefully printed *x*'s. "Kiss Page," she titles it. Along the margin she prints, "that's not even half as much as I love you." In her perfect penmanship she writes that I was smiling "so-o-o big in *Viva Las Vegas*" and that is a "compliment."

Is it possible to be the sister she thinks I am and be myself also?

Who have I become? I'm not sure. I have written a man in Japan for money and he has sent it to me. Fifteen hundred dollars. I have spent nights with Jorge because it was too late to get into my two-dollar-a-day hotel. I have had way too many bottles of wine, pitchers of sangria, multiple martinis, and been attracted to handsome dancing men. I have had one drunken night after another. Worse even since Mary left. If Judye hadn't appeared by magic I would have been completely depressed.

My last day in Madrid I buy a sweater at a shop downstairs, and then repack in Jorge's apartment. No stray girlfriends wander through the rooms this early in the day.

78
July 17, 1964
Paris, France

I am settled in at the International Foyer for Women on Blvd. St. Michel. Annette stayed here in 1958. It is not far from the Alliance Française on Blvd. Raspail where I study French. It is a pleasant walk through the Jardin du Luxembourg, then a few neighborhood streets. I pass by Gertrude Stein's home where I imagine the ghosts of her many famous guests still gather.

I like my French book, *Cour de Langue et de Civilisation Francaises*. I can understand the written work somewhat, but everything is in French. No English hidden at the bottom, giving me a little help. And speaking French might be impossible for me. Trying to mouth French pronunciation seems such a quick and easy way to humiliate myself.

How is it to be in Paris after our long detour around the world?

How does it feel to be here without friends, not knowing anyone, walking alone across the River Seine, leaning over the bridge to follow the *bateaux mouches* (tourist boats) gliding underneath, glancing up at, yes, Notre Dame, and then happening upon the famous, compelling book stalls along the quay? How does it *feel* to walk onto the Right Bank, meander to W. H. Smith Bookstore on the rue de Rivoli, buy *all* of Sholokhov's "Don" books, and put them in my bag with my diary and letters to read later on a quiet park bench? How does it feel to wait in line at American Express and receive a sweet and funny letter from Grandma Lee? To buy postcards of Paris and sit and write to my Grandmother in Tryon, Oklahoma, while having my third expresso of the day at an outdoor café on the Champs-Élysées? I shiver with pleasure.

At last, I am in Paris.

I have mail every day. This week I have heard from my lost friend Tommy, my Oberon from U. of Houston, who is now doing quite well in New York and living his dream. As for me, the long ago Titania, I write him back that each moment I feel as if I am in a dream also and can never predict the wonderful things that happen to me. For instance, this past Saturday, while reading poems by Yevtushenko in the park, I met a young man from Africa named Pap. He was joyful, with lively kind eyes trying to tell me his stories, and never showing the impatience I felt when our English and French words broke apart and scattered in the Jardin du Luxembourg. He read out loud from my poetry book. Even though I could barely understand the words through his accent, his rich happy voice suited the poems. I thought that listening to Russian poetry that had been translated into English and then read with a French accent by a man from Africa to a woman from Texas was a celebration of language. I look for his handsome face on all my walks.

The next day, Sunday, I went to see *A Streetcar Named Desire* in FRENCH. Also I had a postcard from dear friends in Beirut, and they may be here in the fall. Selfishly speaking, I couldn't ask for more.

Each moment I am wildly, quietly, rejoicing. How did I get here? How? Through failed plans, by being in Las Vegas and meeting Kathy and voicing childish dreams, then Annette, then Mary. And this year? Because of Dan, because of Masao, we detoured through Honolulu, Manila, Hong Kong, Tokyo, Bangkok, Calcutta, Agra, Benares, New Delhi, Tehran, Isfahan, Baghdad, Beirut, Damascus, Cairo, Athens, Crete, Rome, Pompeii, Madrid, Seville, and Pamplona in order to arrive in the City of Lights.

I breathe slowly and my coffee cools as cities, rivers, monuments, shrines, palaces, ruins, gardens, dusty hot streets, faces, and promises are resting and settling within me. But how do I feel? I feel like walking. I feel like rummaging through Shakespeare & Co. and then, on the way home, stopping at the first vendor I pass selling little bouquets of flowers tied in ribbons. I'll choose the sweetest and then walk slowly up Blvd. St. Michel studying every shop window full of shoes.

A surprise! Mary shakes me awake and I stumble out of the Foyer with her for coffee and an early Saturday morning walk to American Express. She is thrilled with her three letters from the dashing friend she met in Cairo. I have a letter from Mom, and we find a café to read our mail and catch up on our weeks apart. We laugh till we cry about our first night in Paris together a few weeks ago when the bidet overflowed in our lovely Hotel d'Angleterre and somehow we couldn't get it turned off, and we flooded the hallway and two flights of stairs. So much shouting! We were humiliated.

We both agree Annette will not keep this Houston boyfriend for long since, between the three of us, we haven't many faithful bones. Although I should speak only for myself, since Mary has come quite a ways to pick up mail from this newest boyfriend.

Although I am always moaning and fantasizing about a true love and getting married and all that "catastrophe," I keep flitting from one man to another and having a very nice time of it. I think it is natural to look at someone so irresistible right in the eyes when you pass on the street and hope there is a chance that he will stop and perhaps you will both struggle in English or French or German and maybe agree to have a café together. Then you can laugh at yourselves as the possibility of being lovers or friends is decided. If nothing at all develops, at least the moment wasn't lost.

Anyway, it is my girlfriends that make me happiest. Or unhappiest. Seeing Mary leave on the train again makes me very sad. I had thought we would be together more here in Paris. She is probably right about trying to see all that she can and make full use of her Eurail Pass, but watching her train leave the station does make me melancholy. Why didn't I go with her?

My books come from Madrid the day after Mary leaves. I have been missing them and was afraid they were lost. I lug them all the way down the Champs-Élysées from the train station, through the Place de la Concorde, over to Blvd. St. Michel and at last to the Foyer and up a flight of stairs to my room. I am delighted to see again the Oriental history books I found in Manila; my guidebook for Thailand, which is written on old newsprint and stapled together; the *Hafiz of Shiraz* volume of poetry I bought in Isfahan; the third edition of *Historical Monuments of Isfahan*; and I have the small Egyptian tourist information book covered with bright red flowers that remind me of Houston azaleas.

The book, though, that has caused me grief is the Buddhist Scriptures I bought in Tokyo. I remember skipping to the chapter on meditation and then becoming quite demoralized when I came to the six types of persons. As I begin reviewing this book on its return to me here in Paris, I am reminded that my "type" is described as greedy, hateful, delusional, and a little bit discursive. Discursiveness means, among other things, aimlessly rushing about and being unsettled in all doings. Delusional is being unsettled because of complete confusion: if you are delusion-ruled you stand in a posture which is "bewildered." The Hate-type person stuffs her mouth full, and of course, is hateful. The book includes helpful charts.

If I am ruled by greed, hate, delusion , and discursiveness, I need to meditate on certain ideas: friendliness, even-mindedness, and moderation in eating and sleeping. I remember when we went on to India, I didn't want to read further. I try every day to be moderate in eating, but it doesn't work. I am fairly friendly, though, and my friends, like Mary, are moderate.

My roommate here in the Foyer, Jennifer from Stoke-on-Trent, England, is a model of moderation. She is studying French, speaking French, never overeats, and is tolerant of my habits. We went to see the Leningrad Ballet perform *Sleeping Beauty* this week. It was lush, and for me, near the divine. I left feeling as if I had been in a holy spot, and I wanted everything in the world to be touched by its loveliness. I know I am "ruled" by this kind of euphoria at times. Particular evenings at the ballet, a hushed dance deep in a sun-dappled jungle, fireflies rising in a darkened sky—these are things I can meditate on that surely will edge me into a better place.

The brown-eyed sexy man who stopped me on the street two days ago bumps into me again and makes me laugh. Mounir is an artist from Beirut. We spend the afternoon walking along the river and having too much to drink, coffee, an aperitif, beer even. Much later in the evening we meet at the "cave" on rue Huchette and stay till early in the morning. I tell him I feel sad because I haven't heard from the Italian boyfriend, and he says it is better anyway, that it wouldn't ever come to anything. That makes me indignant, and he laughs at me and kisses my hands. Then I laugh too. The wine, the guitar and its poems, smoke circling through tables, people crowded together, knees and legs demanding more than a nudge, suggestive eyes and mouths quivering...it is too delicious.

He knows well the Hotel Excelsior I lived in in Beirut, its nightclub, the Cave de Roi. We both go on and on about the elegant St. George Hotel and how fulfilling it had been to loaf on the veranda, dreaming with a glass of wine, waiting for the sun to fall into the Mediterranean and the small fishing boats rocking below on the silver blue sea. I tell him about my day touring Baalbek, lunch in a village in the mountains of Lebanon. He has his stories too. We are silenced by our melancholy, longing for Beirut, the voice of Fairouz, a stroll along the Corniche.

The evening is full of heartache and yearning: the guitar with its own memories, the poignant breeze that caresses us outside, and then the couple that pauses in front of us. We are envious of how he takes her face into his hands, kisses her forehead, her eyes, her nose, nibbles at her mouth.

The next day we become tourists together. Mounir wants to see certain things in Paris. The moody Parthenon and the brash Museum of Modern Art, where he detects early on how little I know of the artists he is interested in. It is important to him that I understand what influenced him as an artist. We eat at a Lebanese restaurant, we linger, we drive up and down the Champs-Élysées at all hours. We drive outside of Paris, along the banks of the Seine, for ice cream. He sketches my face in his notebook, my eyes tired with dark shadows. We are together at all hours, Le Select on Boulevard Montparnasse, a favorite of Picasso and Chagall and others, always after midnight. I sit in an old mansion turned into a casino and read Henry Miller for six hours while he gambles. We sit on the quay in early evening, watching light and shadow play in the water. He is always kissing my shoulder or my neck and holding me whenever we pause while walking. He wears me out. Then he stands me up. Then he arrives at midnight at the Foyer, shouting at me from the sidewalk. I am irritable, the week is too rich, too full. I forget my French classes.

At last he is gone and then I wonder about him. We never exchanged addresses. Perhaps he is married, or at least has a serious girlfriend in Beirut. Whenever I pass the café at rue de la Petit Pont, I look to see if he or his friends are there.

My new French teacher keeps asking me out, and it makes me uncomfortable. He's interesting but I need to study. Now that Mounir is gone, I am catching up on my writing, my letters home. I have been gathering all of my sisters' letters and organizing them by date. Also, I now have time with my roommate, Jennifer. On Saturday we have the best outing to the Bois de Boulogne. We go by metro and bus and walk and rest and read and snack and have a perfect day.

This is my fourth week in Paris. I am barely learning any French. I keep up with my daily journal but have written only eight full pages in my writing notebook. First, what am I supposed to be writing? I go to the restaurant next to the Foyer, order coffee and a sandwich and write. I write about the people sitting around me, what they might be talking about. But things that I'm actually thinking about sound so ridiculous when I start to put them on paper that I usually cross them out. I like writing with pencil the best. But if I don't have a sharpener, I can't stand writing with a dull point, and then that's just another excuse. I have to face the truth. I'm not doing what I always thought I would do: learn French and be a writer in Paris. I think I must have been a little crazy all these years.

Do I write about what I am really best at? Getting involved with men, having short interludes of attraction, then moving on and avoiding at all costs studying and writing? Do I write that I like traveling, seeing new places, meeting people, tasting new foods, exploring winding streets, buying books, reading books in hotel rooms, looking out windows onto strange and wondrous sights? That I like flowers, smelling flowers, oohing over their colors? That I like the sky and clouds and sitting on a park bench and watching tree branches tremble in the wind? That at night I love to see the moon and watch clouds cover, hover, near it? What am I going to do for the rest of my life?

I have some, few, serious thoughts. But never original. And my thoughts are never orderly. I can be listening to, and describing in my notebook, the puppet shows in the Jardin du Luxembourg, giggling children and amused parents, and my next thought could be about Grandma Lee and me speeding in my convertible with the top down in Alvin, Texas. So when I try to write what I am reminiscing about, I am not fast enough to get my thoughts down before my mind jumps to something totally unrelated. It would have been helpful if I had had some training in writing in school, but I actually thought that a person just sat down and began writing if he or she wanted to be a writer. How mistaken I've been.

79

I buy the *Herald Tribune* from some young disheveled American on the street corner near American Express. I pounce on the page advertising apartments for rent and read them eagerly. Since Jennifer has returned to England, I notice the rules more often at the Foyer. Sometimes walking along the Seine after midnight seems the best thing to enjoy.

I want a place of my own. I've been hoping for something nearer the Alliance Française but have had no luck. For weeks "Home Mont-Thabor" on rue Cambon has advertised rooms for one hundred dollars a month and I thought that was too much. I make an appointment to look at what is available.

When I meet a tall, young, cute man who works there and speaks fluent English, I think the place may be exactly what I need. He is from Norway, is studying French at Alliance Française, plays the guitar, loves poetry, and is consumed with European and world politics. He asks if I have made arrangements to vote in our elections.

Then I am shown a room. It has a small bookcase, a large window that looks out over rue Cambon. When I first open the shutters and look down on the sidewalk, I swear that I see Jane Fonda walking towards me. I want to wave and call her name but don't. The street is on the backside of the Ritz, and also Chanel is down the block, so it is possible that it really is Miss Fonda. Even though the room is tiny, and there are rules about no overnight guests (how would they know?) and the actual landlady, Mme. Grenier seems aloof, I take the room immediately.

The location is ideal. I am half a block from the rue de Rivoli, minutes from W. H. Smith bookstore, literally six minutes from the Jeu de Paume with all of Monet's Water Lilies and—can this be true?—

Vincent's "Starry Night"! Just being near the bookstore is certainly worth having to share a toilet with a few other people on the third floor. And I do have my own private shower and a bidet and wash basin. Most convenient, too, is that I am a hop, skip, and a jump from American Express. I have to write Mother, because I also am near the rue de la Paix—yes, "where there was once a cabaret, and MiMi," the popular song she played for us so many times years ago. Finally I have a room all to myself. I need to write.

Mary arrived unexpectedly the day after I moved to Home Mont-Thabor. Even though she had left Germany after touring sites with Annette, and made a promise they would meet here in Paris for my birthday, Mary changed her mind. She is going home to Mississippi in two days.

The first night Mary is here she wakes up with a terrible earache, and we stumble to the street and flag a taxi to go to the American Hospital. (Although we are very quiet, we are noticed coming at all hours by my landlady). It turns out Mary had a small insect fluttering around in her ear, and it is several tiring hours before she is taken care of and we are back in my room.

The next morning I make it to class (tired and mumbly) while Mary gets a little rest. At noon we meet and begin our last day in Paris together. At the new Le Drugstore we have disappointing hamburgers for lunch. They are very expensive, but symbolic: a return to America and white, tasteless bread. She stops to have her hair done. I walk over to NBC to leave a note for Frank, my friend from Cairo. Later we window-shop on our way to have a drink at Fouquet's. That is a mistake for me because no matter how cavalier I try to be about her leaving, after one drink I can barely control my sniffles. But we laugh at ourselves for feeling sad since, after all, it has been a remarkable and surprising nine months that we never expected. And so what if we are worn out and confused in Paris? We made it. Not like we planned but a thousand times better, and we have Mr. Aguinaldo to thank for that.

Back in the room, she packs and repacks, and it begins to look like our apartment in Las Vegas, with clothes, underwear, books, letters, magazines strewn about. We talk about this latest boyfriend of hers, the reporter she met in Cairo, and how the whole experience has opened up a new world to her. She says she will never forget the thrill of being part of a historical event, and now she can't read enough about where we have been, and she tries to weave together history with present day events.

She feels an overwhelming need to get to Greenwood for a while to check on her parents and brothers and sisters. Every day we lived together in Las Vegas, she was involved in their daily lives, so I know her concern is genuine. We plan to meet in New York. Annette and I have money, I hope, for a few more months here in Paris, and maybe I will look for a job.

The next morning we have a thoughtful and largely silent bus ride to Orly. Although the streets and life of Paris are on display outside the bus, I see downtown Manila, with Mary and I holding on for dear life in the fanciful painted jeepneys; our horse-drawn carriage ride on a cool night in Benares; our cold and desolate bus trip from Tehran to Isfahan when Mary was shivering and ill and we were loaned a rough woolen blanket by a very kind and brave Muslim lady. Here in Paris, I find myself constantly wandering among these memories.

We have time for two quick drinks at the airport lounge, just enough to make me blubbery at the last minute when her flight is called. Then I am watching her walk away with her heavy, overloaded makeup kit, looking smaller than ever with her very large bulky purse. And Mary, my dearest friend, is gone.

I have the lonely and miserable bus ride home with plenty of time to think of Mary and me and our unexpected adventures. Only a year ago we were Las Vegas Copa girls drinking Black Russians after the last show, taking a Shakespeare class, and planning on sailing to Le Havre on Lykes Lines. Now we have been around the world. I remember our noontime dancing dates in Manila; the long talks until daybreak in Tokyo; sitting at the Nile Hilton at the bar, straining to see the pyramids; and our dusty day at the Hanging Gardens of Babylon. I guess when we are old we will say, "At least we had Hong Kong, or Cairo…" or all the other places we never imagined we'd see.

Back at rue Cambon I put a cold washcloth across my red puffy eyes and intend to sleep for at least a day, but am startled by my ringing phone. Les, a handsome, enigmatic friend we met in Beirut, is calling from London to say he will be in town for the weekend. And just when I have fallen asleep again, Martin, the young man who works here in our apartment, calls to say that I shouldn't be moping in my room over Mary leaving, that we should walk.

So Martin and I stroll along the rue de Rivoli. We meet his Portuguese friends Maria and her brother at the café across from Notre Dame on rue St. Jacques. I listen to their conversation about the dictator Salazar, in French, English, and Portuguese. I hear bits and pieces of their discussion, but below me the River Seine is murmuring, meandering its way to the English Channel. And I think, Mary and me are like a river. Six months, slowly twisting and turning, flowing to Paris.

The next day I have a manicure. I have my hair done. I forget trying to be a struggling French student and a know-nothing writer. I press my black lace Chinese dress from Hong Kong, wriggle into my black girdle, my black merry widow, put on new hose with not one run in them, my black silk high heels also made in Hong Kong, find my long black satin gloves and go out on the town with Les. We have dinner at Le Berkeley, after-dinner drinks at Elle & Lui, then go to New Jimmy's, where—oh, good grief!—we sit one table away from Francoise Sagan and three boyfriends. Or they might be just friends, but who knows the possibilities? The lighting is low, smoky, so I hope she doesn't notice my starstruck, furtive glances. *Bonjour Tristesse* in person.

On Saturday, Les and I stroll the Champs-Élysées and then have dinner and a show at the Lido. There I am in the very room where my friend Kathy Martin began her days in Paris. How stunning she must have been. I imagine her in rehearsals, maybe sitting at our very table waiting to be called up on the stage. Of course, I also try imagining myself on stage, posing in a spectacular costume, breasts bared, and I gasp. Oh, what would my parents think, and at the same time why, oh why, am I such a damn hypocrite? The girls are stunning. I want to be brave and haughty and vamp across stage with a three-foot-high headdress! But I have to lose weight.

The next morning, Annette arrives. I tell her of all the clubs I have been to in two days and that I had seen Francoise Sagan. She is, of course, jealous, and I am happily smug. She wants detailed descriptions of the costumes and dancers, and I do my best at entertaining her and softening the blow that Mary is already in Mississippi. She joins Les and me for lunch at the Rond Pointe and then goes off to see about a room at the Foyer for Women, relieving me of the difficulty of sneaking her past my landlady.

Late afternoon, Les and I go to the bar at Tour Eiffel for my twenty-fourth birthday drink, dinner at Fouquet's, and then to the Crazy Horse Saloon. The show there, I think, is better than any in Las Vegas—so sensual and brash and startling. I envy the dancers with their haughty, sexy attitude. Why can't I be like them? They are beautifully skinny too. I am enthralled, but Les seems detached and slightly amused at me for admiring the performance. But he is always like that.

I recall bits and pieces of the stories I have been told about Les and his family. After the 1958 revolution he was held in a prison for a year in Baghdad. A member of his family was assassinated. He was helped by friends who were able to arrange for food and water throughout his imprisonment. Whatever his experience, of privilege or tumult, his remote and distant gaze adds to his mystery. He is equally pleased by a fine champagne or a pleasant stroll along a boulevard. When we first met in Beirut, he had a gift of fresh mangoes sent to Mary and me at the Hotel Excelsior. When he guides me across a street, it is with a light, affectionate touch to my arm. I imagine his little black book of telephone numbers with many girlfriends from London to Beirut.

Les returns to London. I put away my black beaded purse and lace dress. Annette meets me at Alliance Française each day. We have lunch with Martin. Then we wander through her old streets near St. Germain des Pres. We poke through bins of old postcards, I find a paperback copy of Henry Miller and a used hardback by Kazantzakis about his travels in Japan and China. We always say, "Oh, Mary would love this, wouldn't she?" We shop at Prisunic and Galeries Lafayette for ribbed long-sleeved T-shirts. We visit American Express two or three times a day to check our mail. I receive a book of poetry by e. e. cummings from Bernie and Stella, and we read it together while we drink too many cups of espresso.

We stroll by the tabac shops on Blvd. St. Michel, where many Algerians gathered for protests when Annette was here last.

When Annette leaves for Germany, I go to bed and nurse an eye infection and sore throat. I spend a long time in my writing notebook gathering my thoughts on all Annette had to say about her first year of teaching—how she loved working with her thirdgraders, how eager they were to paint and write, and how excited they were with the little things I sent them from Hong Kong. Annette decorated the room with posters by Kandinsky and Klee and the students' artwork, creating their own new world in their classroom. For the first time, teaching children is appealing to me. It is the deep feeling Annette has for the students, the life they made together.

I catch up in my daily calendar, which means writing in my microscopic shorthand. I did show Annette how well I have kept her advice to record my experiences, that there isn't a day I've missed on the whole trip so far. I try to read it back to myself, but the lighting is so poor I can barely make it out and *Merde*! Ah! Poor me, having to struggle with dim lighting in my own room, on the Right Bank, in Paris.

80

Two weeks later I receive a severe warning from Mary. She writes, "Do not come home, or at least to the South, until after the election." Mary will vote for Johnson, but her family are Goldwater fans. Her parents have asked her not to express her views, and of course she never does, and she can't wait until January, when she plans to move permanently to New York City.

Mary has a lot to sort out, though, besides what she is going to do in life. She is seeing her old boyfriend next month in Chicago, and though she was disappointed in her reunion with the young man from Cairo, she intends to meet him in New Orleans this weekend. Anyway, she has to tell me all this in person because it's too difficult to write it down and everything changes quickly.

Mary isn't sorry she left Paris, but now that she's reassured that everyone at home is well, she's at a loss. She's looking forward to a short trip to Memphis with her dad, and everything on television this season is actually ridiculous, according to Mary. Of course, I don't believe that she has gained five pounds, though that's what she claims. And will I please mail her the world map and bra she left behind? I read her letter over and over, and it is as if we have had the best talk, and I feel happier than I have for days. It must be because she sounds as confused as I feel, and if she feels confused, at least we are still connected.

I will write and tell her about Martin: that he disapproves of my pouting ways; that at the first sign of lethargy or smoking packs of Gauloises alone in my room, he calls up and says we must walk. We walk over to the Jardin du Luxembourg, sit and gaze at the Medici Fountain, wind our way to Notre Dame, go around to the far Square ile de France, and sit on a bench and watch travelers on the Seine. He finds new bookstores to visit. He plays guitar and sings. He has given me the wildly popular poetry book by Jacques Prevert, which he reads in French, then translates for me. He brings me warm wine and honey for my sore throat. Sometimes we go for late night walks to find ice cream to share.

I'll also tell her about Frank, my gentleman friend at NBC. We meet once or twice a week at a café to chat about things I should not miss in Paris, or his next possible assignments. He says probably Vietnam, which I hear more and more ugly talk about all the time.

And, Mary, besides French class and Martin and Frank, my life in Paris also includes Joe from Beirut, who called last week. And, dear friend, you missed the greatest time: dinner at the Crillon, the late show at the Moulin Rouge, then to Le Sexy till the wee hours of the morning. Also, you missed a trip to the horse races, and I know how you love riding and horses, so I truly regret you weren't with us.

But that's not all: Joe was in the company of the Sheiks from Abu Dhabi. They rented one entire floor of the Crillon. When Joe first introduced me to them, they were in western business attire. But even then it was clear to me that I was in the company of Very Important People!

Imagine the following day when we met to go to the races. The sky was a startling blue. Five glossy black limousines waited obediently in front of the elegant Crillon. The doors of the hotel were opened and held in place by polite doormen. Then a parade began of handsome Saudi men clothed in long white flowing robes and white headdresses, a vivid contrast to all of us dressed in drab western style. It was a joyous and curious sight with many of their young male children along looking like small impish princes themselves. I not only saw these men of the desert, but sat with them at the races and enjoyed every moment. Joe and I had the last limousine to ourselves, and he thought it funny that I'd never seen the white flowing robes in all my travels, only in the movies.

At the racetrack, the stream of glossy thoroughbreds and their silky colors made a beautiful sight, but none could compare to the princes in their regal white, with their heads together deciding each bet on every race. I was invited to have tea with them after the races, and I was tongue-tied in their presence. I have oil and gas talk in my background, and so they were very polite when I explained my dad's position with Houston Natural Gas. I know these men do not live in elaborate tents in the desert. They are very clever, progressive business men from Abu

Dhabi who are at home in the world. Nevertheless, in their suite of rooms at the Crillon Hotel, tethered to a perch was a hunting falcon. Can you imagine?

Two letters. A short one from Mary. She has been with her man from Cairo and is totally happy and not to pay any attention to her complaints of the last letter. She is not seeing her old permanent boyfriend, so things have changed.

Grandma Lee sent me a long letter. She took off work to write it. She is making good money with Kirby Company, getting leads for the vacuum sweeper salesmen. She loves having a job and her own money. She's happy, too, with the new home Mom and Dad bought for them. It's big and spacious with a patio and a place for a vegetable garden and a flower garden. Grandma had the whole family over for dinner, and I could smell her homemade hot rolls all the way from Texas. She makes me laugh. She says if I get tired of studying French, come home and she will teach me Cherokee. She says not to bring home a Frenchman because it is too late for her to learn French, even though she loves to talk to good-looking men and she knows French men are handsome. I should be careful, she says, because she has heard that French men have "that soft touch."

Young Cora Lee Abercrombie and her beau, Sylvester Jess Linn

81

Today I threw away forty francs by paying for another month of classes at Alliance Française. I miss at least one day a week, sometimes more. I can barely drag myself to class, then I fight to stay awake, rarely understand a thing anyone says and urgently wait for the hands on the clock to leap to the next minute. I might as well be back in high school.

And now that I have had to live up to my big mouth offer to share everything with Annette, I could kick myself. I was so happy that day when I wrote to her from Bangkok and begged her to come to Europe. And I am glad she is here. But I'm mad at myself for being so frivolous. I had so much money then, so I went right on having my hair done, my nails done, and buying *Harper's* whenever I could find it. I have been reckless from the beginning and never had a grasp on how to live on five dollars a day in Europe, as Mary and I planned.

On top of all that, George in Tokyo has sent me only one of the two boxes of my clothes that I left in his apartment after he sweetly assured me it would be no problem at all to ship them to Paris. In a letter that came later, he apologized that one of his girlfriends must have taken some of my things. I have this vision of some very small, beautiful Japanese or French or Russian woman wearing my very large silver lamé Chinese dress (made in Hong Kong for me). Surely it would drag to the floor like an evening dress on her. There can't be a woman as tall and large as I am in all of Tokyo. Oh, grumpy me. Be thankful for my dear black suede coat with its mink collar intact and my nice leather coat that I need right now. And I did find my red-ribbon, loveliest dress from Hong Kong, which I will certainly wear if I am invited out to the Crazy Horse again—and not complain about that debonair George of Tokyo.

The pressing problem is my dwindling traveler's checks. I keep hunting in my passport billfold for hidden, folded up checks I might have tucked into its various pockets, but there are only the few now. Five hundred, then only four hundred dollars left? And change. So that is my point. Why did I pay for another month of French classes? Is it so I can write home and say I am still studying French and paint a picture of my life as student? A total lie.

Unless a job falls into my lap, my money will be gone by the end of December or at the latest, January. Even though I have written my family that I might be home for Christmas, if anything turned up, I wouldn't hesitate to stay right here and write and try, I swear, to utter, at least once a week, "Merci," or "s'il vous plaît."

And books. Please keep me from buying another book. I will only buy writing notebooks and fill them to the brim. And I'll explain to Martin that we must avoid the bookstores and especially the Globe, with all the Russian art books, and he has to make sure I only browse.

I need to stick to frugal entertainments, like the leisurely outing Martin and I had on Saturday. We had café on the terrace of the Jeu de Paume. We loafed and lingered in the pleasantly nippy fall air. We admired Monet's water lilies after hurrying up the stairs to stand before "Starry Night." (I do this at least every other day.) Afterward, we enjoyed blvd. St. Germain and wandered over to the Rodin Museum and Sculpture Garden, and then just as happily over to the Tuileries and up and down the Champs-Élysées. A perfect day.

Yesterday while taking a shower, I had a frightening experience. Inside my little steamy stall I noticed the shower curtain move but assumed I had touched it with my elbow while rinsing my hair. But the third time the curtain moved oddly, I flung it open and faced a man crouched in front of me with a nylon hose covering his face. I shouted, I chased him out of my bathroom screaming ever louder and followed him as he raced out of my bedroom. I continued screaming, but stopped at my doorway as all of the other tenants opened their doors startled by the commotion. Were they more frightened by my naked, wet, wild self or the intruder fleeing down our three flights of stairs? I immediately withdrew for a towel as a young neighbor offered her help. Another tenant, a young Italian man that I had never seen before, recovered the nylon stocking that the nasty intruder had stolen from my towel rack and hastily pulled off as he escaped. It would never have happened if I had not forgotten to lock my door, and I was very embarrassed by the scene and immediately grateful that he had been scared off. Later, I realized that I'd had a "feeling" after the second movement of the curtain but had not paid attention to it.

Happily, I am comforted by two beautiful and provoking letters from Annette that immediately make me forget looking over my shoulder for some weird stalker. She is in Munich and has confirmed plans to take a train to Algiers to visit her old college friend, Rachid. I would love to go, too, but I haven't been invited, and of course I shouldn't spend the money either. Annette will be here on the tenth or eleventh and then be off. But she is broke, and I must send a money order to Frankfurt.

In her first letter, she writes that her present boyfriend, George, is driving her crazy with wild desire and his intense love of life but that "…he's like an octopus—in all directions only going a hundred mph." She is searching for answers too. Is there a God? She wants to study Catholicism, Judaism, and Buddhism soon. Later in her letter she admits that the architecture of Catholic cathedrals draws her in to sit in silence. Also, she's upset with herself for neglecting the study of languages. She had such a good start with German years ago when she worked in Wiesbaden. And she has been inspired by a multilingual architecture student from U. of Rome (very handsome, of course, from Honduras, and if she stops in Madrid, his family will take her to Seville to see their ranch) who has escorted her to many of the museums in Munich and has encouraged her to become a student again.

In her second letter, she writes these things: She must see Greece, Croatia, Yugoslavia (its language is like music), the Dalmatian coast, and Vienna; she might apply for a teaching job in Frankfurt; why is she so lazy and why doesn't she write more? She must get back to painting or sculpting or "do something with my hands to express the abstract me which cannot be said in words." And she ends with the one thing that we wrestle with the very most: If we leave Europe, will we ever come back, or will we all "settle into security and find a stable life and love and marriage, home and children?" And "would there be satisfaction for us?"

We three, Mary, Annette, and I, discuss these matters casually and often. Yet seeing these questions written in a letter has a nauseous impact on me. They are real, not just frivolous passing comments. We could lose something in the near future if we aren't careful: our personal freedom. Because, once there is a child, a husband, dishes, beds to be made, life for me would forever change. I know it. Every sense I have tells me this is true. And all this stupid guilt I have for accepting money from men will seem a ridiculously small sin when faced with daily washing and ironing. I know my mother's life, and I have never wanted it.

Yet, what do I enjoy here in my little space at rue Cambon? Some mornings Martin has brought me coffee. On our long walks I am content. He pulls me from my self-made angst and insists I read Beckett's *Malone Dies* immediately after I finish Camus's *The Plague*. He pushes me towards the Rouault exhibit and expects some thoughtful comment afterward. He shames me with a chuckle and raised eyebrow when I miss class. We frequent the cave on rue Huchette and listen to guitar music that expresses how we feel. Without a word, he reminds me of why I am in Paris. I am so much better now that we are friends, and more. And what does this mean? We have not burdened each other with our feelings, and he has many plans and maybe someone back home. But I do see the peril of finding someone so companionable. It creates a constant battle between what I know is right for me, travel and work and being single, and this overpowering draw to a more settled life.

But without Mary or Annette or someone like Martin, I could easily become a fat toad by myself, sitting endlessly at my window envying the workmen in their blue uniforms as they pour in and out of the tabac shop across the street, greet one another with rough slaps and punches, spill out onto the sidewalk of rue Cambon as they gulp quick cups of coffee, laugh at rude jokes (I imagine this since I don't know their language), and trail the heavy aroma of Gauloises smoke up to my room. Then they rush off to work.

Work. I need work. This is the first time, since high school, that I haven't had some sort of job.

82

Before Annette went off to Algeria, we had three perfect fall days tramping along the Seine, having drinks and giggling at Harry's Bar, and poking through all the favorite bookstores with Martin. While I will remember those days fondly, I'll long regret a really stupid mistake I made when I let Annette talk me into riding to Madrid with her on the train. The trip was very long and boring and the train crowded and uncomfortable, but the worst thing of all is that I lost my precious writing notebook. Just a few hours before we pulled into Madrid, Annette asked to read the notebook. I handed it to her and went back to sleep. Later, when we were settled into our hotel room, I asked for my notebook. She thought it was in one of her bags, but we never found it. I was, am, so mad at her. She has always been careless with my things, beginning when I loaned her a dress in college and she spilled spaghetti down the front of it. I'm mad at myself, of course. I should have gotten it back on the train. I should have.

I was mean as a snake for the few days in Madrid, even though we stepped right into my old life with Jorge and Flamenco and bullfighters and angry girlfriends. For me, though, I couldn't wait to be back in Paris and be alone in my very own room. And nothing could distract me from the loss of the writing notebook or how discouraged I felt about Annette and me. Most of the time we are so in tune with all our feelings about the important things in life: travel and art and literature and music and mountains and rivers and being outdoors and close to nature. Then she does these things, extremely careless where I am concerned. Such as accidentally running off with that guy I liked in Las Vegas. But this is the worst by far. A boyfriend is replaceable, my writing notebook is not.

After spending an afternoon admiring Notre Dame and then Sainte Chapelle with two visiting friends (Art and Rita, whom Mary and I met in Isfahan), I stay behind while they continue to other sights. I am drawn to the trembling fall light inside Sainte Chapelle and cannot leave. I feel like writing Mary a little note and begin with a sly complaint about Annette and the loss of my notebook. After several sentences to Mary in Mississippi I pause. Am I actually pouting? Surrounded by the delicate atmosphere of Sainte Chappelle? On the lovely Ile de Cite, in the middle of the rippling Seine, with all of blvd. St. Michel waiting to be explored for the thousandth time after I wander aimlessly through the irresistible maze of St. Severin? I scribble instead how I wish she were with me and that I am reading the "Short and Happy Life of Frances Macomber" and that Annette had thoroughly enjoyed the flamenco in Madrid and meeting my sweet friend, Jorge.

Am I crazy? Why have I wasted so much money on foolish things and am always trying to figure out what I should be doing?

Tell me, what is more important in my life right now than wandering freely through the Left Bank on a cold October evening? Probably nothing. Sometimes, when I'm in the Jardin de Luxembourg reading or writing or staring at the trees and watching leaves tumble and float, I'm the happiest person in the world. And other times, doing the exact same thing, I feel ridiculously sad. I have no control over feeling hopeless. I see my grandmothers shaking their heads and I know what they are thinking: I better find a job or at least quit this moping. If only Mary and I could talk a little.

Then I fantasize: if I could lose eight or nine pounds I would go to the Lido and see about work. If I could wear big pasties, and maybe jewel chains over some of my fat waist, I could be a nude model. Actually, I don't think I look terrible without my clothes on. I probably wouldn't look too bad at all with high heels. I think being half, or mostly, naked on stage would be easier than selling the *Herald Tribune* in front of American Express. I would be a total failure at calling out to people to buy a newspaper. I would definitely look more ridiculous waving newspapers at people than being a little bosomy and mostly nude onstage. I must get up the nerve, and energy, to see about a job at the Lido.

On a visit to American Express, I run into a beautiful girl I worked with for a month or two at the Sands, Lisa W. We've talked nonstop for days. She is modeling and has an introduction to a famous photographer in London. Lisa is energetic and full of plans. When we are deep in conversation, either gossip from the Sands or her excitement over going to London, I am aware that I am not energetic or full of plans. I am envious of her enthusiasm and her certainty.

I do know, though, that since coming back from Spain I am totally unsuited for French classes and will not pay for November. I've lost interest in being a student. It's as if going to Madrid and connecting with old boyfriends and the nightlife has derailed me. And losing my dear first writing pages.

I have a new writing notebook, but it's not the same. I'm not the person I was when I first came to Paris. I miss all my happy pages and hate to think of them all tossed out into the trash in Madrid: my first gushy impressions of the café next to the International Foyer; the descriptions of my girlfriends there, Barbara from Amherst, Jennifer and her friend; and then the children's faces delighted and hypnotized by the Punch and Judy shows in Jardin du Luxembourg. I want all that back, all those sentences I wrote when I had my good plan for being here in Paris.

I would like to think that it is normal to feel slightly sad on cold, dark, rainy autumn days in Paris. The huge falling yellow leaves carpeting whole stretches of blvd. St. Michel are crushed daily and to me they express beauty and fragility. I am comforted by a caress from the warm fleeting whoosh of the metro rattling underground. I linger on a cloudy corner, drugged by the smoky aroma from roasting chestnuts.

Les Parapluies de Cherbourg is a new film this year, and it is like an opera. All dialogue is sung. I saw it alone. The two young characters so in love don't end up together. Stories like that shouldn't be allowed. When I walked outside there was a slight drizzle to compound my silly disappointment. But the music won't leave me alone. I will be happy when Annette returns and we do these things together.

Annette Hillman. Paris, France, 1964

83

My blue woolen suit and a few books and the black sweater Annette and Mary brought me from Sweden are on their way to Houston. I know I will be leaving Paris soon. In a month. I was horrible to Madame Grenier when I left Home Mont-Thabor. She wouldn't give me my full deposit back and that sent me into a rage. I kicked a bottle of ink and it splashed over the wall and carpet. So I'm out of 5 rue Cambon, and I've been shaking off and on, wondering if I might be in serious trouble. I've never done anything like that before. What in the hell made me so mad about the money? Madame Grenier never liked me. And when I think of how I've been—like having that kitten for a day when I knew I wasn't supposed to, then Mary and Annette spending the night several different times when that wasn't allowed either, then dragging in at all hours of the morning, tiptoeing around like an alley cat, then the episode with Martin when the maid suspected we were in my room together, which was scary since he was in trouble and almost lost his job....

As a tenant, I was a pain in the ass.

I have felt guilty for taking money from men, but that seems small compared to vandalizing property. In my dialogue with myself I can twist taking the money to something I had to do to get to Paris. But I've been mean and cross for weeks now. I stood Martin up the other day. And when I saw him later at the bar down from W. H. Smith's bookstore, there was nothing to say except, "I'm sorry, Martin." And that is a useless phrase to say to someone you've been reckless with.

Today Martin spent the entire day helping me find my three-dollar-a-day hotel. We were looking for a two-dollar or less but Hotel St. Severin will do. We tried several hotels on rue des Ecoles, then wandered to Place de Contrescarpe and asked prices around there. Then we walked along the Seine and wandered through the Ile St. Louis but found nothing. Finally we stopped for a café, and with my mood as dark and gray as the day was, Martin shook his head at me, like he does, and said I should take the room at St. Severin. So I did.

I didn't want him to leave. Martin, who has seen every lazy rotten part of me and still takes my arm to guide me across the street, and now I won't see him in his office on the second floor every time I come in from American Express. And now I have no phone. I can't pick up my nice room phone and talk to him when I am lonely. And what if this sore throat comes back and no Martin to bring me a warm glass of wine with honey?

Before I lugged myself and my belongings upstairs and unpacked, I stood for several minutes in the lobby, surprised that I was there, after the daylong search. Inside Chambre #12, I first notice that the overhead light is weak and wobbly. And there is no bedside lamp for reading. Then, I'm sure it's not because of my black mood, but indeed, the floor slants. It feels slanted, or buckled. It's a very sad old room. We are a perfect fit.

Everywhere Martin and I walked today were headlines: JOHNSON WINS BY A LANDSLIDE! My dad must be dejected, Grandma Lee elated, and all my friends, especially Bernie and Stella, celebrating. I'm glad, too, but this hasn't been a good day. Before we began looking for a hotel, Martin came with me to American Express while I paid for Annette's train ticket, and so I am mad at myself for saying I would share half of my money months ago. And madder still when I see she spends it on perfume. But what can I say? When I read in my diary—any random day—I see that I have supported beauty shops and manicurists from Hawaii to Paris. And random bookstores. I bought *Notebooks 1935–1942* by Camus today, and one last writing notebook, and why? I am still dreaming.

I have a pastry on the street, rattle and shudder on the metro with other dejected people to the Champs-Élysées station, and walk to Pan American. Another message there from Masao. He thinks I should fly to Tokyo. Over a coffee, I wonder what am I doing here, staring at this rain-slicked boulevard without one person to see, no class to go to, not one friend nearby like Mary or Annette or Martin to tell me to get up and quit moping. What kind of person feels sad and mad and confused when there is the choice to pay for coffee, wander down the Champs-Élysées and enjoy window shopping on the way to the Jeu de Paume, or maybe just find a corner in Sainte Chapelle and huddle there in colored rays of dim light and see what happens after an hour or so? I have any part of Paris to stumble through.

I go to Bon Marche for a look around, then to my hotel. Martin comes by with the last of my books. He says the ink came out of the carpet. I cringe and there is no way to get away from myself. We walk up blvd. St. Michel to my old café by the International Foyer for Women, where I lived three long months ago and had my good roommate Jennifer. Martin says I should begin classes again at Alliance Française.

I examine my "Carte D'Etudiant" from Alliance Française and see the telling progression of dismal performance. I began classes at 8:30 a.m. in Aout. In Septembre I arrived at 10:30 a.m. for studies. I recall that in Octobre I was often late to my class beginning at 12:30.

At noon at Cluny Self Service I meet a funny-talking American guy. We walk over to the mosque and have mint tea and he tells me his stories. I don't hear them really, or don't remember them, but I don't mind him either. All day I feel like I have a hangover and can barely stay awake. Last night I felt like I might roll off the bed and fall to the floor.

This guy and I decide to meet later for dinner at the same place

Mounir and I liked with the jukebox. And after that we go to the Cave on rue Huchette, which is crowded and smoky and full of interesting looking men and women. We both have a good time commenting on anyone who catches our eye. Every person who walks by, he has an opinion of their dress and look. It isn't necessary to respond. He speaks for both of us, and I am free to watch smoke float and climb. He thinks *I* am peculiar and strange.

We spend most of the day and part of the evening together, and do we ever say our names? I tell him goodbye. I edge my way around tables and make it out to the cold and mist and no cigarette smoke. Then I think how pleasant it was to spend time with my nameless acquaintance, to have no ties except the sunlight and mint tea and the mosque. I walk around the corner to my new residence, Hotel St. Severin. I feel much happier tonight in my sad room. My eyes are adjusting to the light, and I don't mind my bed feeling like one side is higher than the other.

84

Is there such a thing as a happy melancholic? If so, I am one. I am a little lonely. I did enjoy having my hair done this morning. I had an interesting conversation with two Greek boys at the Select Latin for several hours. I walked back to St. Severin and sat on my bed and had my books and letters around me, and my notebooks. I thought to myself that I need to have *some* companions, but not a lot, and no lingering boyfriends to distract me from settling down and writing.

I write about the large yellow leaves stuck to the pavement up and down boulevard St. Michel. And can I explain logically how it feels to be alone in this dear crooked room with roughly three hundred dollars, and not be concerned (at this hour) about next month or going home or staying here? Should I worry that after reading the first five pages of any book I forget what I've read each time? What do I do with this tan and faded card that my uncle Bob sent me advertising his favorite bar in Versailles? The *Bar de la Reine, 8 rue de la Chancellerie, VERSAILLES.* I think I should live here another year. I think I should leave Paris in December. All these things I think at the same moment.

I leave the Monoprix on St. Germain with a carton of yogurt and a baguette. I walk towards blvd. St. Michel. It is rainy and cold. I feel raindrops on my face. I pull my scarf further over my forehead. I notice two men walking towards me. One is tall, the other a little less. They are both dressed in dark suits, overcoats, and of course, dark wool scarves just so, as all the men wear here. The tall man is slender, has a slight and mouth-watering olive complexion and thick black hair. Dark eyes, I think. They are closer now. He is in deep conversation with his friend, and so I am bold and in my private thoughts I imagine standing in front of him and loosening his tie and tasting his mouth. I have to look down at the sidewalk when we pass. I walk on. Why can't I meet someone like that? I keep thinking of him and the rain dribbles down my neck and then I feel a slight touch on my right elbow.

He is next to me. For once, I am embarrassed. I didn't expect this though I wished for it on my rainy way to Hotel St. Severin. He says several things to me in French, and I wait until he finishes to reply, "I'm so sorry, I only speak English." And because he is soft-spoken, has a polite way about him and is so unconsciously handsome, I am lost in his face and eyes and we look at each other and I hope, that he is lost, too, and feeling exactly like I am.

"Ah…. So…. could you join me and my friend for coffee at Deux Magots?"

I nod. We turn around. We walk in the light rain and drizzle. He is Jacques. When I am able, I turn my head, feast on his dark eyes and thick black eyelashes and a mouth I can barely wait to trace with my fingers. I give my name in a shaky voice. At Deux Magots it is easier with the friend Jean. They are interested that I am from Texas. They speak of the election and Johnson and they regret the sad death of President Kennedy.

We make plans for dinner. Jacques escorts me to my fine hotel. I tell him about the crooked floor. I do not take his face in my hands and kiss his mouth, but he does take my hand to say we'll go for Chinese food. And he will be in the lobby of St. Severin Hotel at eight.

I freshen up in my sink. Now that I have mailed my blue suit home (the one mother bought me years ago when I was Miss Houston, which would have been perfect for tonight), I decide to wear the plum wool knit dress and matching sweater, my black merry widow in hopes of containing my midsection, and search for black hose with no runs. My black leather high heels are almost finished, but the black silk beaded ones made in Hong Kong would look ridiculous. My damp hair must be fluffed, or towel dried or disguised somehow so it doesn't stand out around my head in its usual scary wild way. My pearls might be too much, but I wear them tucked into my scooped neckline. A Chinese restaurant? I don't know what to order at a Chinese restaurant. I can wear my long elbow-length leather gloves and black suede coat with the mink collar and hope to stay warm. I should have a scarf like everyone else wears here, warm and heavy. Martin gave me his, a green and black plaid, but it won't go with my coat.

That evening, Jacques looks beautiful. But for the first few hours he must have thought I was a moron, for every time I looked at him, even for a second or two, I had to study the white table cloth, the candle on the table, and catch my breath. Jacques and I go hours without touching and that is hard for me. After dinner we go back to Deux Magots and meet Jean and sit amiably and chat. Then, instead of leaning up against a building and pressing into each other, we go to his tennis club for a drink. I have no idea about French men and how they think. Then, at last, it must have been after midnight, he says we are near his apartment and would I like to come for a drink? Did he think I wouldn't?

He has a large red Moroccan carpet and a fireplace. He brings little glasses with a swallow or two of something that burns my throat, and I try not to cough.

I don't know. He touches my face. I stroke his irresistible eyebrow, I nibble his closed eyes, his nose and along his cheekbone right to his mouth.

85

Four days disappear. For the first time this year I didn't write in my journal. I had no sense of time, of walking along the Seine, or admiring the Medici Fountain one more time, my arm linked with his, standing close together, cold air on my face coming out of Harry's Bar. Three and a half months in Paris walking the streets and now they are all new. Everything is new.

A Thursday morning, and we get up late. We walk from rue Croulebarbe to rue Mouffetard. We walk for hours and hold hands and if you want to know about walking and not remembering anything or any street or any marketplace or any fascinating window displays or even what it is like to walk by a bookstore without having any desire to go inside, ask me how that is. I am in danger, walking trance-like, not knowing that we are on boulevard St. Michel.

Suddenly, this drug wears off. I have a shock. Jacques and I pass my old Internationale Foyer for Women, heading to the Closerie des Lilas. I see a face. I think about the passing face. I turn quickly, and that person with the face has turned also, and we exclaim to each other in disbelief, "Dale!" "Judy!"

The friend I always wanted to know better, Dale MacConathy from my first semester at Central in Oklahoma. Five years since we last spoke, when he insisted that I must read *Dr. Zhivago* immediately. "What are you doing here?" We both want to know. I introduce him to Jacques. He introduces us to his friend. Can we meet? Where? We hold hands, hug each other. My God. Of course, Dale would be here in Paris. He is a real writer.

It is good to be reminded that I am a person connected to a past. I am not the floating ghostly particles of a dandelion, like I have felt these past three days. I begin to recognize the Jardin de Luxembourg, the bench I claimed in August. I know a little later that we are in the Tuileries, then the Champs-Élysées. Ah. This is my hotel. This is my room, and I dress for dinner. Jacques arrives and we drive to the home of his friends, Claude and Bernadette. We are joined by his vivacious phantom roommate, Jean-Louis D. I have a pleasant evening and recognize the red Moroccan carpet when we return to his apartment. I feel like I have materialized, returned to myself.

Jacques's parents are retired in Biarritz. His father is Moroccan, his mother French. Jacques works at the Ministry of Finance. He says he and his wife are divorcing. They live apart. He has a small son he misses. Jacques is eight or nine years older than I am. He worries that maybe he is too old for me. I don't think so. He has a group of friends who look right through me at dinner. It's because I don't speak French and they don't want to speak English, and probably we don't have a lot to say to each other anyway.

One beautiful blond woman is always kind. I recognize a little melancholy in her movements. She looks like Joanne Moore in *Walk on the Wild Side,* the movie with Jane Fonda about men and women and how they are ruined by desire. Her name is Annie, I think (I can't understand them...the French). But Annie is interesting to me because she is friendly, and maybe, I keep asking but never quite understand the answer, maybe she's related to the writer Andre Maurois. How I got that impression, some obscure conversation, I don't know. At one time I thought it was Andre Malraux but no, Maurois. I don't pursue the conversation because I don't want to appear nosy, or that I am impressed with her connection and not her. One evening I venture forth and mention that I have read several of his books and found them fascinating. Annie is surprised, and I tell her my favorite is *Desert of Love.* Later, I wonder if she was surprised because I had read a book or that she has no idea why she should care about this writer she has no connection to. Each time this group meets she has a different handsome date.

I sit next to Jacques, watch and look and study faces and expressions. I notice that Jacques's close friend, Francis, always sits at the head of the table. Francis has a girlfriend who flits around and among the group. She hangs casually over his shoulder. In my mind I call her the "Mistress of Ceremonies" since she seems in co-command of our events. Jacques's close friend rarely acknowledges me. I put together the story that Francis has heard from Jacques about me and imagine his impression: "Jacques meets girl on street. She more or less moves in with him immediately, probably to save on cost of cheap hotel. She is a former chorus girl or 'something' from Las Vegas. Then she is from Texas, not New York City. Worse, has cowboy and Indian connections to Oklahoma. Barely speaks English, certainly no French." Surely he's heard I don't cook or recognize anything in a kitchen. What, he thinks, has happened to my best friend?

I stand my ground. "To hell with them," I repeat over and over to myself, and smile at each encounter. On one of those days I am walking in a cloud, Annette arrives from Germany. I barely notice. She and Jean become friends, so she also saves on a hotel bill. Gold-digging American floozies. But in a week's time I am friends with Jean-Louis, my brotherly, refreshingly happy-go-lucky roommate. We go shopping, I find flowers, we laugh, tell stories.

86

It's a Saturday. Jacques works all day. When he comes home we have the soup he made the day before. We pack his car, and by 8:30 p.m we are on the rain-slicked road to Normandy, moonlight smacking into one tree branch after another. We arrive around eleven at an ancient sprawling farmhouse, creaky stairs, large blazing crackling fireplace with old stuffed sofas covered with heavy quilts. On one sofa, under quilts, Annette and Jean are having drinks from pewter mugs. She is more than tipsy. In a corner, the usual evening crowd sings and laughs.

By midnight I am warm and cozy and fuzzy. I look across the room and wonder, does the Mistress of Ceremonies have her arms around Annie? And why is Jacques's good friend Francis leaning over the sofa and caressing both women at the same time? People are disappearing into bedrooms. It is very late.

Jacques leads me upstairs to our room. Inside it is very cold. At least the bed is piled high with blankets. Jacques says that his friend Francis has certain ideas about relationships. Okay. I learn that the lovely lady Annie is married. Furthermore, her husband arranges for her escorts each evening. And Annie's *husband* is Francis, the boyfriend of the Mistress of Ceremonies.

I stare at the ceiling in the dark, see my breath in the moonlight. I can't imagine that situation even though my own life, without a doubt, raises eyebrows. I shiver under a foot of comforters and quilts. I listen to creaks in the floor. But what, I wonder, does Jacques want? The wind gives me no answers, even though the tree branches are whispering around us.

Church bells ring, the sun is shining through our ancient wrinkled window and "to each his own" is my first thought. Who cares who someone wants or desires? We are euphoric that this morning is cold and bright and crisp. We eat apples. We tromp through old and tottering cemeteries where tombstones lean and fade and are barely readable since they've been rained on for seven hundred years. Everyone, I mean everyone, is released and breathes deep here in the countryside. We are delighted by the village, peek into dark shop windows. We drive a short distance and crowd into an inn for lunch. We are shown a place upstairs, where our table barely fits into the room. Huge windows surround us. Light and more light; we can't get enough.

Hot hearty food. Bread. Carafes of wine. Annette is across from me. She smiles, arches her eyebrows, leans across the table. She has something to tell me. She has tears coming.

"I had an affair with Jorge in Madrid," she stage-whispers across the table.

"What?" It's noisy in our small place. Did she say she had an affair with Jorge in Madrid? When? "What," I ask her again.

She repeats, "I had an affair with Jorge in October."

This is not the place for a somewhat private conversation. I am with the man I hope is the love of my life. Annette is next to Jean, who is trying to understand the drama and intensity of our dialogue. Even Jacques seems to notice we are leaning across the wide table whispering. I'm okay with this news. It is irrelevant but I don't understand the choice of location for the revelation. Is this boasting? Maybe it's wine in the afternoon, the emotion of cemeteries, memories of traipsing through forgotten meadows.

Jacques is not feeling well. He is quiet. We have been at home for the past two evenings. Tonight he asks Jean and Annette over for a partridge dinner. Jean-Louis joins us at 8:30. We have the fire too. It is an easy evening. Annette and I do dishes. We talk about home. Going home. I tremble at the thought and as Annette details the steps she must take to leave on Icelandic Air, I know that I prefer washing dishes in Paris.

We have a letter from Mary. She is headed for New York City. She is waiting for us. I have a letter from my sister, Linda. She says it's urgent that I come home. That I must come home, everyone *expects* me home, and won't I come for her birthday, December 15?

On Sunday, November 22, we drive to Epernay in champagne country. Jacques is quiet and he must see Dr. Bas again tomorrow. He is not himself. I feel uncomfortable. While we enjoy hot soup and compare our thoughts on sips of champagne, I remember my crooked room at Hotel St. Severin. I need a quiet room to sit and stare out a window and figure out what to do next. I am afraid of the feeling I have for Jacques. I am not my old self...or the person I have been for these past months. And I have never been so happy washing and drying dishes until now.

Yesterday I met his little boy. We took him to the zoo. We walked through Jardin du Luxembourg. This sweet boy, who is beautiful like his father, probably his mother too, is a quiet child, somber. Well-behaved. How about my behavior? I do not want to come between a mother and father and child. Having a child, and a wife that maybe you are divorcing, and a young woman from Texas living in your bedroom off and on for fifteen days—this is a dilemma. It could make you sick, quiet, sad, remote.

It is one year ago today that President Kennedy died. I think of Mary and me studying for our Shakespeare test. So much has happened since then.

87

Jacques comes home for lunch. He prepares two fresh artichokes and we have a pleasant hour. He tells me stories of growing up in Rabat, Morocco. His happy years there hiking, fishing, and skiing with his friends. He moved to France in 1954, so each year he meets these boyhood friends in Corsica. I agree that it is vital to keep in touch with friends who have known our early dreams.

Around three or so Annette calls and wants to borrow my suede coat. I say I am wearing it tonight, and we argue over it. We are all going to Shakespeare and Co. for a poetry reading. Annette and I fight like this over clothes, and then I get moody and pout. I guess I imagined that we would be living together more and trying to find a way to stay here in Paris, but it hasn't been like that.

I think Jacques is perfect for me. He reads, he likes poetry, we walk and poke around in shops while I cling to his arm and refrain from kissing him at every corner. We lean over the Pont Neuf and discuss our lives and families. At the kitchen table I tell my stories of Grandma Lee cooking steak and eggs and bacon and biscuits and gravy for breakfast, and recite the names of her Cherokee cousins and her stories of Belle Starr, the infamous outlaw, hiding out on their farm. He tells me that he might come to the United States to work on a project. He loves his tennis so I am free to idle away my time as I please.

But haven't I interrupted his life? Is he really leaving his wife? I am carried away by this emotion for him, but reality creeps in and I'm unsure what I want. I want to have romance. On the other hand, this year has probably ruined me for life. I want to travel and have the absolute freedom of living in a hotel with no chores to do. It is safer, I think, for me to be free and a little sad than to risk being hurt and, worse, being caged up in one place forever.

Yet I have to be something more than I am. I don't want to think of myself as a gypsy. I need to work and make my own money and travel and write as I go along.

Later, at Shakespeare and Company, I wear my suede coat and Annette laughs and says for me not to be mad at her. I never stay mad with Annette. A Mr. Jack Hirschman reads poetry to us. I buy a thin blue book of poems by Robert Bly. Jacques asks everyone to come to the apartment after the reading.

It's all a blur now. We had the usual group plus others I had never seen before. Jean and I were listening to Annette tell about her trip to Sweden, about watching the rehearsals of a work by Ingmar Bergman and her crazy attempts to see him in person. And then little by little the crowd vanished, and I was there by myself.

Jacques came home many hours later. He had given someone a lift. I was sick. I acted like I wasn't hurt that he had offered to drive a fascinating, chic-looking French woman home who must have lived outside of Paris somewhere near the Swiss Alps.

This is what *I* usually do. *I* leave a date for someone else. This is awkward since I am a squatter in his bedroom. I want to pack and leave, but it is difficult to do that in the middle of the night.

The next day, I call Hubert, a wealthy, crazy guy I spent a few days with in September. He has an elegant apartment on the Ile St. Louis. We meet at Deux Magots at four in the afternoon. He is the perfect French playboy to help me adjust my attitude. I am such a silly American, he assures me. His gallant and louche presence reminds me of how many lovers, interludes, dalliances are possible each day. No need to get tangled up in a serious love affair and a broken heart. Annette joins us. She is delighted with Hubert. We are inside and we have a corner to ourselves. For once, it is a quiet place, Deux Magots. We watch the waiters watch for customers. We have a conversation, the three of us, for several hours. How awkward it is for me to be in the apartment since Jacques seems interested in another woman. And why didn't I leave today and go back to St. Severin? Silently, I know that I don't want to leave Jacques. And although, to Annette and Hubert, I appear nonchalant one moment and petulant the next, underneath I keep thinking over and over, I *thought* we were having a love affair.

I don't remember. Somehow Annette and I decide to go to New York City and join Mary, *in a few days*. Why do I agree? I am hurting, but Jacques and I haven't had a chance to talk about last night. Maybe it was nothing and I am making much ado about nothing. But should I go home? So much has happened.

What have I done? Why don't I move back to Hotel St. Severin and think about things? These weeks have been too intense. I need a place to live, so we can slow down. I can enroll in classes again, and I'll learn French. I am ready to work as a nude model at the Lido if they will have me. I can do this. Tomorrow I will move to a hotel. Tomorrow, I promise myself I will go to the Lido and apply for the job, and I will write Linda and everyone at home that I will come home sometime next year. And then Jacques can breathe in his place and I will love my hotel room again.

I find a taxi. I am overcome looking out the car window. I'm startled at the empty, forlorn chair sitting on top of a table on blvd. St. Germain. Rain-soaked trees, streaked and drooping, crying. A woman struggling down the damp street dressed in black and carrying a black umbrella and string bags that bulge at her side. I hear the moan and steam of the metro. My throat burns and aches. Have I really agreed to leave Paris?

At Jacques's apartment I am sweet-acting and sincere and say that it's time for me to leave Paris, that Annette and I have to get back to Houston and we are leaving Sunday. Jacques becomes extremely upset. He is very sad and doesn't understand at all why I should leave. And don't I remember that Jean-Louis has a new posting and is leaving shortly for Brussels and I will have a room of my own then, so please, please stay. He needs me. He doesn't feel well, and can't I stay a few more weeks?

I never expected this. I expected him to be sweet-acting and sincere like me and say, of course, your family is expecting you for Christmas, and then we would both save face and be diplomatic about our failed situation. We sit on the red Moroccan carpet and hold hands. I am miserably heartbroken by his face, his solemn face, his silence.

I wake up thinking "I love him." I have fallen in love with this man and I want to stay here with him. At breakfast he is sweet and sad and asks again why am I leaving. I feel this terrible falling sensation. I shake my head and somehow mumble, "I really have to go." He comes home early at lunchtime. We find our melancholy bedroom. I am barely breathing as I memorize our bodies, this room, his suit placed just so over a chair. Some fear takes hold of me.

Later we have lunch at his table for two in the kitchen. It looks new to me today, this table we have been sharing for nineteen days.

Do I have any idea at all of what being in love means? My judgment is unreliable, and I am suspicious of myself in this matter. Or is it that I am suspicious of other people because I am so unreliable?

88

We meet at eight in the evening at La Boucherie. We are better now. Tomorrow is our last full day together, and we have planned our walk. We will walk from Croulebarbe to the book stalls on the river, have a long look into the Seine from the bridge, continue on to Place de la Concorde, stroll past the Crillon, linger along the Champs-Élysées all the way to the Arc de Triomphe. Or we might meander through the Jardin de Luxembourg and end up at Deux Magots. And it is not goodbye. I will be back soon, and we will vacation in Spain next summer. He says he will wait for me "tenderly."

On Sunday he carries my suitcase to the hallway. I tell him I will be there in a second. I walk through the apartment once more to memorize each room. The red Moroccan carpet. The courtyard beneath the window and the lonely bare-limbed trees. I gather my rosy cosmetic bag that is not ready to return to Texas. My black plastic book bag weighs two tons. My purse, my passport folder, my round-the-world Pan American ticket, thick with carbon copies and red ink marked for arrival in New York City, then Houston.

At the airport bar I lean close to him, memorize his face, touch his mouth.

When the plane lifts I fumble through my purse, then my book bag, find my journal, but no pen or pencil. I start all over again, find a pencil. How many plane, train, boat and bus rides did it take to get to Paris? I have made three hundred and nineteen entries in this 1964 Journal. I have hours to figure out how I arrived in Paris on July 13. Why I am leaving now I will never understand.

89
New York City

In New York City, Mary is ecstatic. She is living at the YWCA. Annette and I are sharing a small room in a hotel, blocks away from Mary's apartment. Annette met some guy in a coffee shop and thinks she might go to Colorado with him. Mary and I do not approve. We find a place to sell earrings from Hong Kong and have a little extra money. It is so cold we sit in a coffee shop for hours trying to think, plan. It is futile. I leave in the morning for Houston. Mary insists we must be back here in New York City within a month. She must be crazy. I freeze walking along the cliffs and valleys of this city, wind howling, my throat aching within fifteen minutes. Martin's green-and-black wool scarf protects my throat against this icy blast.

90
December 28, 1964
Houston

I've made some decisions. I will sell my diamond ring and gold Rolex watch and probably my pearls in order to get from here to New York City, then back to Paris. That is, if I don't have anything from Masao or Dan within the next few weeks. My parents have a friend here in Houston who is a jeweler, and he can tell me what I can sell them for. But they must be worth eight or nine hundred dollars, enough for bus fare to New York and an Icelandic Air plane ticket like Annette had.

My dearest Kathy Martin did call me only a week ago and said there was an opening at the Desert Inn for me. They are rehearsing a new show, *Hello, America*, and the costumes are lovely, just bosoms showing. Of course there are pasties. I protest that I am too heavy, but she says not to worry about my extra weight. So working there for a while could be an option.

I have many letters from Jacques. My sisters Janet and Beth just snatch them out of my hands, and there is no privacy here.

We have had changes. Linda has married, and at the wedding I had a run-in with that Walter Jones, my boyfriend from college, who fell down laughing when I told him I had someone in Paris and couldn't go out with him. Since when did having one absent boyfriend preclude a date with another one? He just doesn't believe me, and it's not a lot to brag about, but I have been faithful for twenty-seven days.

We've had Christmas and seen my "movies." It's hard to believe, but Dad actually went to an Elvis Presley movie to see the Sands Chorus girls in our white fan number. My dear Copa sisters! And seeing myself in *Zorba* was a surprise. I was there, I think, but now I'm not, and yet

I have proof. It wasn't a dream.

Annette and Mary and I are happy to be with family, but we also think that home can be a foreign place too. I know I would be happiest walking on blvd. St. Michel. I am always thinking, What time is it in Paris?

Tomorrow, though, I leave with Grandma Lee and Grandpa and Uncle Toss for Oklahoma. I've written Jacques to expect postcards for a week while we are on the road. We'll cross the Red River in Grandpa's old white Plymouth, telling stories all the way to Edmond to see Uncle Bob and Aunt Dorothy. I will tell Bob that I never made it to Versailles and the Bar de la Reine. He won't care because he'll be off and running on his story of being in Paris in 1953 and working at SHAPE headquarters, making films with Sam Goldwyn Jr. and how he met General Eisenhower.

In the morning we'll head to Route 66 and meander the old roads to Tryon. We might find Headquarters Creek a couple of times. That's where my dad went swimming before and after school. I'll watch for Cow Bell Creek because I know we're close to Tryon when I see that sign.

Grandma Lee and Toss and Grandpa will drop me off at Grandma Johnson's and will head to the cemetery outside of Cushing to pay respects to little Dicema, Grandma Lee's first daughter. That was in 1919, but it seems like I've known that baby myself, the way we always visit her in the cemetery. Then they will head to Stroud to see Grandma Lee's brother Herman, and his wife, Delores. They will sit at the kitchen table and ask each other "remember when?" a thousand and one times.

Grandma Johnson and I will read over all the postcards I sent her this year.

She and Papa will want to know exactly how it felt to stand in the desert when we visited the Hanging Gardens of Babylon. Hot and still, so quiet you could almost imagine ghosts passing by. And I'll tell them about the little goat I led down the path in the mountains of Crete. They will love that story.

I'll have two days with Grandma and Grandpa Johnson. She'll fix fried chicken and make mashed potatoes and gravy, and we'll go deep into the cellar and maybe find beets or something good she's put up. I can hardly wait to smell that old musty place. It's cold in Oklahoma. For sure, we'll take a quick look up at the sky, see if the moon is fat, or just maybe it will be a perfect curved slice, with Venus or Mars or Jupiter placed just so, making us stand still and shake our heads at such a sight.

A Lot of World to See—Acknowledgements

One day I woke up. It was 1980. I was forty years old, married, two children, two dogs, one cat, and I was a teacher in Manassas, Virginia. What happened? Hadn't I been a glamorous Las Vegas showgirl, gone around the world with Mary, lived in Paris with dreams of being a writer? And did I ever thank the two men who made it all possible? Mr. Aguinaldo and Mr. Kubo? No. I took their money and Mary, Annette, and I spent it in no time. But thank you. It did change my whole life. Thank you.

But forty? Was it too late to be a writer? By chance there was a writing class for teachers with Mr. Sandy Lyne in D.C., and my friend Janet Wheatcraft and I were fortunate to be there. We were swept up in his kindness, the idea of "moving" into a journal, filling it with poems and stickers and favorite quotes from beloved authors. Janet and I began writing together, reading books by Carolyn Heilbrun and Catherine Bateson, and feeling nourished by their words. And in our fervor we made journals for our friends and parents. We decorated with photos, stickers, writing prompts. We encouraged our students to do the same. I found writing with my schoolchildren was immensely gratifying. To be surrounded by authors, poets, artists—the life I dreamed of! Thank you dearest first, second, and sixth graders. Thank you.

Shortly after turning forty, I was, believe it or not, fifty, and surrounded by my sixth graders. Around that time a fellow teacher rushed into my room to ask, did I have a copy of *Gilgamesh*? I did not. But inquiring about Gilgamesh led me to Mary Washington University, where I entered into a program that required me to complete a project of my own choosing. I thought of my 1964 journal and wondered if I could make something of it. Yes, I could, announced my two sponsors,

Bulent Atalay and Carol Manning. Yes, write about those long-ago adventures. Thank you. Thank you. Carol has been encouraging me for twenty-five years. She is my friend. I hear her voice, and I am grateful.

In 1992 Brian McDonald, a former student who was attending U. of Virginia at the time, informed me of a Writers Conference titled "Returning the Gift" to be held that summer in Norman, Oklahoma. Native American writers, poets, singers, and dancers from all American continents were present. At early morning coffee, lectures, and meetings, I attended as a shadow. I was intimidated but proud, nevertheless. N. Scott Momaday, Kiowa, winner of the Pulitzer Prize in 1969, was revered and honored. Emotions ran high. Each dance, song, poem, or story was an expression of anger, beauty, loss, grief, and separation. Huanani-Kay Trask, activist professor from Hawaii, demanded attention to the never-ending struggle of the island natives in her poems and essays. The solemn family of Leonard Peltier (American Indian Movement member and participant in the 1975 shoot-out at Pine Ridge, convicted of the murder of two FBI agents) gathered to protest his imprisonment. Family affairs figured prominently in stories and poems. Seated in the kitchen with my family, remembering old times, poems by Joy Harjo and Luci Tapahonso come to mind. Thank you

As a novice writer, I was assigned a mentor, Jean Starr, Cherokee. Thank you, Jean, you beautiful spirit, for your fierce encouragement. And Suzanne Rancourt, after Jean left us too soon. Lee Francis, upon reading early pages, assured me that having my hair done so often in 1964 reminded him of his mother and sister and the braiding and grooming each day, and I was caught off guard. Yes, it is a ceremony between mothers and daughters. Lee, the first National Director of Wordcraft Circle of Native Writers and Storytellers, thank you. You gave me courage.

The year before I turned sixty, 1999, I was awarded a three-week residency at Norcroft, a writing retreat for women, in Lutsen, Minnesota, sponsored by Joan Drury. She was strict, wise, and generous with her encouragement. No talking until 4:00 in the afternoon. My fellow residents and I had a writing goal of five pages a day. I treasure those efforts, on faded yellow paper, all in pencil. The twenty minute dip each day into the icy Lake Superior. Oh! See: Each day your purpose is to write. Oh, Miss Drury. You are gone now, but thank you for those days. I see them, clear as the water, sharp, full of purpose. Thank you.

In 2000, after recovering from a surprise sixtieth birthday given by my daughter-in-law Cathy Alice (so shocked to see my mother and friends, I cried and blew my nose endlessly throughout), I began evening writing classes at the Bethesda Writing Center with Lynn Stearns. I was grateful for her page, sometimes two, of detailed notes on our weekly assignment. "The protagonist is trustworthy." She is! I am? "Pay attention to tenses. Are you writing in past or present tense, that is the question." Thank you, Lynn. A class with JoAnne Biggars helped me with my travel chapters. Also a class with Philip Gerard gave me new ideas and confidence about my story. To my teachers at Bethesda Writers Center, I thank you.

I met Matt Klam at a weekend poetry and fiction writing workshop, where fellow students assured me I should write a memoir, not a fictional account of my journey. Matt said listen to Nat King Cole, Judy Garland, Frank, and Dean. Imagine the dressing room, recall the clink of silver dollars in the casino. I renewed friendships with the Copa ladies, especially Charlotte Nort, Rowena Buttonweiser, Carolyn Collette, and Joy Blaine. I began research in the University of Nevada Las Vegas Special Archives where I met a young archivist, Su Kim Chung, who would become a best friend. Mary and Annette and I met in Las Vegas to search through the Sands files in Lied Library. We found many photos of our prior life. We participated in the Oral History project conducted by Claytee White. I found that the library was my connection to the Sands Hotel, faded memories safely preserved by devoted archivists. Through friends, I found my long-lost friend Kathy Martin. We met at the Paris Hotel in Las Vegas after a fifty-year separation. Thank you, Matt Klam, for the research that you encouraged. Instead of the Sands dressing room, I now hang out at the UNLV Library, discovering proof of my recollections. Thank you, Copa ladies, we are so rare! Thank you, Su Kim: You made the archives my Place in the Sun.

Before I left teaching in 2002, our school secretary, Sue Mauck, had typed hundreds of pages for me. After translating my journal from shorthand to longhand, Sue typed them, and returned them with no raised eyebrows. Thank you, Sue. You were busy, gracious, and so kind. To Jonathan Gilbert, our grandson, who put my scattered chapters into a book on my computer and has been on call daily for fifteen years of IT help. There would be nothing here at all without you. Thank you, Jonathan.

In January of 2005, I met a young woman at our book club who invited me to an upcoming two-day writing workshop she was conducting. Held in a cozy beach house setting, I was immediately drawn to the participants and the young author, Maribeth Fischer. For the past fifteen years that small group has grown into the Rehoboth Beach Writers Guild. It has been a safe place to grow as a writer. The guild is unique because of the coordination between artists, writers, singers, and musicians for many presentations. For me, to work with Maribeth, Amy Felker, and Stuart Vining in our one-hour show featuring songs and excerpts from my memoir was thrilling. And to the many who attended those five events and received us so warmly, thank you. Maribeth, my friend, you deserve so much more than these poor words, but thank you forever and ever for your generous attention to my story. Thank you.

In 2008, I drove to Southampton to be in a class taught by Frank McCourt. That week was one long exuberant celebration of writing, acting, performance, and inspiration. Although Mr. McCourt gave me an F on my first assignment, I made progress. Thank you Southampton Writers Conference, my fellow classmates, Matt Klam, and the entire cast of generous teachers that gather there year after year.

Protests and demonstrations in the Middle East were regular features in the world news of 2011. Thus, the six-day literary event in Aspen, Colorado, in July of that year was of great interest to me. First, I was in class each day with a writer and poet I had admired for many years, Erica Jong. My fellow writers were a joy to be with. After class, writers Khaled Hosseini (author of *The Kite Runner*), and Mona Eltahawy, journalist and public speaker, were part of the lectures on the politics and literature of the Middle East. It was a privilege to attend those events and listen to poets and writers describe their countries in terms we would never see or hear or read about in the news. I am thankful for that week, to our teacher Miss Jong, and the friends I made there. Thank you, Aspen Writer's Summer Words literary festival.

Between ages seventy and eighty I traveled to Guatemala to write with the vivacious Joyce Maynard and swim in the incredible Lake Atitlan; I traveled to Florence, Italy with Matt Klam and the Southampton writers again. To Cania, Crete, to explore that once small village, now a thriving resort, where I recalled those weeks in 1964 wandering its solemn quiet streets. Later, my husband and I joined Jemma Kennedy in Loutro, and the writing group Espiritao for swimming in the deep clear Libyan sea, wandering among ancient ruins, and dreaming about writing. In 2019, Walter and I joined Roland Merullo in Orvieto, Italy at Locanda Rosati. Thank you Roland, for bringing us together for good food, conversation, support, and perfect weather. Your reading of my memoir and the suggestions you made were invaluable. Thank you.

Crystal Heidel, thank you for your support and enthusiasm for this book.

During this writing journey I have called on my sisters, Linda, Janet, and Beth many times for help in remembering. My Aunt Betty read an early version of the story and liked it and gave it a seal of approval. My Uncle Toss was always there to verify train schedules and family stories. My cousins have answered my calls for photos and to read chapters, and I thank them. Bobby, Karen, Claude, Rita, Donald, Ronald, Shannon, Robin, Glenda, and Tracy Linn, thank you. To Jacques Barat, for names and places that I didn't remember, thank you. Kathy Martin's daughter, Elaina Eller, has sent me the lovely photos of her mother. Ana and Seth, Annette's children, thank you for your help. And Nina, Mary's daughter, found the photos Mary took on our trip through the Middle East. Thank you. Emily Kolp, at a crucial moment, you took my hand and guided this book to the finish line. I am deeply grateful for your invaluable expertise. Thank you.

To my dashing husband, Walter, who has indulged my love of travel these last years of our long life together, I am forever grateful. Thank you for encouraging me to "Get that book finished!" And to our children and grandchildren, Jess and Kathleen, Jonathan and Jemalyn, Roger and Cathy, Ethan, Rachel, Brady and Erin, thank you for your support. Most of all, thank you for traveling with your Mimi.

To Kathy Martin, keeper of my childish dream, to Annette and Mary, who made dreams possible, thank you.

Read and Travel, Or, Travel and Read

Anthology. *The Poetry of Living Japan*. New York. Grove Press Books, 1958.

Arcellana, Francisco. *Selected Stories*. Manila. Alberto S. Florentino, 1962.

Beevor, Antony. *Crete: The Battle and the Resistance*. Boulder. Westview Press. 1994
(First published in United Kingdom by John Murray Publishers, 1991.)

Burati, Robert M., Burati, Robert M. and Harold Pettelkay, photographer. *Hong Kong*. New York. Kodansha International/ USA, 1971.

Burke, Andrew, and Mark Elliot. *Iran*. Oakland. Lonely Planet, 2008.

Conde, Bruce. *Byways of Byblos*. Beirut. Al-Bayan Press, 1962.

Carson, Rachel. *Silent Spring*. New York. Crest Books, 1962.

Conze, Edward, Translator. *Buddhist Scriptures*. Harmondsworth, Great Britain. Penquin Books Ltd., 1960.

Dalton, David. *The Rough Guide to the Philippines*. New York. Rough Guides, 2007.
(p. 395. A description of Daniel Aguinaldo's Pearl Farm. Now a resort.)

Durrell, Lawrence. *The Greek Islands.* New York. The Viking Press, 1978.

Fodor, Eugene, and William Curtis, Editors. *Fodor's Guide to India.* Tokyo. Tosho Insatsu Printing Co., 1962.

Frommer, Arthur. *Europe on 5 Dollars A Day.* New York City. Crown Publishers, Inc., 1959.

Geis, Darlene, Editor. *Let's Travel in Thailand.* Chicago. Childrens Press, Inc., 1965.
(Original copyright 1961 as *A Color Slide Tour of Thailand.*)

Gerrard, Mike. *National Geographic Traveler GREECE.* Second Edition National Geographic Society, 2007.

Gibran, Kahlil. *The Prophet.* New York. Alfred A. Knopf, One Hundred and Third Printing, 1979.

Gonzalez, N.V.M. *Look, Stranger, On This Island Now.* Manila. Benipayo Press, 1963.

Hafiz. *Hafiz of Shiraz. Thirty Poems.* Translated by Peter Avery and John Heath Stubbs. London, John Murray Ltd., 1952.

Hemingway, Ernest. *A Moveable Feast.* London. Jonathan Cape, 1964.

Honafar, Lotfollah. *Historical Monuments of Isfahan.* Isfahan. Emami Press, 1964.

Hopkins, Jerry. *The Hula.* Hong Kong. Apa Productions (HK) Ltd., 1982.

How to Visit the Beauties of Rome. Firenze. Bonechi Edizione Il Turismo. (This book had no identity that I could see, 55 years.)

Huxley, Julian. *From An Antique Land.* London. Max Parrish & Co. Limited, 1961.
   ("The cover design is from a photograph of the Arch of Ctesiphon by the Author." When I found this book at a used book store I hugged it like an old friend. Published just a few years before we arrived in the Middle East, it was a perfect reminder of our travels there. These words and photos are dear to me. Thank you, Julian. I wish we had met.)

Japan Travel Bureau. *Japanese Arts-What & Where? Vol.11.* Tokyo. Tosho Insatu Printing Co., 1962.

Japan Quarterly January–March 1964. Tokyo. Asahi Shimbun Publishing Co., 1964.

Jimenez, Juan Ramon. *Platero and I.* Austin. University of Texas Press, 1957.

Karnow, Stanley. *In Our Image: America's Empire in the Philippines.* New York. Ballantine Books, 1989.

Kazantzakis, Nikos. *Zorba the Greek.* Translated by Carl Wildman. New York. Simon & Schuster Inc. Scribner Paperback, 1996.

Kramer, Samuel Noah. *History Begins At Sumer: Twenty-seven 'Firsts' in Man's Recorded History.* New York. Doubleday Anchor Books. Doubleday & Company, Inc. 1959.

Lawrence, D.H. *Lady Chatterley's Lover.* New York. Pocket Books, Inc., 1959.

Lee, Mary Alice, *"Artists in Beirut,"* MID EAST: A Middle East-North African Review 8, no. 6 (November/December 1968): 34 and 38.

Interview with artist's commentary. Photos: Ian Rawson. Critique: Helen Khal

Lorca, Federico Garcia. *The Selected Poems of Federico Garcia Lorca.* Norfolk, Connecticut. New Directions Paperbook, 1961.

Martin, Andre, Photographer. *Paris.* London. Spring Books, 1960. (Introduction by Andre Maurois.)

Matheson, Sylvia A. *Persia: An Archaeological Guide.* London. Faber and Faber Limited, 1972.

Mattson, Marie. *Orient Holiday: A Guide to Travel in the Lands of the Orient.* American President Lines, 1957.

Mauriac, Francois. *The Desert of Love.* New York. New Bantam. 1960

Mishima, Yukio. *The Sound of Waves.* Tokyo. Charles E. Tuttle Company, 1963.

Papiomitoglou, Vangelis. *Wildflowers of Crete.* Rethvmnon, Greece. Mediterraneo Editions, 2006.

Sagan, Francoise. *Bonjour Tristesse.* New York. Dell Publishing Company, Inc. 1955.

Sands, William, editor. *The Middle East Journal* 22. (Summer 1968).

State Tourist Administration. *Tourist Information U.A.R. Egypt.* UAR Institute Graphique Egyptien.

Steinberg, David Joel. *The Philippines: A Singular and a Plural Place.* Boulder, CO. Westview Press, 1990.

Stevens, Georgiana G. *Egypt: Yesterday and Today.* New York. Holt, Rinehart & Winston, Inc., Vol. 9, no. 1, January–February, 1963.

Schneps, Maurice. Editor in Chief *The Death of a President: An Editorial.* Orient/West Magazine. Yokohama, Japan. 1964.
> p. 19.   "......The violent times we live in are, perhaps, no different in their violence from other times, but this is no consolation. .....Improvements and progress have been made—in science and technology—but Man remains, as before, the victim of his own irrationality. When the assassin's bullet struck down President Kennedy, all the evil forces of hate and murder rose to torment men of reason and good will. Neither the mighty nor the weak are spared; there is no safety in our times. .....His passing has left a deep ache, an emptiness, and the fearful question, where will the madness strike next?"

Trask, Haunani-Kay. *Light in the Crevice Never Seen.* Corvallis, Oregon. Calyx Books, 1994.

Tretyakov Gallery. *Our Museums.* USSR. Government Publishers of Graphic Art Reproductions, 1963.
Thank you, Albina Gilaeva, for this translation, and Spaska Hadzhiyska for your help.

Wilson, Henry. *Benares.* New York. Thames and Hudson, Inc., 1985.

Villa, Jose Garcia. *Selected Stories of Jose Garcia Villa.* Manilla. Alberto S. Florentino, 1962.

Yevtushenko, Yevgeny. *Selected Poems.* Harmondsworth, Middlesex. Penquin Books Ltd., 1964.

Don't Forget!

Durrell, Lawrence. *Justine.* New York. Pocket Books Inc., Giant Cardinal Edition, 1961.
>   p. 250.   "….the summer Mediterranean lies before me in all its magnetic blueness.   …..lies Alexandria, maintaining its tenuous grasp on one's affections through memories which are already refunding themselves slowly into forgetfulness: memory of friends, of incidents long past."

Notes

Chapter 2

Page 7. When he left Bellaire High School, Mr. Pickett (Cecil) taught at the University of Houston for eighteen years and ensured his students were ready for hard work and disappointments. He beguiled us with humor and surprises, instilled dedication and teamwork. We feared disappointing him. We became more responsible because of him. Dennis and Randy Quaid studied under Mr. Pickett.

Chapter 3

Page 11. According to information found in the University of Nevada, Las Vegas, Southern Nevada Jewish Heritage Project, digital library, Al served in the Army and "received numerous accolades for his service including: five Battle Stars, Legion of Merit for his service in combat, the Purple Heart and three clusters." My husband said Al was a hero.

Chapter 17

Page 68. The Civilian Conservation Corp, part of Franklin D. Roosevelt's New Deal "to provide jobs for young men and to relieve families who had difficulty finding jobs" according to Wikipedia. Mom and Dad always spoke highly of these young men. They were the same age as my parents. Stephenson Park, to this day, is a place to walk under green trees, swim, and enjoy a summer day.

Chapter 27

Page 91. Houston's Tommy Tune, ten Tony Awards! What an honor to have been on stage with him. I speak for myself and Rusty Spicer, our Puck, thanks for the memories Tommy, it was the grandest time.

Chapter 32
Las Vegas. March 1963

Page 107. The Nelani Kele Polynesian dancers at the Stardust Hotel enjoyed many years as a top draw in Las Vegas. The dances were energetic, original, and their Tahitian numbers were thrilling. I haven't forgotten them.

Chapter 50

Page 153. "Fire shooting from endless crevasses in the earth" is inspired by the poems of Huanani Kay-Trask, the fearless advocate for the preservation of Hawaiian culture.

After Paris

I met Matt Klam at a weekend poetry and fiction writing workshop. The poetry teacher was Billy Collins. With these two creative writers and performers it was an uplifting literary treat.

Top left to lower right: Easter with our cousins and Grandmother Johnson. Tryon, OK; My sister Linda; Uncle Jess and Aunt JoAnn, Wedding photo; Uncle Bob in Morocco, Uncle Bob and Aunt Dorothy

Top left to lower right: Kathy Martin; Annette Hillman; Italy Summer 1959; Mary and Judy; photo Collage.

Top left to lower right: Copa girls 1963, Photo credit: Mary Marx. Dancers; Mary's passport photo; Mary and Annette in Sweden 1964; passport

Top left to lower right: Mary's photos
of Thailand; Bottom right: Walt Jones
USMC

Judith Lee Jones
Photo credit: Janet Wheatcraft

After working at the Sands Hotel in Las Vegas and her year of traveling the world in 1964, Judith taught in public schools for 28 years. She continues to travel with her family and friends and divides her time between Virginia and Delaware.

"As for you, wise one, I have a feeling that you too perhaps have stepped across the threshold into the kingdom of your imagination, to take possession of it once and for all. Write and tell me—or save it for some small café under a chestnut-tree, in smoky autumn weather, by the Seine."

"Clea."
Lawrence Durrell